Dad

Happy Birthday

love,

Mike and Julie

Talking *on* Tour

Talking *on* Tour

The Best Anecdotes from Golf's Master Storyteller

Don Wade

Foreword by Matt Lauer

CONTEMPORARY BOOKS

Library of Congress Cataloging-in-Publication Data

Wade, Don.
    Talking on Tour: the best anecdotes from golf's master storyteller/Don Wade;
Foreword by Matt Lauer.
        p.   cm.
    Includes index.
    ISBN 0-8092-9473-7
    1. Golf—Anecdotes.

GV967.W275   2001
796.352—dc21   00-52383

Contemporary Books

A Division of The **McGraw-Hill** Companies

Illustrations by Paul Szep

1 2 3 4 5 6 7 8 9 0   LBM/LBM   0 9 8 7 6 5 4 3 2 1

ISBN 0-8092-9473-7

This book was set in Sabon
Printed and bound by Lake Book Manufacturing

McGraw-Hill books are available at special quantity discounts to use as premiums and
sales promotions, or for use in corporate training programs. For more information, please
write to the Director of Special Sales, Professional Publishing, McGraw-Hill, Two Penn
Plaza, New York, NY 10121-2298. Or contact your local bookstore.

This book is printed on acid-free paper

DEDICATION

Sometimes there's a certain symmetry to life.

In October, my mother died peacefully in her sleep, and while we all miss her terribly, we keep our memories of her close by so we can revisit them—and her—in those times when memories mean so much.

Ironically, my mother died on my 50th birthday, but then she always had a good sense of timing.

About three weeks before her death, I appeared on CNN to discuss the Supreme Court's decision to take up the Casey Martin matter. The discussion was, as they say, lively. The next day I spoke with my parents.

"Geez, Don, you were terrific," my father said. Of course, he would have said the same thing if I had acted like one of the Three Stooges.

My mother, as always, was a bit more critical.

"Donnie, next time mind your manners and lose ten pounds," she said.

About a week later she was hospitalized. Her heart was failing, and our family rallied to her side. Early one evening, my father and I sat on either side of her bed. The room was dark except for the soft lighting above her head, and she was resting comfortably as my father and I talked.

"Don, you don't look so heavy," my father said. "How come you looked bigger on television?"

I explained that television makes you look heavier and that the lighting wasn't all that great and so on. There was a pause. My mother opened her eyes slowly and looked at me.

"Lose the 10 pounds anyway," she said.

Beautiful.

I'm thankful for that memory, and for everything else she and my father have meant to me, my brother and sister, and our families.

Mom and Dad, this one's for you.

Contents

IX

x

Foreword

I guess I was eight or nine when my father first took me to the public golf course at Christopher Morely Park, on Long Island. My parents were divorced, and the weekends spent with my dad were cherished. They were made even more special by those days when we would add our names to the long list of starting times, head off for breakfast, and return two hours later to find we were still five or six slots away from the tee.

But the wait never bothered us. It was a necessary prequel to the main event: four hours of quality golfing time—father and son, teacher and student, one generation passing on a passion to the next. Those moments and memories sealed my fate; I was hooked!

Today, I'm certifiable. Which is what you have to call a golfer who can shoot 72 one day and 92 the next. I love almost every aspect of the game: the drive to the course, the walk to the first tee, the dew on the greens early in the morning, the light on the fairways late in the day. I love the smell of the glove and the feel of new grips, the simplicity of a white golf tee, and the complexity of my oversized, somewhat cavity-backed offset irons. I love basic scorecards without pictures, pencils without erasers, and the number 3 in any of those 18 little boxes. Oh, and there's something else: I love great golf stories!

Years ago, someone gave me a copy of *The Golf Omnibus*, by P. G. Wodehouse, an amazing book filled with the kinds of stories that make up the fabric of the game of golf, that draw all golfers together through shared experiences, thoughts, and emotions. But that book dealt with fictional characters, and my love of the game and of the great stories it held made me thirst for more. I wanted the real thing!

It's in the great tradition of that Wodehouse book that Don Wade brings us his *"And Then Jack Said to Arnie . . ."* series. When I picked up the first installment in 1991, I felt like someone had allowed me "inside the ropes," given me the chance to walk the course with the greatest names in golf, and invited me to lean in and listen as they spoke just out of the gallery's earshot. Some of the stories are as legendary as the players they describe; others are as surprising as a chip in from the rough.

Reading these books will not—I repeat, will not—improve your swing! But they are guaranteed to make you the life of your weekly foursome. Don Wade's stories and Paul Szep's magical drawings will remind you of why you fell in love with the game of golf in the first place.

So enjoy *Talking on Tour* and its many smile-filled pages—golfers both great and ghastly can tee it up together!

—Matt Lauer

PREFACE

By a happy coincidence, this series of books coincided with a remarkable period of growth in golf, which certainly helps explain why the books have been so successful.

People often ask why golf has become so popular, and there are certainly a number of good reasons. For one thing, members of the baby-boom generation are finding themselves with time on their hands and pain in their knees, which makes golf more attractive than an afternoon spent killing yourself in a game of full-court basketball (or even half-court, come to think of it).

A more important reason, however, is that golf is the last pure sport. At a time when kids in other sports are taught to, if not break the rules, then at least twist them beyond recognition, golf can point to a string of role models that run from Bobby Jones to Tiger Woods.

Then there is the addictive nature of the game. Once people take it up, the sheer beauty of the courses and the friendship and camaraderie of the game touch something deep in most people.

Occasionally, I'm asked why I think these books have been so successful, and I think the best answer stems from something the late Dave Marr told me. When the first book came out, Dave called to say how much he enjoyed it. Then he said that if you had friends who didn't understand why golf has such a hold on people, they should read *"And Then Jack Said to Arnie . . ."*.

"It's all in there," Dave said. "The humor, the drama, the courage, and the sadness. Every part of the game. You got it just right."

I thanked Dave then, and to the extent he was right, I hope it has remained true in all the books that have followed—especially in this collection.

I hope you enjoy it.

ACKNOWLEDGMENTS

This series of books owes its success to a large number of talented people who I'm also happy to call friends.

First, I want to thank the incomparable Paul Szep, whose caricatures have graced every single one of these books. Szep has won two Pulitzer Prizes for his editorial cartoons in the *Boston Globe* and is a passionate golfer. But his true measure, at least to me, is his fierce and undying loyalty and friendship. Millions of people have been enlightened by Szep's remarkable work. Those of us who count him as a friend are truly blessed. Thanks Szeppy. You're a beaut, eh?

Next, I want to thank Nancy Crossman, the editorial director at Contemporary Books who took a chance on the first book and then lovingly nurtured the books that followed until she decided that she wanted to devote her professional life to doing the same thing for other writers as a literary agent. I hope the writers she represents know just how lucky they truly are.

When Nancy left, these books were put in the hands (or fell into the laps) of Matthew Carnicelli and John Nolan. Matthew is a senior editor at Contemporary Books and is in charge of the day-to-day challenge of dealing with writers like me. This is no easy task. John Nolan, who replaced Nancy as editorial director and then became publisher, gets to oversee both Matthew and me and others like Matthew and me. Sainthood awaits them both.

Steve Szurlej has shot the covers for this series and, in doing so, has magnificently captured the spirit and flavor of the game. Steve and I met early on in our careers at *Golf Digest*, and my respect and admiration for his particular genius are unflagging—as is my thanks.

I'd be more than remiss if I didn't give thanks to Bob Rosen, who has been one of my agents since the mid-1980s. In 1989, I was working as an on-air analyst for the USA Network at the Ryder Cup. Over dinner on the eve of the first day's matches, I told Bob and his partner, Craig Foster, some stories I hoped to use on air. Bob immediately suggested we do a collection of anecdotes, and *"And Then Jack Said to Arnie . . ."* was born. Bob has represented clients who have far higher profiles than I do, but in his heart of hearts, he takes a special pride in this series of books, and for that, I thank him.

Bob handed the project off to Chris Tomasino, who handled the literary side of the agency, and Chris was magnificent in pushing, prodding, cheerleading, handholding, and ego massaging. Chris eventually left to strike out on her own, but I cannot thank her enough for her help and friendship. I wish her every single happiness.

Jonathan Diamond took over from Chris and helped keep the series moving along smoothly until the call of southern California became too much for him and his wife, and they fled the friendly streets of New York City for L.A. At that point, the magnificent burden fell to the great Jennifer Unter, who has been just that—great. Thanks to you both.

Any number of players, writers, television guys, and The Boys from Stanwich have been more than generous in sharing their stories, as have a surprising number of readers. But I want to give special thanks to the people who have graciously written the Forewords for this series. More precisely, I want to thank them for their friendships. To Lee Trevino, Gary McCord, Ken Venturi, Curtis Strange, Peter Jacobsen, Amy Alcott, Sam Snead, Nancy Lopez, and Matt Lauer, thanks so much for everything.

Finally, thanks very much to the Concord Wades, who got me off and running, and Julia, Ben, Darcy, and Andy, who are the best family anyone could possibly imagine.

Stamford, Connecticut
September 10, 2000

TALKING ON TOUR

AMY ALCOTT

Amy Alcott is one of the great characters in women's golf—or in all of golf, for that matter. Not the least of her attributes are a wicked sense of humor and a great sense of comic timing.

One day she called a writer friend to tell him that she'd just been named the top female Jewish athlete in the United States.

"Congratulations, Amy," the friend said. "That's great. Who'd you beat?"

"Some fencer from Brandeis," she deadpanned.

Amy's nine-shot victory in the 1980 Women's Open is generally considered to be one of the great wins on any tour. In the searing heat and humidity, she was the only player to break par.

In the final round she was paired with her longtime rival Hollis Stacy. As Amy, on the verge of exhaustion and dehydration, approached the last green, Hollis walked over and said, "Amy, whatever you do, don't fifteen-putt."

ARCHITECTS

It's been said that every great artist is at least a little eccentric. Maybe it's because they see the world from a slightly different slant or perspective. Whatever the reason, it can fairly be said that architect A. W. Tillinghast was eccentric—to say the least.

The man who designed such masterpieces as the two courses at Winged Foot and its neighbor, Quaker Ridge, was born to wealth and then managed to accumulate a fortune of his own. As befits a man of his stature, he both dressed and acted the part.

He invariably dressed in expensive, three-piece suits and was driven to his New York City office by chauffeured limousine. If his plans called for him to visit a course site that day, it didn't alter his choice of clothes. He'd motor out to the construction site, march imperiously into the woods and fields, find a shady spot, and begin shouting orders to the laborers—interrupting his instructions just long enough to sip whiskey from a silver flask he always carried with him.

Eccentric? Sure. But in what was surely the golden age of American golf course architecture, Tillinghast's designs were unsurpassed.

Architect A. W. Tillinghast came from a wealthy and well-connected society family. He could be imperious at times, was known to take a drink, and had a certain roguish quality about him. On top of these laudable qualities, he was positively a genius when it came to designing golf courses, having created masterpieces like the two courses at Winged Foot and at neighboring Quaker Ridge.

It's not surprising, then, that when his daughter brought a boyfriend home to meet her father, the poor boy was more than a little nervous. It didn't help that Tillinghast didn't have much patience for small talk.

"Young man, there's only one thing I want to know about you," Tillinghast said.

"Yes, sir?" the man stammered.

"The results of your Wassermann test," he said.

Tillinghast was, among other things, a talented writer, and his gift with language is revealed in his description of his work at Winged Foot, where he built two of his finest courses.

"As the various holes came to life, they were of a sturdy breed. The contouring of the greens places a premium on the placement of drives, but never is there the necessity of facing a prodigious carry of the sink-or-swim sort. It is only the knowledge that the next shot must be played with rifle accuracy that brings the realization that the drive must be placed. The holes are like men, all rather similar from foot to neck, but with the greens showing the same varying character as human faces."

Tillinghast had little patience for critics of his courses—or of himself, for that matter. When the U.S. Open came to Winged Foot's West Course, Tillinghast was at the championship to accept the praise he was justifiably due for creating such a great test of golf.

As he sat in the clubhouse talking with friends, a man came up to him and said, "There's something wrong with your bunkers. A player just took four shots to get his ball out of one."

"Did it ever occur to you that the problem might not be with the bunkers?" Tillinghast sniffed.

Donald Ross was born and raised in Dornach, Scotland, and his religious roots ran deep. One day a writer ran into Ross and praised him for his brilliant masterpiece, Pinehurst #2.

Ross thanked him—and then corrected him.

"God created those holes," Ross said. "All I did was discover them."

On another occasion, he famously summoned the Almighty while surveying the property where he would design the South Course at Oakland Hills near Detroit. He climbed a slight slope and gazed down upon what are now the 10th and 11th holes.

"God intended this to be a golf course," he said, no doubt to the considerable relief of the club's founders, who had not only Ross but the Lord Himself on their side.

Donald Ross came to America from Scotland and quickly established himself as one of the premier golf course architects—a man whose works are revered today, and many of which are the standards against which others are measured.

Ross was fiercely proud of his work and not above promoting his efforts. He once telegraphed a player following a tournament at one of his courses, congratulating him on winning.

"Excellent. The greatest," reads Ross's cable.

"Undeserving of such praise," the player wired back.

"Was referring to the course," Ross replied.

"So was I," the player shot back.

The education of golf course architects comes in a fascinating variety of fashions. This was particularly true until recent years; today, more and more architects are learning their craft in college.

To be sure, Dr. Alister Mackenzie's education was unusual by any standard. Mackenzie, a Scotsman, was serving with British forces in South Africa during the Boer War of the late nineteenth century. He became fascinated by the Boers' use of camouflage to hide their defensive emplacements from British artillery.

"I came to understand the remarkable resemblance between the use of military camouflage and the design of a good golf hole," he once observed.

Following the war, Mackenzie put his knowledge to work in his designs for some of the world's greatest courses—courses like Augusta National, Royal Melbourne, and Cypress Point.

Dr. Alister Mackenzie is best known for his designs of Cypress Point and Augusta National, but he also designed a wonderful course in Michigan named Crystal Downs. His partner in this project was Perry Maxwell, who was a distinguished architect in his own right.

At one point in their collaboration, Maxwell left the site for a while, expecting Mackenzie to complete a routing plan in his absence. When he returned, Mackenzie proudly showed him his design.

"Well, tell me what you think," Mackenzie said.

Maxwell diplomatically pointed out that while it was a splendid effort, it had only seventeen holes.

When Bob Jones decided to build Augusta National he selected Dr. Alister Mackenzie as his collaborator. He admired the design work Mackenzie did at Cypress Point. Together they produced a course that is fair and challenging for players of every skill level.

At one point, a gentleman approached Mackenzie to tell him about a course he had recently played.

"It's very difficult," the man said. "No one has ever broken par there."

"My goodness, what's wrong with it?" asked Mackenzie.

No golf course architect has been as prodigious and, until Pete Dye, as controversial as Robert Trent Jones. He is credited with making course architecture a modern profession and, indeed, a lucrative one. Jones combined an artistic eye with a keen grasp of finances and public relations. As is evidenced in the following story, Trent Jones has a knack of being in the right place at the right time—and making the most of it.

"I was commissioned to modernize the Lower Course at Baltusrol for the 1954 U.S. Open," Jones recalls. "Some of the membership felt I had made the course too difficult, particularly the 4th hole, a 194-yard par 3 over water. Of course, the last thing I wanted was an unhappy membership, so I went over to Baltusrol and played with Johnny Farrell, the professional, C. P. Burgess, the tournament chairman, and another member. When we came to the 4th hole, all three fellows hit the green with their drives. I pulled out a mashie and, as luck would have it, made a hole in one. As soon as the ball went into the hole, I turned to my hosts and said, 'Gentlemen, I believe this hole is eminently fair.'"

7

Robert Trent Jones has designed courses all over the world and over the years has rubbed elbows with some of the world's most powerful leaders—although not always without incident.

In the early 1970s, he designed forty-five holes at Royal Golf Dar Es Salaam in Rabat for King Hassan II of Morocco. Jones soon struck up a friendship with the King, who invited him to one of his palaces for a birthday party.

When he reached the palace, he tried to enter the grounds in his rental car but was turned away by guards and directed to a public lot. When he reached the course where a tournament was being played, he was confronted by a group of soldiers, who soon began firing in the direction of the palace.

Jones assumed it was part of the festivities, until the troops ordered him and some other guests to a remote part of the property at gunpoint. In the background they could hear gunfire and grenade explosions.

A soldier approached Jones and demanded his passport.

"Diplomat?" he asked after studying the document.

"Yes, American diplomat," Jones said, trying to maintain his composure.

With that he was led away from the others. An hour or so later, a second group of soldiers came along, shouting, "The King is alive! God save the King!"

It was only then that Jones learned that he had been caught up in the middle of an attempted coup.

8 Architect Robert Trent Jones, Jr., learned many lessons from his father, who is perhaps the most well-known of all the golf course architects of the modern era. Not the least of those lessons was that golf is a universal game and that sometimes means building courses in out-of-the-way places—as long as the money is right.

One such place was Malaysia, where the younger Jones was commissioned to carve a course out of the steaming jungle. As he was doing his preliminary site research, he and a local guide had to wade through a swamp. Midway through, he saw a snake slither past as his guide quickly pulled out his machete.

"What kind of snake is that?" Jones asked.

"It's a krait snake," the guide answered.

"What happens if he bites you?" Jones said.

"You smoke one cigarette and say good-bye," the guide replied.

Robert Trent Jones, Sr., was hired to build a course near the pyramids in Egypt. Early on in the project he was asked if he had any suggestions for naming the course.

"We could call it 'The Sphinx Links,'" he quipped.

Today, golf course architects routinely use computers and all sorts of state-of-the-art technology to design and build courses. That was far from the case with early architects. For example, Charles Blair MacDonald, who designed several of the world's greatest courses, including the National Golf Links on Long Island, had a unique method of determining the contours of his greens.

"I would take a number of smooth, round pebbles in my hand and drop them on a small space representing the putting green," he once explained. "I watched as they dropped on the diagram and then placed the undulations accordingly."

Whereas today's architects often learn their skills in college, MacDonald—who was a man of some wealth—went back to his roots. Literally. For five summers he traveled to Great Britain and studied all the great courses, taking careful notes. It's not surprising, therefore, that several of the holes at the National resemble holes in the British Isles—particularly those at St. Andrews, where MacDonald attended university as a youth.

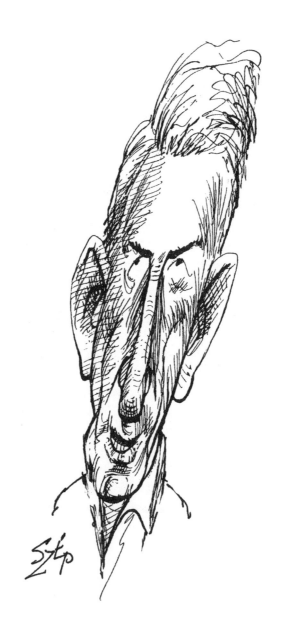

TOMMY ARMOUR

Tommy Armour, who won the U.S. and British Opens as well as a PGA Championship, enjoyed a reputation as an outstanding teacher. He was best known for the years he spent teaching at Winged Foot, but he also taught for a time at Medinah, the huge and celebrated gold mecca in the Chicago suburbs.

For all his skill as a teacher, however, Armour was far from the touchy-feely teachers we've grown so accustomed to today. For example, the mind boggles at the thought of the irascible Armour saying something as cloying as "What we want to feel in our golf swing is a sense of freedom. . . ."

And on and on.

No, Armour was one tough guy. The Scottish-born Armour had served valiantly in the British army during World War I and had been badly wounded, losing the sight of one eye to shrapnel.

While Armour was undoubtedly a fine teacher, his methods were unorthodox, to say the least. He would sit in a lawn chair under a large umbrella, usually with a gin buck resting on a table within handy reach. From there, he would issue curt instructions to the string of wealthy swells who sought him out for a miracle cure.

At Medinah, he also had the unnerving habit of dispatching nearby squirrels with a round from his .22 pistol. Despite his war injury, he was an excellent shot.

Still, celebrity or no celebrity, this particular habit didn't always sit well with his pupils, and finally one complained.

"Say, when are you going to take care of me?" the offended pupil complained.

"Don't tempt me," Armour said, fingering the revolver.

Armour faced down the likes of Bobby Jones, Gene Sarazen, and Walter Hagen in his playing career. After he was retired, a writer asked him whom he liked playing against.

"Rich guys with fast backswings," Armour said.

Armour knew the pressures of competition fully as well as anyone who has ever played the game. And he also understood that, unless you have been under that pressure, it is impossible to appreciate what it is like.

Armour was playing in a tournament in California in the early 1930s. He was paired with Johnny Revolta, who was fighting for a share of the lead. When Revolta left a four-footer a bit short of the hole, a man in the gallery yelled, "Gutless!"

Armour wheeled around and confronted the man.

"I'll bet you any amount of money you want that you couldn't make that putt," the icy Scotsman said.

"Don't be ridiculous," the man replied.

They settled on a $5,000 bet—an enormous amount of money in those days. The man went to the bank and withdrew his $5,000. Armour collected the same amount from his fellow professionals, who joined him and a growing gallery on the 18th green. Both men placed their cash on the green near the hole, and a ball was placed on the same spot from which Revolta had putted.

As the gallery closed in around him, the man addressed the ball and then backed off, sweating heavily and his hands visibly shaking. When he finally hit the putt, the ball wound up both wide and short of the hole.

"I want to apologize to Mr. Revolta," the man said. "When I got over the ball I couldn't even see the hole. I had no idea."

"In that case," said Armour, "the bet is off. Pick up your money."

One reason Armour was such a brilliant teacher was that he understood just how complicated it is to make the game simple. Witness his thoughts on putting:

"All there is to putting is keeping the head steady and the face of the putter moving squarely across the line to the hole," he said. "The problem is there are at least a thousand different ways of doing these two things."

On another occasion, Armour summed up why he felt it was so difficult for people to master the game.

"It is ridiculous to think that a person with physical, temperamental, and manner-of-living limitations is able to play subpar or even par golf. He might as well expect to become a great painter or sculptor, master the violin or piano, or even become a scientific genius or a millionaire simply by taking lessons and practicing. No, there's more to greatness than that. If there wasn't, greatness would be meaningless."

Another time a man came to Armour complaining that he had come down with a case of the yips and his putting had been ruined. He asked Armour what he could do to solve the problem.

"Nothing," said Armour. "Once you've had them you've got them."

Tommy Armour was born and raised in Scotland and attended the University of Edinburgh. He served as a machine gunner with British forces in World War I, suffering shrapnel damage that would pain him for the rest of his life. In addition, he lost the sight in one eye. In one battle, Armour single-handedly captured a German tank. When the commander of the tank refused to surrender, Armour strangled him to death with his bare hands.

Armour remained a viable tournament attraction into the 1950s, when George S. May tried to get him to play in his World Championship of Golf, a Chicago-area tournament that offered far and away the richest purse in the world. Armour was agreeable enough until he learned that May required players to wear numbers pinned to their backs so that the large but generally golf-ignorant galleries could identify the players.

"The last number I wore was in a [World War I] German prisoner-of-war camp," he said. "I won't wear another."

Late in his playing career and for the rest of his life, Armour had a healthy—some would say unhealthy—thirst. For a long period of time, his routine of choice would be a scotch and soda, followed by bromo seltzer, a chaser he'd determine as the mood struck him, and finally a gin buck. After pausing to catch his breath, he'd start all over again. Naturally, his friends became concerned.

"Tommy better watch it," said Walter Hagen. "That bromo seltzer is going to kill him."

Whatever his particular fancy in drink was on any given day, Armour would never let plain, unadulterated water pass his lips. Why not? he was often asked.

"Fish **** in it" was his reply.

Following a brilliant playing career that saw him with a British Open, a U.S. Open, and a PGA Championship—just for highlights—Tommy Armour became a celebrated teaching professional, most notably at Winged Foot Golf Club, outside New York City. Armour could be gruff and imperious, but he had a keen eye for both talent and the golf swing. Beginners and pros alike sought out his advice and opinions.

One day a promising young player on the PGA Tour visited Winged Foot, and Armour went out to check out the man's game. After watching the player spray one drive after another, Armour had seen enough and went back to the clubhouse.

"What do you think, Tommy?" he was asked. "He's got a beautiful swing, doesn't he?"

"Oh yes, it's beautiful," Armour replied. "The problem is, it doesn't work."

Tommy Armour was a machine gunner in the British army during World War I. During one engagement, he suffered a shrapnel wound that cost him his sight in one eye.

One day, playing a tournament in the States, he drew a young man for a caddie who was nervous about working for such a great player. At one point during the match it began to rain, and the caddie pulled Armour's umbrella from his bag. As he did, he hit Armour in the face with the umbrella.

"Son, I only have one eye as it is, and if you poke that one out I'm going to have a hard time finding my wallet," Armour said.

AUGUSTA NATIONAL GOLF CLUB

Clifford Roberts is widely, and justifiably, credited with making Augusta National and the Masters the golf institutions they are today. When it came to the tournament, Roberts was a man who seldom took no for an answer.

One year he wanted to shift the tournament's dates, so it was played slightly earlier in April.

"The problem, Cliff," a committee member said, "is that means we'll finish on Easter Sunday."

"Well, who's in charge of scheduling Easter this year?" Roberts asked. "We'll get them to move it."

One year during the Masters, Clifford Roberts heard reports that some people in the gallery were making a lot of noise and bothering the players. Roberts drove out to investigate; when he got there, he discovered that the culprits were comedian and television star Jackie Gleason and some of his friends. Roberts took their badges and ordered the Pinkerton guards to escort them off the property.

"This is the Augusta National, not Broadway," he told Gleason.

Augusta National and CBS operate under a series of one-year contracts. This gives the club enormous leverage when it comes to making suggestions on how the telecasts might be improved.

One year it occurred to Roberts that someone of unusual stature was needed to open the telecast. But whomever he had in mind was a far cry from the person CBS proposed: Ed Sullivan, whose variety show was one of the longest-running hits on the CBS schedule.

"Ed Sullivan?" Roberts replied. "Never. Why, the man has monkey acts on his show."

Roberts was a brilliant investor who made millions in the stock market. Because he was very fond of Byron Nelson, he offered to help Nelson with his investments. When Nelson told him of his plans to eventually retire from golf and buy a ranch in Texas, Roberts was skeptical. Still, Nelson was determined, and in 1946 he virtually retired from competitive golf.

Several years later, he got a phone call from Roberts.

"Byron, somebody just told me that Ben Hogan and some partners are building a golf course a few miles from your ranch," Roberts said. "Is that correct?"

Byron said that it was.

"They tell me that Ben and his people bought twenty-five hundred acres and they paid $3,500 an acre," Roberts said.

"I believe that's right," Byron said.

"Didn't you once tell me that you paid just $82 an acre for your ranch?" Roberts asked.

"That's right," Byron said.

"Byron, the next time we sit down to discuss your investments, remind me to treat you with more respect," Roberts said.

Even his friends used words like "stern" and "autocratic" to describe Cliff Roberts, but the bottom line was that he loved Augusta National and the Masters and was willing to do whatever he thought best to improve both the club and the tournament that made it famous.

During one Masters, Roberts walked up toward the clubhouse and started through the front door. He was stopped by an imposing security guard.

"Excuse me, sir, do you have a badge?" the guard asked.

"I'm Clifford Roberts," he said and started to walk around the guard, who again blocked his path.

"Yes, Mr. Roberts, but do you have a badge?" the guard said firmly but politely.

"You don't seem to understand," Roberts said icily. "I'm Clifford Roberts."

"Yes, Mr. Roberts," the guard said. "I understand that, but do you have a badge? If you do, I'll be happy to let you into the clubhouse."

With that, Roberts turned and walked back to his cabin. He returned a few minutes later with his badge and showed it to the guard.

"Yes sir, Mr. Roberts," the guard said as he opened the door. "Thank you very much, and you have a nice day."

Roberts stared at the man, his face pinched and his eyes narrowing.

"What's your name?" Roberts demanded.

The guard answered, no doubt with more than a little nervousness in his voice.

"Fine," Roberts said as he walked past the man. "This job is yours for as long as you want it."

Masters champions—by club policy they are never referred to as "past champions"—are allowed to play the course whenever they like. But there are certain limitations, as Arnold Palmer found out after his 1958 victory when he brought his father, Deacon, down to play.

When they arrived, Cliff Roberts took Arnold aside and gave him the facts of life, so to speak, at Augusta National.

"Arnie, we're glad to have you play anytime you'd like, but your father can't play unless he has a member with him," Roberts said. "I'm afraid that's one of our rules."

Of course, it's fair to say that they didn't have a tough time scraping up a member to show the Palmers around the place.

On another occasion, Roberts even overruled Bob Jones when it came to a question of the club's rules.

One year, on the day after the Masters, some writers who were his close friends stopped by to see Jones. As their visit wound down, Jones invited the men to go out and play the virtually deserted par-3 course. As they were preparing to leave, Clifford Roberts arrived. When he learned of Jones's invitation, he begged to differ.

"Bob, surely you know the rule about guest play," he said. "All guests must play with a member."

Jones, confined to a wheelchair because of his illness, asked if an exception couldn't be made just this once. Roberts was not a man for making exceptions, especially when it came to the rules at Augusta National.

That left just one alternative. Roberts, who was recovering from surgery, would play with the writers.

Six holes later, he'd had enough and walked in, leaving the writers to finish unchaperoned.

Once again, history had been made at Augusta National.

Clifford Roberts had a reputation as a dour, stern autocrat who believed in the old maxim that there are only two ways to do things. "My way or no way."

In truth, Roberts was remarkably open to suggestions about how Augusta National and the Masters might be improved. And while it's certainly true that he wore neither his sense of humor nor compassion on his sleeve, there is evidence that he occasionally was capable of exhibiting both virtues.

On one occasion, in answer to a question from a writer, Roberts began by noting, "As Jesus said, and I agree . . ." and then went on and offered up a story from the Bible to make his point.

At the time, writers didn't think it was odd that Roberts would invoke Jesus' name, although some were surprised that the answer wasn't "As I've said, and Jesus agrees. . . ."

Nevertheless, at the club's annual Members Jamboree that year, a brief film was shown that made light of Roberts's biblical reference and put his standing at the club in perspective.

The film showed Roberts hitting a shot from the 16th tee, followed by the ball going into the hole for an ace. Roberts and his caddie then walked toward the pond fronting the green, where a narrow deck had been placed just under the waterline.

With Handel's "Messiah" playing in the background, Roberts walked out onto the submerged deck; in the film he appeared to be walking on water. A few steps out, he motioned for his skeptical caddie to follow. Naturally, the caddie began dropping deeper and deeper into the water as Roberts looked on from above. Just as it appeared that the caddie was about to go under, a graphic reading "Oh, Ye of Little Faith" came on the screen.

It brought the house down, and no one laughed longer or harder than Clifford Roberts.

One year British writer and television commentator Henry Longhurst fell ill and was taken to a local hospital. While in the hospital, he told some of his fellow writers that he was worried he would be unable to pay for his treatment.

Like everything else at Augusta, word of Longhurst's plight got back to Roberts, who quietly called in one of Longhurst's friends.

"Please tell Henry not to worry about his hospital expenses," Roberts said. "They will all be taken care of."

One of the biggest stories in the early days of the Masters was the Calcutta, where people would bet—often enormous sums—on their favorite players.

In 1946, Herman Keiser went to the big Calcutta party and saw that the odds on his winning were 20 to 1. A frugal man by nature, he sprang for a mere $20. He shot 68-69 in the first two rounds to take a five-shot lead over Ben Hogan, who was in second place.

The next morning, the two men running the Calcutta approached Keiser and told him there had been a huge amount of money bet on Hogan. One member alone had bet $40,000 on Hogan.

"They asked if there was anything they could do to help me out," Keiser remembers. "I thought about it for a minute and then asked them if I could get $50 down on me at the same 20-to-1 odds. I told them that if I couldn't hang on to a five-shot lead, I didn't deserve to win, Hogan or no Hogan. They let me make the bet."

He was paired with Byron Nelson in the final round and hit the pin with his approach to the final hole. The ball stopped thirty feet from the cup.

"Herman, is it true that you haven't three-putted once this week?" Nelson asked as they walked toward the green.

"Yep, but I've still got some work left," Keiser said.

Naturally, he three-putted the hole.

"Poor Byron was beside himself," says Keiser. "He was sure he'd jinxed me and cost me the tournament. He must have apologized a dozen times."

Keiser was sitting with his friend Henry Picard in the clubhouse as Hogan played the 18th, tied with Keiser for the lead.

"Let's go watch and see how Ben does," said Picard.

"No, thanks, you go watch and let me know," said Keiser. A few minutes later, Picard came back into the clubhouse.

"He made a heck of a putt, Herman—for a five."

Keiser won $1,500—and a healthy Calcutta payoff.

One year at the Champions' Dinner, a player was discussing the short but difficult par-4 3rd hole with Bob Jones. He said the hole bothered him because he felt he should come off of it with a birdie, and yet he was always relieved to make a par.

"But you're not supposed to make a 3 there," Jones said, grinning. "There are just some holes that are supposed to be par 4s, no matter how short they might be."

The Masters is known as the "toughest ticket in sports," and with good reason. The club stopped taking names for the waiting list several years ago. Scalpers can make a fortune selling tickets. People resort to all sorts of schemes to get their hands on a badge.

A few years ago, a man was whiling away an evening at one of the many bars that dot Washington Road near Augusta National. As the night wore on, he struck up a conversation with a woman and, naturally, one thing led to another. Soon they were back at his hotel room.

After a few minutes, he excused himself and went into the bathroom. When he came out, the woman was gone. In a panic, he quickly searched his room.

His wallet was there and no money had been taken.

His car keys were still on the dresser, and so was his gold Rolex watch.

He assumed the woman had simply gotten cold feet and left. For a moment he began to relax. Then he realized what was missing. His clubhouse badge for the Masters.

The Masters wasn't always so popular. In the first year, the members had to pass a hat to cover the purse. For many years the tickets were priced at $3, which Clifford Roberts felt wasn't enough. He wanted to raise the price to $5, but other members of the tournament committee were afraid that might be too steep an increase. To no one's surprise, the prices were raised.

On the first day of the tournament, Roberts and another committee member stood on the clubhouse porch and watched the galleries jam their way down Magnolia Lane.

"Five dollars, five dollars, five dollars," Roberts said as the people walked past.

The greens at Augusta National, with their severe slopes and undulations as well as their traditional speed and firmness, are what make the course such a great test of golf. Every year, it seems, a new horror story is written during the Masters by some poor player who comes to disaster on the putting surfaces.

Bill Hyndman, one of America's most successful amateurs, is surely a case in point. In the 1959 Masters he putted his ball off the 11th green and into the water.

"Bill," said his playing partner, Lloyd Mangrum, "that was the dumbest putt I ever saw."

In 1972 Ben Crenshaw came to Augusta National to play in his first Masters. He was twenty-one years old and one of the finest amateurs in the nation.

The traditions of the game had always been important to Ben, and playing in the Masters—where fellow Texans Ben Hogan, Byron Nelson, and Jimmy Demaret had dominated—was the culmination of a long-held dream.

Ben opened with a first-round 73. As he left the scorer's tent and made his way to the clubhouse, he ran into Clifford Roberts.

"How did you enjoy your first round in the Masters, Ben?" Roberts asked.

"Very much, Mr. Roberts," Crenshaw replied.

"That's fine, Ben," said Roberts. "And I think you'll enjoy it a lot more if you'll go get a haircut."

The caddies at Augusta have long been recognized as a colorful bunch. One time a new member was hosting a group of guests and was being a little hard on the caddies. His mood wasn't helped any by the swarms of gnats that seemed to follow him around the course.

"What the hell are these things?" the man finally raged in frustration.

"They's called jackass flies," said one of the caddies.

"Why's that?" the member asked.

"'Cause they's usually be around jackasses," explained the caddie.

"Are you saying I'm a jackass?" said the member.

"No, sir," said the caddie. "I'm just sayin' they don't seem to know the difference."

Until 1990, when Ron Townsend became the first African-American member of Augusta National, the club had been widely criticized for the lack of diversity among its membership. Even a few years later, members would occasionally make embarrassing faux pas when it came to the matter of race.

In 1995, there was a lot of speculation concerning how Tiger Woods, then the U.S. Amateur champion, would fare at the Masters. A longtime Augusta member was standing near the clubhouse when a tall, dark-skinned player approached.

"Hello," said the member, extending his hand. "You must be Tiger Woods. We've heard a lot about you, and I want to personally welcome you here to Augusta National and the Masters."

"No, sir," said the player, shaking the man's hand. "I'm Vijay Singh from Fiji."

People collect all kinds of memorabilia from the Masters. They leave the course loaded down with shirts, sweaters, photographs, and all sorts of other wonderful stuff. In 1997, Masters rookie Paul Stankowski was no different. Well, actually he was a little bit more creative than most.

After missing the cut, he took a cup with a Masters logo on the side, went out to the course, and filled it with sand from one of the bunkers.

"I mean, you never know if you'll be invited back, right?" he told a reporter.

Jack Stephens, who succeeded Hord Hardin as chairman of the Augusta National Golf Club in 1992, is one of the wealthiest men in America. His fortune is measured in the billions of dollars, and yet he has never forgotten his modest upbringing in Arkansas.

One day Stephens set out to play at Augusta with a foursome that included a guest who had just met Stephens for the first time. When they got to the first tee and agreed to a match, the guest was astonished that Stephens insisted on playing a $2 Nassau.

"Two dollars!" the man said. "Why, I never play for less than a $100 Nassau."

He remarked on it more than once during the match, and when they returned to the clubhouse to play gin, he was even more incredulous upon learning that Stephens played for a penny a point.

"Usually we play for a dollar a point at my club," the man said.

"How much are you worth?" Stephens asked the man in his slow Southern drawl.

"About $12 million," said the man.

"Let's cut the cards for it," said Stephens, absolutely serious about the bet.

The game proceeded smoothly from there . . . at a penny a point.

One of Jack Stephens's predecessors as chairman of Augusta National was the autocratic Clifford Roberts, who, along with Bobby Jones, founded the club in the early 1930s.

One of Roberts's closest friends and a prominent member of Augusta National was President Dwight D. Eisenhower. Ike, a passionate if not terribly skilled player, was particularly vexed by a large tree that blocked the left side of the 17th fairway not far from the tee. The President drove into it so often that it became known as "Ike's Tree." He wanted it cut down. Roberts wouldn't hear of it.

One year, at a meeting of the club's membership, Roberts gave a brief report on the state of the club and then asked if there were any questions.

"Cliff, about that tree on 17," Ike began.

"If that's the only question, I move we adjourn," said Roberts, interrupting Ike and ending the meeting. At Augusta, after all, there are presidents and then there was Clifford Roberts.

In 1959, in the midst of Arnold Palmer's remarkable string of wins in the Masters, a quiet unassuming player named Art Wall won the Masters by making birdies on five of the last six holes. Wall had already won eight tournaments in his career, but he was best known for his uncanny record on par 3s.

On the evening before the final round that year, Wall attended a cocktail party and was approached by a local resident.

"Ain't you Art Wall?" the man asked.

"Yes," said Wall shyly.

"Ain't you the guy what's made all those holes in one?"

"Yes sir, thirty-four of them," said Wall.

"Who you tryin' to kid," said the man. "Bobby [Jones] ain't made but three."

In the 1978 Masters, Japan's Tommy Nakajima was playing well until disaster struck on the par-5 13th hole. By the time he was finished with the hole, he had used up thirteen shots and had managed to shoot himself out of the tournament. Later, in an interview, he was asked if he had lost his composure.

"No lose composure," he said, ruefully shaking his head. "Lose count."

Finally, in 1963 Tony Lema came to the 12th after missing a short putt on 10 and three-putting 11. His tee shot stopped eight feet from the hole, but he missed the putt, which prompted a glittering display of verbal pyrotechnics. Embarrassed by his outburst, he turned to his playing companion, Chen Ching-po from Nationalist China, and apologized.

"It's all right," said Chen. "If I only knew those words I would use them myself."

Here's a good trivia question: Who was the first player to win a Green Jacket? If your answer is Horton Smith, who won the first Masters in 1934, you're wrong. The first year the winner received a Green Jacket was 1949, and it went to Sam Snead for the first of three Masters victories.

AUSSIE RULES

The 1988 World Cup of Golf was played at Royal Melbourne, whose two wonderful courses were designed by Dr. Alister Mackenzie. The tournament attracted writers from around the world, who were naturally charmed by their Australian hosts.

One afternoon, as an American writer followed Ben Crenshaw—the eventual winner of the individual title—he fell into a conversation with a group of locals. Before long, they had extended an invitation for the American to join them at their club for a round of golf.

"Thanks a lot," the American said. "What time should I be there?"

"Oh, we don't play 'til after four or five," one of the Australians said.

"In the afternoon?" the American asked.

"No, mate," said another of the Australians. "Beers."

It's no secret that golf is a good way for businesses to promote their goods or services. But at the 1985 New South Wales Open in Australia, a local official, Paul Smith, came up with a unique way to pick up a little publicity for his firm.

Mr. Smith sponsored a hole-in-one contest on a par 3. Anyone making an ace had a choice between winning £5,000 or a complete, prepaid send-off by Mr. Smith's highly regarded funeral home.

Talk about a decision that will weigh heavily on your mind.

SEVE BALLESTEROS

According to those who know him, Seve Ballesteros has burned to be a champion almost from the moment the youngster picked up an old 3-iron and began hitting golf balls along the beaches near his home. It was beyond ambition, even beyond the considerable ambitions that drive other champions to succeed. It was as though he had to prove something—to himself and to others. Maybe he wanted to prove that a Spanish golfer could beat the best the rest of the world could offer. Maybe it had its roots deeper than that, in Spain's fairly rigid caste system.

Whatever the reason, Seve was uncommonly driven and competitive. After his first big tournament, the Spanish PGA Championship, one of his brothers found him sobbing and disconsolate in the locker room.

He had lost.

He was seventeen.

When Seve Ballesteros tied for second at the 1976 British Open at Royal Birkdale, the nineteen-year-old Spaniard was instantly billed as the "Next Great Player." And while he was certainly talented and charismatic, the verdict remained out for more than a few writers—at least until he went head-to-head with a forty-seven-year-old Arnold Palmer at the Lancome Trophy tournament in Paris a short while after the British Open.

After falling 4-down, Ballesteros staged a magnificent comeback over the final nine holes. He birdied 12 and 13 and, after making another birdie on 15, the match was all square. After he birdied 17, he knew he had broken Palmer's spirit.

"I knew I had won the match when I saw him shake his head and look at the ground," said Ballesteros later. "That was when I knew I finally had him beaten."

For his part, Palmer was both gracious and prescient in his praise of Ballesteros—who would go on to win three British Opens and two Masters.

"I threw everything I could at him," said Palmer. "I hit every green on the back nine and he never flinched. Not once."

Seve Ballesteros is nothing if not an inventive scrambler. It's fair to say he can hit shots most other players can't even imagine. Very often, it's been the key to his success.

At the 1980 Masters, Seve hit a towering hook on the 17th hole that came to rest on the 7th green.

"Nice drive, Seve," joked David Graham, who was preparing to putt when Seve's ball bounced past. "Would you like to play through?"

Typical of Seve, he lofted a 7-iron over the bordering trees. The ball wound up fifteen feet from the hole, and he made a birdie.

He wound up winning his first Green Jacket by four strokes.

Seve Ballesteros's genius for shotmaking, particularly around the greens, is unchallenged. But there are times when he leaves even the most gimlet-eyed professionals shaking their heads in awe and admiration.

"I was playing with Seve one year at Augusta," remembers Raymond Floyd. "He missed the 4th green and had to come over a bunker, land the ball on the downslope, and try to keep it on the green. Not only did he pull the shot off, he actually stopped it short of the hole. I couldn't believe he even tried the shot. I dropped my club and applauded him. To this day, I tell people I was there and I saw it, but I still don't believe my eyes."

Even in his prime, Seve's driving left something to be desired. Witness the final round of the 1979 British Open at Royal Lytham and St. Annes, when he beat Ben Crenshaw and Jack Nicklaus by three strokes.

On the 16th hole, Ballesteros blew the ball way down the right side, through the rough, and into a car park some twenty-five yards wide of the fairway.

He made a birdie three, threading his second shot—a breathtaking pitch-and-run between two bunkers. Lee Trevino called it one of the greatest shots he's ever seen.

On the 18th hole, Ballesteros ripped a drive to the left side of the hole.

"What's over there?" he asked his caddie, Dave Musgrove.

"I don't know," Dave said. "It's the only place on the course we haven't been this week."

During a round in the 1988 Masters, Seve Ballesteros—one of the game's finest putters—somehow managed to four-putt the treacherous 16th green. When he was brought into the pressroom for his postround interview, he was asked how the disaster occurred.

"It was easy," he explained. "I miss the hole. I miss the hole. I miss the hole. I hole it."

"Seve has a particularly mischievous sense of humor," the late Peter Dobereiner once recalled. "One day I had happened to mention in my newspaper column that Seve was driving the ball wildly, even by his unusually erratic standards. That I had the statistics to prove this mattered little to Seve. The day the column appeared, he sought me out after his round to inform me that he had missed just two fairways, and those by merely the smallest of margins. These updates continued daily for what seemed like weeks, until he had made his point—with tiresome regularity."

Although Seve was born and raised in Spain, his English is exceptional. Occasionally his accent has created some confusion among the press. A case in point was the time a CBS Sports crew interviewed him following a round at the Masters. He had been penalized for a mistake on the 13th hole and was asked to explain what happened.

"I hit the ball into the hazard but I did not know it was a hazard and when I ground my club it was penalty," he said.

With his accent, "hazard" came out sounding like "cazzard." This led to a frantic phone call to the Butler Cabin studio from one of the editing trucks just before CBS's late-night highlights show was set to begin taping.

"Does anybody up there know what the hell a 'cazzard' is?" asked one of the crew.

BRIAN BARNES

There never has really been any question about Brian Barnes's ability—although his ability to focus on the job at hand has occasionally come into question. But on September 21, 1975, Barnes proved just what he could do when he set his mind to it.

The scene was the Ryder Cup matches at Laurel Valley Golf Club in Ligonier, Pennsylvania. Barnes faced Jack Nicklaus in the morning matches and won 4 and 2. This was considered an upset of enormous proportions because 1975 was the year Nicklaus had won both the Masters and the PGA Championship and finished a shot back in the British Open and two shots back in the U.S. Open.

"When we came to the first tee for the afternoon matches, Jack said to me, 'You've beaten me once but there ain't no way you're going to beat me again.' He started out birdie, birdie, birdie, and I didn't think that I would. But I did. I know how bloody mad he was, but he never showed it and congratulated me very warmly when it was over."

THE BAUER SISTERS

Alice and Marlene Bauer, daughters of a teaching professional from Eureka, South Dakota, were charter members of the LPGA. They joined the Tour in 1950, when Marlene was only sixteen and her sister was twenty-two. Their talent, along with their youth and striking good looks, made them immediate drawing cards on the fledgling tour.

A few eyebrows, however, were raised when Marlene married her sister's ex-husband shortly after their divorce. The sisters' marital ups and downs, although painful for them, at least kept the struggling tour on the sports pages of the country's newspapers.

Not long after her divorce Alice remarried, but this marriage wasn't destined for a long run either.

"We were incompatible," she says. "We both loved spectator sports. The problem was he was a spectator and I was a sport."

37

Patty Berg

By any standard, Patty Berg is one of the greatest players in the history of women's golf. She was one of the founding members of the Ladies Professional Golf Association and won fifty-seven tournaments.

More important than her victories, however, were her tireless efforts in promoting golf. Under the sponsorship of Wilson Sporting Goods since 1940, she traveled the country—indeed, the world—giving exhibitions. No audience was ever too small, and her enthusiasm never failed. Even into her eighties, she's capable of delivering stem-winding speeches that would do any old-time politician credit.

When World War II broke out, Patty Berg served as a lieutenant in the Marine Corps. When the war ended, she resumed her playing career and won the inaugural U.S. Women's Open Championship in 1946.

At the awards ceremony, she was handed a trophy and a check for $500. She kept the trophy but returned the money.

"Please use it to help promote junior golf," she said.

TOMMY BOLT

Leading the 1958 U.S. Open, Tommy Bolt stormed into the press-room one day looking for Tom Lobaugh, who was covering the championship for a local paper, the *Tulsa World*. Summoning all his righteous indignation, he berated Lobaugh for reporting that Bolt was forty-nine instead of thirty-nine.

"Sorry, Tommy, it was a typo," said Lobaugh.

"Typo, my ass," said Bolt. "It was a perfect four and a perfect nine."

Tommy Bolt was playing in a tournament in Philadelphia when he came to a particularly difficult par 3, with the pin tucked to the back left of a two-tiered green. Most players were willing to settle for a par by playing a 6-iron, landing the ball on the front of the green, and then taking two putts and moving on to the next hole. Not Bolt, one of the game's finest shotmakers. He knocked down a 4-iron, landing the ball short of the green and watching it run up within a few feet of the hole. There was a large gallery around the green but very little reaction to what was plainly a work of art.

"Son," he said to his caddie, "old Tom's hearing's gone but I can still see. Now you just go on up there and pick up that ******* ball. We're through. If they don't appreciate old Tom here, old Tom ain't playing."

Tommy Bolt never believed he got as many good breaks as bad. One day, after missing yet another short putt, he tossed down his putter and glared at the heavens.

"So it's me again, huh, Lord?" he grimaced. "Why don't you just come down here and we'll play? And bring that kid of yours. I'll play your best ball."

Bolt had a well-deserved reputation for throwing clubs, although he always protested that if he threw and broke as many clubs as people claimed, "the entire damned equipment business in this country would have spent their time making clubs for old Tom, don't ya see?"

Anyway, the story goes that in one tournament Tommy came into the final hole facing a 120-yard shot to the green. His caddie handed him a 3-iron.

"What the hell is this, son?" he fumed. "I can hit this club almost 200 yards."

"I know, sir," the caddie said. "But it's the only iron you have left. You broke all the rest."

By the way, Tommy always takes credit for giving Arnold Palmer a valuable lesson when Palmer first came out on tour.

"I had to take the boy aside and teach him how to throw a club," recalls Tommy. "He was so innocent he'd toss them backwards. I had to explain that you'd get worn out walking back to pick them up. You have to throw them in front of you if you're going to be a professional."

Tommy Bolt was born in Haworth, Oklahoma. One day a reporter asked him what city Haworth was near.

"City!" exclaimed Tommy. "Hell, it was so far out in the sticks that we had to pipe sunlight in."

"One year Tommy was playing at Colonial and he hit a bad approach to one of the greens," Dave Marr remembered. "That was all it took. He snapped the club over his knee and sent both ends flying. Dan Jenkins wrote about it, and when Tommy read Dan's piece he took issue—and let Dan know about it. When Dan pointed out that he was right there when Tom erupted, Tommy had an answer for him.

" 'It was a 5-iron, not a 4,' he said. 'Why can't you guys ever get your facts straight?' "

Like anyone else, occasionally the frustrations of a round would build up and get to be too much for Tommy Bolt.

At one tournament, the poor conditions of the greens, coupled with some uninspired play on his part, sent him over the edge. On one of the closing holes, his ball came to rest on the edge of the green, near the gallery.

As Tommy knelt behind the ball, lining up his putt, a man in the gallery kept moving from side to side, trying to get a better view. Unfortunately, his shadow kept moving back and forth over Tommy's ball.

"Could you stand still?" Bolt asked the man. "Even old Tom can't read weeds in the dark."

One day, while playing in a pro-am, Bolt drew a partner who was not a very good player in the first place. Naturally, playing with Tommy made him nervous, which only made things worse. The man shanked every shot on the first hole. Embarrassed, he turned to Bolt and apologized, asking if Tommy had any advice for him.

"Yes," said Tommy. "Just aim left and allow for it."

It's not that Tommy didn't try to help his amateur partners. One story holds that Tommy once tried to fix a pro-am partner's poor grip.

"With a grip like that, I don't expect you hit it very straight," Tommy said.

"Well, yes, Tommy," he replied. "As a matter of fact, I'm very straight with every club."

"Then you can't possibly hit it very far," said Tommy.

"Actually, I'm one of the longest players at my club," came the reply.

"Well, you must play a lot then, son," said Tommy, becoming increasingly frustrated that his attempts at instruction were getting so complicated.

"No, Tom," said the amateur. "I hardly play at all."

"Well, that explains it," said Tommy walking away. "The more you play with a grip like that, the worse you're going to get."

When Tom Weiskopf came out on tour, Tommy took him under his wing. Once, when playing in Ohio, Weiskopf arranged for a friend from Ohio State, Ed Sneed, to join them for a round.

When they reached a par 3, Sneed hit a draw that landed on the green, bounced once, and ran into the rough.

"My, my, Edgar, that was a fine shot you played there," Tommy said, as he strolled off the green. "Those old right-to-lefts will run on you, won't they Ed?"

Along with his uncanny shotmaking ability and his mercurial personality, Bolt was one of the game's finest dressers. He once told a young Tom Weiskopf that "if you lose your crease, son, you're allowed to walk in."

Tommy proved he was as good as his word one year in the Houston Open, which, as is often the case, was played in unremitting downpours. In the second round, Bolt turned to his playing partners and said, "Here I am ruining a $100 pair of shoes, a $110 cashmere sweater, and a $65 pair of slacks. Hell, I'm ruining more than I can win." With that, he walked in.

45

Tommy Bolt always took a lot of pride in his sense of style. In fact, the easiest way to get a rise out of him was to tell him how much you admired Doug Sanders's kaleidoscopic sartorial sense.

One evening Tommy arrived for a Legends of Golf dinner in a magnificently tailored, white silk, double-breasted jacket, dark slacks, and a matching tie and handkerchief.

"Tommy," a friend told him, "I just want your old clothes."

"Can't have them, son," said Tommy. "I give my castoffs to Doug Sanders."

One time in a pro-am, one of Tommy's partners faced a particularly difficult shot. He motioned for Tom to come over and asked how he should play the shot.

"Under an assumed name," Tom said.

"Tommy never thought he was a good putter, and he never believed that the breaks evened out," remembers Bob Rosburg. "I was paired with Tommy and Bud Holscher one year in Las Vegas. Tommy had hit it close all day and never got anything out of it. Every time he missed a putt, he got hotter and hotter. Finally, near the end of the round, Bud had a two- or three-footer for par. He tucked the putter under his arm and was fishing around in his pocket for a coin to mark his ball with. The putter dropped out of his arm, hit the ball, and knocked it into the hole. It was all Tommy could do not to just walk in."

During a rain-plagued tournament, Tommy, along with many of the other players, protested that the final round should be called off because of the soggy conditions. Finally, it got to be too much for him, and he walked off the course after missing another in a series of short putts.

"It's not that I'm a bad putter," he explained. "It's just that I've never been very good at reading mud."

Tommy was playing in the Crosby one year when the weather was particularly bad, even by the freakish standards of the Monterey

Peninsula. Playing along through the rain, sleet, and high winds, Tommy spotted Bing Crosby's house just off the 12th green.

"I wish I had a .45," Tommy said. "I'd go in there, put it to that old crooner's head, and force him to come on out here and see how much he enjoys making all these 6s, 7s, and 8s."

Jimmy Breslin, the celebrated New York City–based newspaper columnist, got his start as a sportswriter by covering the 1958 U.S. Open—probably one of the few times he ever set foot on a golf course.

He followed Tommy Bolt in the last round of the Open, and after Bolt hit his drive on the final hole, Breslin approached him with a suggestion:

"You're going to win anyway," he said. "Go ahead and throw a club."

Tommy Bolt's greatest win came in the 1958 U.S. Open at Southern Hills. He had been playing very well coming into the tournament, and as the Open went on he seemed to gain confidence. It wasn't until later that he revealed he had been carrying a card on which was written this message: "God, grant me the serenity to accept the things I cannot change, the courage to change the things I can, and the wisdom to know the difference."

Whenever he got a bad bounce or hit a poor shot—and there weren't many that week—he would quietly pull out the card and ponder its message.

THE BOYS

I can't prove this, but I'm willing to bet that every club in America has a group of guys like "The Boys" at my club in Connecticut. The Boys are mainstays of the place. They rarely miss a round of golf on the weekend. They're rarely lacking for an opinion on how the place is being run. The club's restaurant/bar budget couldn't come close to balancing without them, and they provide whatever club they belong to—whether it's a Winged Foot, a Garden City, or wherever—with much of the club's character. You don't have to be single to be one of The Boys—although it helps. Failing that, an understanding wife will do. My friend, Dennis Powell, is one of The Boys.

At one time we had a locker-room attendant who, it's safe to say, didn't specialize in the care and upkeep of shoes. Given his job description, this was something of a problem.

One afternoon, Dennis arrived with three guests. Since he worked on Wall Street and these were important clients, he wasn't taking any chances.

"Hi," he said to the attendant as they entered the locker room. "Here's $20. Don't touch the shoes."

All this might seem excessive, unless you understand what he had been through when he visited another club for a tournament. I should note here that The Boys spend much of their time playing in tournaments all over the place. The host pros love them because they always spend lavishly on shirts, sweaters, bags, and all that stuff. It helps to have discretionary income if you're going to be one of The Boys.

"I showed up at this tournament with a shirt from Pine Valley, a belt from Merion, and a hat from Shinnecock," Dennis said. "When

I was changing my shoes, the locker-room guy asked me how everything was at my club. I asked him how he knew what club I was from.

" 'Your shoes,' he said."

If you're one of The Boys, there are few fates in the world worse than playing golf with a woman. In fact, there may be nothing in life—short of an IRS audit—that holds more terror. For them, just being around a club during a mixed tournament is a near-death experience.

One day Dennis and some friends were out on Long Island where they came across a place that offered bungee jumping. Now, even though it was late in the day and more than a few beers had gone by the wayside, even Dennis could see that bungee jumping wasn't a pastime designed for a middle-aged man. And no amount of cajoling or insulting was going to change his mind—until he received the ultimate threat.

"Dennis, you wussie, either go up there and jump or you've got to play golf with me this weekend," said a woman friend.

And that was Dennis Powell's introduction to bungee jumping.

The Boys love almost everything about golf, except that it sometimes involves playing with women. It's not that they have anything against women, per se. It's just that in the best of all worlds, the golf course would simply be an extension of the men's locker room. Or better yet, the men's grill.

One day my friend Dennis Powell was asked if he'd be willing to fill a spot in a mixed tournament. He politely declined.

"There's two things I don't do," he said. "Dance with boys and play golf with girls."

If you're one of The Boys, the highlights of the golf season include the big three-day member-guest tournament and the club championships. Not so much because of the competition, but because they're perfect times to party.

One day a friend approached Dennis Powell and asked him how he stood in his match.

"I've got him right where I want him," Dennis said. "He's three up with three holes to go, and I'm out of beer."

It's not true that to be one of The Boys you have to work on Wall Street, but apparently it helps. And since Wall Street is, at its core, legalized gambling taken to the highest level, it only follows that The Boys love to have all sorts of bets and side bets going on the golf course. In fact, sometimes the betting scarcely leaves room for the golf itself.

"I was playing with Dennis one day, and when we finished the front nine he let us know how all the bets stood," remembers Tim Cassidy. "There was the front nine, the presses, the sandies, greenies, Watsons, Hogans, and everything else. When he got finished, I asked him what I shot.

" 'I don't know,' he said. 'There wasn't any room left on the card for the scores.' "

For The Boys, the fun and games don't end on the 18th green. Grillrooms and patios from coast to coast echo with the sound of dice landing on tables as players roll for drinks, sometimes for hours on end.

One afternoon I brought my son, Ben, then in second grade, to the course for some quality time together. We stopped by the patio to visit friends, and Ben became fascinated by the dice games.

The next day at school, his teacher asked the class if anyone had done anything over the weekend that they wished to share during show-and-tell. Ben raised his hand.

"Mr. Vanneck taught me how to roll for drinks," he said proudly.

For The Boys, the ideal club would have a course, a men's grill, a locker room, and not much else. A couple of tennis courts, perhaps, but definitely not a pool.

"I went to the pool once, but I hated it," Dennis Powell told a friend. "It reminded me of Vietnam—hot, noisy, and crowded. I never went back."

In recent years, the growing popularity of golf and the maturing of the baby-boom generation have led to longer and longer waiting lists at country clubs, particularly in the larger metropolitan areas.

Increasingly, many clubs have begun admitting "limited golf" members, who can play only at certain days and hours of the week. Eventually, as older members either leave a club or give up their golf privileges, people move up the waiting list to full golf status. Naturally, some people are more patient than others.

One of The Boys was on the waiting list for a full golf membership at a club in one of New York City's wealthiest suburbs. As he drove past the club on his way back from the train station early one summer evening, he noticed that the American flag was flying at half-mast. He turned into the parking lot and walked into the clubhouse. At the front desk he asked the receptionist the first question that had popped into his mind:

"Was he a golf member?"

JOHNNY BULLA

Johnny Bulla grew up in a strict Quaker family in Burlington, North Carolina. The family didn't have much money, so when the eleven-year-old learned he could make twenty-five cents a round caddying at a nearby golf course, he leapt at the chance—to the dismay of his parents.

"I'd go to church in the morning and then tell my parents I was going off to meditate in the woods," Bulla remembers. "I'd go off into the woods all right, and right to the golf course."

Soon he was hooked on the game and began playing in tournaments, often hitchhiking to the courses. This not only angered his mother, it worried her as well.

"If you play in a tournament and get killed in a car accident on Sunday when you should be at church, I'll never get over it," she told him.

"Well, if I get killed on a Monday, will you get over it?" he asked, logically enough.

53

Sam Snead and Johnny Bulla frequently traveled together. On one of their trips, they drove through Phoenix, which should in no way be confused with the Phoenix of today. It was basically a small outpost in the midst of a very large desert.

"Sambo, I'm gonna live here one day," he said.

"Are you crazy?" Sam said. "Rattlesnakes can't live here."

WALTER BURKEMO

Walter Burkemo was a marvelous player who won the 1953 PGA Championship and lost in the finals twice. One year, during the PGA, he was approached by a fan who asked a perplexing question.

"Mr. Burkemo," the fan said politely, "I was just wondering how come when you address the ball you sometimes take four waggles and other times you take five?"

Burkemo bogeyed the next three holes as he tried to figure out the answer himself.

Caddies

When Ben Hogan arrived at Carnoustie for the 1953 British Open, he drew a caddie by the name of Cecil Timms. While they were a successful team, it wasn't exactly a marriage made in heaven.

Hogan seldom spoke on the course. Timms never shut up.

Hogan put tins of hard candy in his bag to keep his energy up. Timms ate most of the candies.

Worst of all, when Hogan settled over a putt, Timms would cover his eyes.

Finally, it got to be too much for Hogan.

"Cecil, I want you to do three things for me," he said. "Stand still, keep your eyes open, and keep your mouth shut."

An American traveled to Scotland to try to qualify for the 1927 British Open at St. Andrews. When he reached the course, he was assigned a weathered, wizened old caddie who, despite the relatively warm weather, was wearing an old Chesterfield coat he claimed had been given to him by former British prime minister David Lloyd-George.

After a few holes, the American began to worry about the caddie's health and asked him if he was going to be able to finish his round.

"I'll be fine, sir," the caddie said. "I'm afraid I had a wee bit too much of the drink last night. It's funny how the drink creeps up on you sometimes. By the time I got home I was so drunk me own dog bit me."

An American came to St. Andrews and was looking forward to the experience of hiring one of the caddies he had heard so many stories about. Sadly, the experience didn't work out quite as he'd hoped.

For starters, the caddie was particularly dour and his obvious hangover wasn't helping matters. Standing on the first tee, he took one look at the American's large bag and slowly shook his head.

"Did you nae leave anything at home?" he growled.

Trying to be accommodating, the American took out his rain jacket and extra sweater and left them in the clubhouse.

So off they went, but despite the caddie's advice, the man was clearly baffled by the mysteries of the Old Course. To make matters worse, storm clouds blew in off the water and it began to rain heavily.

"Here, I'll take the bag," the American said. "You go back to the clubhouse and get my rain jacket and sweater."

That was the last straw.

The caddie dropped the bag and glared at the American.

"Get it yourself," he said. "I'm a caddie not a bloody Rin Tin Tin that you can send to go fetch."

Brad Faxon is a player who truly loves the game's traditions and its venerable old courses. Several years ago, he traveled to Scotland for the British Open, and while he was there, he took a side trip to Prestwick, the site of the first twelve British Opens. In fact, only Augusta National has hosted more major championships than Prestwick.

When he finished his round he asked his caddie, who had caddied there for decades, which was his favorite pub.

"The nearest one," the caddie said.

A group of wealthy Arab businessmen wearing traditional head-dresses arrived at the Old Course at St. Andrews for a round of golf. At the completion of his round, one handed his caddie, an elderly Scotsman, a generous tip.

"Thanks very much, your excellency," said the caddie. "And I hope your head feels better."

The greenside bunker on the 17th hole at the Old Course is one of the most feared and noteworthy hazards in the game. Years ago an American tourist came to the 17th at the close of what had already been a long and frustrating round. That he managed to wind up in the bunker came as no surprise to his caddie. Neither did the fact that he couldn't manage to extricate himself.

"What should I take?" he asked the caddie.

"How about the 7:30 train to Dundee?" came the reply.

Bobby Cruickshank came to Muirfield for the 1929 British Open and drew a seventy-year-old caddie, Willie Black. After hitting a good drive on the first hole of a practice round, Cruickshank asked Willie for a 2-iron.

"See here, sir," said Willie. "I'll give you the club, you just play the bloody shot."

On another occasion, Cruickshank was set to play his approach with a fairway wood. Suddenly, at the top of his backswing, Willie shouted, "Stop! We've changed our mind. We'll play the shot with an iron."

The Scots have a much simpler, almost reverential, approach to the game, unlike Americans, who complicate the game by mimicking the things they see the pros do on television—stuff that doesn't help their games but only manages to slow down play.

Take the story of the American who showed up at St. Andrews with his huge, heavy bag, high-tech clubs, and most fashionable clothes.

Upon reaching his opening drive, he reached down, clipped a bit of grass, and tossed it into the air to check the wind.

"What do you think?" he asked his caddie.

The caddie responded by mimicking the player and tossing the few blades of grass into the air.

"I think the wind's come up, governor," said the caddie. "You'd best take out your sweater."

Tip Anderson has achieved a certain renown as Arnold Palmer's longtime caddie in the British Open. It's not uncommon for players to ask Tip what Palmer would hit in a certain situation and then try the shot themselves.

In one case, a friend of Palmer's came to St. Andrews and drew Tip as a caddie. When they came to the 4th hole, he faced a long, difficult approach to the green. He asked for the same club Palmer had hit from that spot, but his ball came up forty yards short of the green.

"I can't believe Arnold got there with this club," he said to Tip.

"Oh, he didn't, sir," Tip said. "He came up well short, too."

Mad Mac was a Scottish caddie whose wardrobe consisted almost exclusively of a long, woolen overcoat that he wore regardless of the weather. He also favored a pair of binoculars without lenses, through which he'd study the line of a putt before announcing that it was "slightly straight."

A golfer was playing the 10th hole at Prestwick in Scotland—the Arrain hole—and as he stood on the tee he asked his caddie how long the hole was.

"It will take three fine shots to get there in two, sir," said the caddie.

60   An American arrived at St. Andrews anxiously looking forward to his first round on the Old Course. He had heard much about the course's infamous old caddies and was somewhat disappointed when he was assigned a youngster without much experience. Still, he resolved to make the best of it and was pleased with the boy's enthusiasm when the American hit a good drive on the opening hole.

When they reached his ball he asked the youngster how far he had to the green. The boy carefully studied the situation, a look of grim concentration on his face.

"I'd say about a two-minute walk, sir," he replied.

An American journeyed to Scotland on holiday, looking forward to experiencing all the pleasures of playing golf in the game's birth-place. One of the things he had heard much about were the Scottish caddies, who are well known for their eccentricities and their knowledge of the game.

Naturally, he was somewhat disappointed when he arrived at one course and was told that the only available caddie was a recent immigrant who didn't speak much English.

However, off they went, and for several holes the golfer and the caddie barely spoke. The caddie was polite and worked hard, but his inability to offer advice began to frustrate the golfer. Finally, after hitting a pretty good shot, the golfer turned to the caddie and asked what he thought. The caddie thought long and hard, trying desperately to come up with just the right words. Finally it all came together.

"Bloody fluke, sir," he said, beaming.

The Jigger Inn, next to the 17th hole at the Old Course at St. Andrews, is a favorite gathering spot for local caddies and tourists alike. One evening during the 1990 British Open, one of the former was regaling a group of the latter with stories about the Americans for whom he had caddied over the years. One story concerned a Yank whose interpretation of the rules was pretty liberal.

"He hit his drive off into the rough on the Road Hole over there," the caddie said. "We'd had a fair bit of rain and the rough was a little thicker than usual, so the ball was sitting down. He got to the ball before me and was pacing all about, testing the lie. I slowed down a bit to give him time, and when I finally reached the ball he asked me whether I thought it was a 4- or a 5-iron.

" 'Sir,' I said, 'you'd best hit the 5-iron. You're at least three stomps away from a 4-iron.' "

An American traveled to St. Andrews on holiday for a little golf. Although he enjoyed the Old Course, he was mystified by some of the bounces and breaks he witnessed around the greens. And although his caddie tried to help, there were times when he was as baffling as the greens themselves.

On the Road Hole, his approach missed the green, leaving a delicate and dangerous pitch. If it was misplayed there was a good chance the ball would run off the green and into the Hell Bunker. The man studied his shot from every angle, then asked his caddie what he thought the ball would do once it reached the hole.

"Well, sir, there's one thing for certain," the caddie said, peering over the golfer's shoulder as they both read the line. "When it slows down, it's really going to speed up."

Two American couples traveled to Scotland in September, usually the most beautiful time of the year to play the classic seaside courses. But as luck would have it, the weather was awful—cold and rainy with nothing encouraging in the forecast. Midway through yet another sopping-wet and chilly round, one of the women said to her caddie, "Isn't this weather unusual for this time of year?"

"Aye, that's the problem, ma'am," he said. "This isn't this time of year at all."

The final day of the Ryder Cup matches is always tense and exciting, but that was particularly true in 1995 at Oak Hill, when the Americans watched their lead disappear in the singles competition.

As one match came to the tee on the par-3 15th hole, the caddie for an American player searched for the yardage plate set into the ground. He finally located it, under the foot of a man wearing the blue European team jacket.

"Get the hell off that marker," the caddie said, glaring at the man, who immediately apologized.

After the players hit their tee shots, a man walked up to the caddie as he prepared to leave the tee.

"See here, young man," he said. "You can't talk to Prince Andrew that way."

After playing a round with a caddie who he thought was particularly incompetent, Tommy Bolt asked for a tour official to come give him a ruling.

"I know you can get fined for throwing a club," he said. "What I want to know is if you can get fined for throwing a caddie."

Dow Finsterwald, the 1958 PGA champion, was one of the favorites going into the 1960 U.S. Open at Cherry Hills. Playing the 16th hole in his first round, he asked his caddie what club he should hit for his second shot.

"Why should I bother?" the caddie said. "You haven't taken my advice yet."

Finsterwald glared at the caddie and then pulled a club from his bag.

"That's not enough," the caddie said.

Finsterwald used the club anyway, and he wasn't any too pleased when his ball came up short of the green.

The caddie never saw the 17th hole. Finsterwald fired him on the spot.

As twenty-year-old Francis Ouimet prepared to tee off in his historic playoff with Harry Vardon and Ted Ray in the 1913 U.S. Open at The Country Club in Brookline, Massachusetts, a friend, Frank Hoyt, tried to convince Ouimet to let him replace ten-year-old caddie Eddie Lowery, who had been with Ouimet throughout the championship. Despite offers of money and all sorts of pleading, Lowery tearfully insisted on being allowed to stay. Ouimet—facing the chance to not only win the Open in his own backyard but to become the first native-born American to win the championship—didn't have the heart to hurt the youngster.

As they stood on the first tee Ouimet was understandably nervous and more than a little overwhelmed. When it was his turn to play, Lowery handed him his driver and offered this simple piece of advice:

"Francis, be sure to keep your eye on the ball," he said.

"I had this boy caddying for me one year in Las Vegas," recalls Sam Snead. "He was a nice enough kid, but he didn't know beans about golf. I was playing a little money match in the practice round. I think it was Jerry Barber and me against Arnold Palmer and Dow Finsterwald. We were playing along just fine until we got to about the 7th hole. We all drove into the fairway, and when we got to my ball the kid was holding it in his hand, cleaning it off."

" 'What the hell are you doing?' Arnold asked him.

" 'Mr. Sam said he wanted me to clean his ball on every hole,' said the kid.

" 'Well, goddamn it, at least wait until he gets on the green,' said Arnold."

"I've had some pretty interesting caddies over the years, but one of the tops was O'Bryant Williams, who used to caddie for me at Augusta," Sam remembers. "He was a hell of a character. Had about eighteen or so kids. And he was a good caddie, except you couldn't count on his clubbing you. He'd be all right most of the time, but sometimes you'd wonder what the hell he was thinking about. In 1949, when I won the Masters for the first time, I got so fed up with it, I told him, 'O'Bryant, if I ever ask you what club to use, you just say I don't know. That's all. Just say, "Sam, I don't know." You don't need to make any excuses. Just say you don't know.'

"Well, the weather was tough that year, and in one round we got to the 6th tee and the wind's a-howlin' and it's just as cold as can be. Old O'Bryant was just miserable. He was standing there holding my bag and shivering away. Now, the key to that hole is the wind, just like at number 12. It can trick you and send you off to a big number. I asked him, 'O'Bryant, which way was the wind blowing yesterday?'

"'I ain't talking, Mr. Sam,' he said.

"I told him, 'O'Bryant, I'm not asking you what club to use. I just want to know what the hell way the wind was blowing yesterday.'

"He said, 'I know what you're up to, and you ain't gonna give me hell. I'm not talking.'

"And you know what? He didn't."

O'Bryant was on Snead's bag five years later when Snead beat Ben Hogan, 70-71, in a playoff capping what Bob Jones later called one of the "most memorable Masters."

"O'Bryant was what you'd call excitable," Sam remembers. "He'd be pullin' real hard for you, and not just because of the money. I had this one long putt and O'Bryant was tending the flag. As the ball got up a rise and headed towards the hole, it looked like it might come up short. O'Bryant set to wavin' on the ball, trying to help it get to the hole. He damned near hit the ball. Lucky for him he didn't, and it went in the hole.

"As we walked to the next tee, I told him, 'O'Bryant, it's a damn good thing you didn't touch that ball. I'd have buried you right in this green—and the last thing it needs is one more big hump.'"

For several years Raymond Floyd had a caddie, Golf Ball, who was one of the best in the business—most of the time. But every now and then there would be a problem and Golf Ball wouldn't be up to his usual high standards. This happened one year in Memphis.

Players and caddies on tour keep books for each course they play. The books show distances, hazards, and other relevant information. In most cases, the books vary very little from year to year.

Floyd and Golf Ball began the first round at Memphis on a particularly bad note. The 1986 U.S. Open champion missed the first four greens in a row—something, it is safe to say, he hadn't done since his boyhood. On the 5th hole he got his yardage from Golf Ball and proceeded to hit a 7-iron twenty yards over the green.

"Golf Ball, let me see that book," he said. "Are you sure that's the book for Memphis?"

"Memphis?" asked Golf Ball. "I thought we were in Fort Worth."

Years ago, the caddies on the tours weren't nearly as professional as they are today. In fact, often they were just local kids without much experience or knowledge of the game. Julius Boros ran into just one such kid.

After hitting his approach to the first hole, Boros pointed to his divot and told the caddie to pick it up. As the round progressed, the boy fell farther and farther behind. Boros, thinking the caddie had become ill, asked him if he was feeling all right.

"Yes, sir, but I was just wondering what you want me to do with all these?" he said, opening the side pocket of Boros's bag, which was filled with divots.

The Quaker Ridge Golf Club in Scarsdale, New York, is an A. W. Tillinghast masterpiece that is occasionally overshadowed by the thirty-six holes at its neighbor, Winged Foot. But Quaker Ridge can more than hold its own, as was evidenced when it hosted the 1997 Walker Cup matches, won by the United States.

Quaker Ridge can also hold its own when it comes to some of the characters they've had for caddies over the years.

One day, at an interclub match, one of the guests happened to be playing very well and made the turn at 1 under par. As he and his caddie headed to the 10th tee, the caddie decided it was time to tell the man just how impressed he was by his play.

"Man, I'm gonna start calling you 'Doc' because you've been operating on this course," the caddie said, no doubt figuring that such lavish praise couldn't hurt at the end of the round.

Bogey, bogey, bogey went his man over the next three holes.

"We need a birdie here," the man said to his caddie as they reached the tee on the long, par-3 13th.

"No, Doc," the caddie said, as he slowly and sadly shook his head. "What we need is some of that malpractice insurance."

For many years, the late Phil Harris used to have a friend caddie for him. They were a perfect team, in large part because the caddie enjoyed taking a drink every bit as much as Phil did, and Phil always enjoyed the company of kindred spirits.

One morning they showed up for their early tee time, and it was hard to tell who was in worse shape. If anything, the nod probably went to Harris, who had to at least try to hit his opening drive. All the caddie had to do was keep an eye on it—although in the end, even that proved to be too much for him to handle.

Harris wobbled to the tee and managed to get his ball on a peg without falling over. After steadying himself, he made a lurching swipe at the ball and somehow managed to make contact, however glancing.

"Where'd it go?" Harris asked his caddie.

"Where'd what go?" the caddie replied.

A man and his longtime caddie were walking back to the clubhouse after the player had just been roundly trounced in the club championship.

"This is the worst beating I've ever had," the man said. "I'll never be able to lift my head around here again."

"I don't know, sir," the caddie said, trying to raise the man's spirits. "You had plenty of practice at it today."

The caddies at Pine Valley are renowned for their remarkable ability to find shots that spray off into the course's abundant trees, shrubs, and waste areas.

One day a guest, playing in the fading twilight, hit a shot that sailed off into the gathering darkness.

"Did you see it?" he asked his caddie.

"No, sir," the caddie said. "But it sounded pretty crooked to me."

Years ago, the caddies at Seminole were known to gamble a little bit on the outcome of the matches their players were involved in. One such match involved President John F. Kennedy.

Kennedy was taking his time reading a putt. Customarily, people are pretty generous when it comes to giving putts to presidents, but this was a delicate little putt at a crucial point in the match. As Kennedy approached his ball one of his opponents said, "That's good. Pick it up, Mr. President."

"No," one of the caddies inadvertently called out.

Kennedy looked over at him and started laughing.

Caddying has long been a popular way to make a living for immigrants to this country, particularly in the large urban areas along the East Coast.

Winged Foot Golf Club outside New York City was one club that benefited from a ready pool of men new to this country. They might not have known much about the game, but they were willing to work hard and enjoyed being outside instead of in a factory.

One day a new caddie was walking up a fairway on the West Course. As he approached the green, his golfer asked for his sand wedge. The caddie seemed to ignore him, walking stoically ahead with his head down. The man asked again for his sand wedge and again got no reaction. After the third request the caddie stopped, laid the bag down, and reached inside one of the pockets, pulling out a brown bag.

"All right," he said in his heavily accented English as he reached inside the bag and pulled out a sandwich wrapped in paper. "But only half. I've got to eat too."

When George Archer won the 1969 Masters, his caddie approached him prior to the start of the tournament and told him, "Boss, if you want to win this tournament, you just listen to me."

"If you want to keep carrying this bag, shut up," said Archer.

"Yes, sir, boss," he said.

Much has been written about Ben Crenshaw's emotional victory in the 1995 Masters, coming as it did just after the death of his long-time teacher and friend, Harvey Penick. The emotion of that victory is vividly captured in the photos of Crenshaw collapsing in tears and being consoled by his caddie, Carl Jackson, after holing out on the last green. As it turned out, Jackson's role in Ben's win went far beyond merely carrying his bag.

Ben Crenshaw is, at heart, a fervent traditionalist. So it is no surprise that when Augusta National changed its rule requiring players to use the club's caddies, Crenshaw stayed with Jackson, a local caddie who had packed his bag since 1976.

Crenshaw had come to Augusta struggling with his swing and with little real hope of duplicating his 1984 victory. But Jackson, after spending some time with Crenshaw on the practice tee, gave his friend some advice.

"Look, you've got to get that ball back a little bit in your stance and then just tighten up your backswing," he said. "Just keep your left arm right there close to your body and turn those shoulders like you used to."

Almost immediately, the crispness returned to Crenshaw's ball-striking and he felt his confidence return—so much so that he told his brother that he truly believed this might be his week. Something he rarely, if ever, did.

In the final round of the 1960 Masters, Arnold Palmer found himself locked in a battle with Ken Venturi. The pressure mounted on the back nine, and when Palmer hit a poor chip on the 15th hole, he lost his temper and tossed his club to his caddie, Ironman.

Ironman glared at Palmer.

"Boss, are we chokin'?" he asked.

"Par, birdie, birdie," answered Palmer, who went on to win his second Masters by a single stroke over Venturi.

In the 1971 Masters, Charlie Coody had a caddie named Cricket Pritchett, an Atlanta bus driver. As they walked down the 7th fairway in contention on Saturday, Cricket turned to Coody and asked him what time the telecast was supposed to begin.

"I don't know, Cricket," Coody said. "Why? What difference does it make?"

"Well, to tell you the truth, I didn't expect us to be doing this good," Pritchett explained. "I told my boss that my grandmother back in Texas was sick and I had to go see her. He doesn't know I'm here."

By the time they reached the 13th hole, Coody had made five birdies and had taken a three-shot lead. But Cricket wasn't taking any chances. On the 11th hole, he draped a towel over his head and put on a big, floppy hat and sunglasses.

In 1961, Gary Player came to the par-3 16th hole at Augusta National in contention to win his first Masters. As he looked over his par putt on Sunday, he told his caddie he thought he should play it on the left edge.

"No, Mr. Player," the caddie replied. "It's right edge all the way."

Player disagreed.

"Trust me, Mr. Player," the caddie insisted. "It's right edge. If you put it there and it doesn't go in, I'm working for free this week—and you know I can't afford that."

Player started the ball at the right edge and it dropped into the cup.

"It was the most important putt I made all week," Player said later.

One time a guest came to Augusta, and as he walked down the first fairway he asked his caddie what the other caddie's name was.

"Cemetery," he replied.

"How'd he get that name?" the guest asked.

"One night he was with a woman and her husband came around and slit his throat," the caddie explained. "We thought he was dead, so when he got out of the hospital we started calling him Cemetery."

"Is that true?" the guest asked Cemetery.

"No, sir," Cemetery protested. "It wasn't his wife."

ANDREW CARNEGIE

One afternoon in 1901, Andrew Carnegie was playing golf with J. P. Morgan. The two had been discussing the sale of Carnegie's corporation for some time, and in mid-round they finally agreed on a price of $250 million.

This, naturally, is often cited as irrefutable proof that the business of American business is golf.

At about this time, Carnegie—a passionate if mediocre golfer—somehow managed to make a hole in one. A few days later a friend—who had read about the deal with Morgan—came up and roundly congratulated Carnegie.

"Thank you," Carnegie said. "It's my first hole in one, but how did you hear about it?"

JoAnne Carner

JoAnne Carner excelled at match play—witness her amateur record—but in truth she was even more dominating than the record shows.

"One night we were talking over drinks, and I said I thought you had to have a real killer instinct to be successful at match play, much more so than medal play," remembered Carner's late friend and teacher, Gardner Dickinson. "I told her that when I played Ryder Cup, if I had a guy 3-down I couldn't wait to get him 4-down. I might be the guy's best friend off the course, but once we teed it up, I wanted to grind him into the ground. JoAnne told me that when she got somebody she knew she could beat down early in a match, she'd let them back in the game, then come back and beat them. From that point on, I always figured that the secret to her success was that she played the game for the sheer joy of it—and humiliating another player would take some of the joy out of the game for her."

CHURCH AND STATE

Boston is arguably the most Irish community in America, and the influence of the Catholic church runs wide and deep in the city.

One day, during the 1988 U.S. Open at The Country Club in Brookline, a writer was having lunch after a round of golf at one of the nearby clubs. As the weekend was approaching, he asked the waiter where the nearest church was.

"A Catholic church?" the waiter asked.

"No, Episcopal," the writer said.

"Oh, junior varsity Catholic," the waiter replied.

WINSTON CHURCHILL

By any standard, Winston Churchill was a man of uncommon courage. He risked death as a young man in escaping from prison during the Boer War, and then personified British resolve in leading his nation against the Nazi assault in the early days of World War II. And while he was an avid sportsman, he never much fancied golf. Alistair Cooke, the graceful British writer and commentator, knew enough about both Churchill and golf to hazard a guess as to why Churchill avoided the game.

"He was not willing to suffer public displays of humiliation," Cooke said, in a brief but brilliant description of the game of golf.

Although Churchill was not an avid golfer by any stretch of the imagination, he enjoyed a membership at Walton Heath, the exclusive club in Walton-on-the-Hill outside London. In the years prior to World War I, Churchill was one of twenty-four members of Parliament who had memberships at the club.

One day he chanced to play with David Lloyd-George, then the prime minister. As was the custom there was a small wager on the outcome of the match, but as Churchill stood over his putt on the final green, he upped the ante.

"I shall now putt you for the prime minister's office," Churchill said.

He missed, but the rest, as they say, is history.

FRED CORCORAN

A woman approached Fred Corcoran and asked if it was true that
he'd been inducted into golf's Hall of Fame.

"Yes, it is," replied Corcoran.

"That's wonderful, but could you tell me what the honor is for?"
she asked.

"Not at all," said Corcoran. "It's because I've three-putted in
forty-seven different countries."

"One year Sam [Snead] and I were traveling through Europe, and
he thought it would be a good idea if we had an 'audition' with the
pope. I arranged it, and when we got ready to leave the hotel for
the Vatican I suggested that Sam bring along his putter and have it
blessed," said Corcoran. "We were met in the vestry of St. Peter's
by a monsignor who proceeded to tell us that he was a 100 shooter
who was having putting problems. Sam quickly put away the putter.

" 'If you're that close to the pope and you can't putt, he ain't
gonna be able to do anything for me,' he said."

HENRY COTTON

When England's Henry Cotton won the 1934 British Open at Royal St. George's, it was a particularly welcome and popular victory in England. For the past decade the championship had been dominated by Americans, most notably Bobby Jones, Walter Hagen, and Gene Sarazen.

Cotton breezed to the title, winning by five shots despite a 79 in the last round. After the awards ceremony, Cotton excused himself and went to the nearby Guilford Hotel. There, he made his way to one of the rooms where an elderly man lay in bed. The man had gamely traveled to the golf course in each of the first two rounds, sitting by "The Maiden," a short par 3, until Cotton had played through, and then returned to the hotel. The man had desperately wanted to be at the championship for Saturday's two-round conclusion, but illness had kept him bedridden.

Cotton knocked softly on the door and then entered. He handed the old man his newly won Open trophy without saying a word. The man pulled the trophy close to his failing eyes, his fingers poring over every detail of the silverwork. Softly, the old man began to cry, and soon Cotton joined him.

The old man was Harry Vardon, who had won the championship a record six times. He died three years later.

Cotton was hospitalized late in 1987. While gravely ill, he maintained his sense of humor. A friend had brought him a small golf club that he could wear so that the shaft appeared to be sticking through his head. One morning his doctor arrived and was greeted by the eighty-year-old Cotton sitting up in bed with a toy golf club running through his skull.

"To be very honest with you, Doctor, I don't think all these pills you are giving me are doing any good at all," said Cotton.

The next day, Christmas Eve, Cotton died.

THE COUNTRY CLUB

The Country Club, in the Boston suburb of Brookline, is one of the founding members of the United States Golf Association, so it is fitting that it has been one of the most popular—and successful—sites of that organization's national championships and other competitions. It has hosted three U.S. Opens, each of which resulted in playoffs that produced Francis Ouimet, Julius Boros, and Curtis Strange as champions.

The Country Club was founded in 1882, but golf wasn't a part of club life until 1893 when a three-hole course was laid out. A group of interested—and bemused—members turned out to watch a brief exhibition of a game they knew little, if anything, about.

As luck would have it, the first ball struck rolled into the hole—a feat that met with overwhelming indifference from the gallery.

"Isn't that the point of this game?" asked one of the members.

The Country Club is a bastion of classic Yankee propriety and reserve, as a new member once discovered.

As he approached his ball on the first tee, near the clubhouse, he was greeted by an indignant member, who chastised him.

"See here, good man, move back behind the markers," he huffed. "These are the rules of golf, and if you can't play by them I'll see that the Board hears about it."

"Look, I've been a member here for six months, and you're the first member who has even spoken to me," the man replied. "And by the way, this is my second shot."

In the 1963 U.S. Open, Tony Lema came to the difficult par-3 16th and tried to determine what club to hit. He checked the tops of the tall trees near the green. He checked the flag. Finally he reached down and pulled up a few blades of grass, gently letting them drop from his fingers. The grass was blown straight back up into the air. That's when Tony Lema realized this was no ordinary golf course.

Throughout his life, Francis Ouimet maintained a special affection for The Country Club. He had grown up across from the club, spent his childhood as a caddie there, and scored his greatest victory there. Some years later, he offered this elegant testimonial to the place he loved so deeply:

"To me, the ground here is hallowed. The grass grows greener, the trees bloom better, there is even warmth to the rocks . . . somehow or other the sun seems to shine brighter on The Country Club than any other place I have known."

FRED COUPLES

One of the most poignant moments in Masters history came in 1992, when Fred Couples won the tournament—his first major championship.

After he signed his scorecard, tournament officials brought him to the CBS studio in Butler Cabin, where he would be interviewed by Jim Nantz and awarded the Green Jacket by the 1991 winner, Ian Woosnam.

What made the moment so special was that Nantz and Couples had been through this many times before in mock interviews. As suitemates at Houston, Nantz—who dreamed of covering the Masters for CBS—would "interview" Couples—who dreamed of winning the Masters one day.

After CBS went off the air, Couples and Nantz embraced, both with tears in their eyes.

"The thing that is so amazing is that all those years ago, we always knew it was going to be the Masters that Fred would win," Nantz said.

Fred Couples is one of the game's most popular players, and with good reason. He's easygoing and genuinely friendly, and if he has a reputation for not taking life too seriously, that's fine with him. Jim Nantz, who went to the University of Houston with Fred and is one of his best friends, tells a story about a phone call he once had with Fred.

Couples had taken six weeks off in 1995 to rest his back. In the course of their conversation, Nantz asked Couples if the time off had been boring.

"No, not really," said Couples. "I've almost finished my book."

"I didn't know you were writing a book," Nantz said.

"I'm not," Couples said. "I'm reading one."

BEN CRENSHAW

Ben Crenshaw is one of those rare players, like Sam Snead and Seve Ballesteros, who has a genius for the game. More than almost any other top golfer, he plays by feel and instinct. And although his play has been praised ever since he was a teenager growing up in Austin, Texas, he is self-deprecating about his abilities.

One day in the mid-1970s a writer asked him how far he felt he was from being a great player.

"About five inches," he quipped. "The distance between my right ear and my left ear."

A writer asked Ben if it was different winning the Masters for the second time.

"I got a lot more mail than ever before," said Crenshaw. "Somebody sent me a pair of underwear and asked me to autograph them. I wrote back and thanked them for their interest, and I didn't want to seem rude, but there was a limit to what I'd sign."

"Ben was always such a likable youngster that the boys on the University of Texas golf team enjoyed having him around," recalls Harvey Penick. "One day he came out to watch the team practice. We were standing on the tee when these two real long hitters from west Texas came along and teed off. They just crushed the ball about three hundred yards each. I could see that Ben was in awe of those boys, so I leaned over to him and, in a soft voice, said, 'Ben, always remember—the woods are full of long hitters.'"

BING CROSBY

Bing Crosby was a fine golfer who played in both the U.S. and British Amateurs. His son, Nathaniel, won the 1981 U.S. Amateur at San Francisco's Olympic Club under circumstances that were positively spooky.

At nineteen, Nathaniel was a very good player but, in all honesty, was not given much of a chance in a field that included players like Jay Sigel, Hal Sutton, Brad Faxon, and Willie Wood as well as many members of the Great Britain/Ireland Walker Cup team that had competed the previous week at Cypress Point.

But as so often happens in match play, the favorites faced each other in early rounds, setting up a thirty-six-hole final between Crosby and Brian Lindley—a relative unknown from southern California. Crosby was down after the morning eighteen but fought back. As he was walking along the rough on the 7th hole in the afternoon, something happened to ABC's Bob Rosburg that made him think that Crosby just might pull it off.

"I stepped on something in the rough, bent down and picked it up, and was amazed to see that it was a pipe just like one of the pipes Bing used to have," says Rosburg. "I kind of thought, 'Geez, it's like Bing is here someplace.' I told [producer] Terry Jastrow about it. I said it was like an omen."

Sure enough, the match was even after thirty-six holes, and Nathaniel ran in a long putt on the first playoff hole to win.

"Two of my favorite celebrities are comedian Bing Crosby and singer Bob Hope. Or is it the other way around? I always forget which one thinks he's funny and which one thinks he can sing."
—JIMMY DEMARET

Crosby played most of his golf at the Lakeside Golf Club in Los Angeles. One day he came out on the short end of a close match with a guy named John "Mysterious" Montague. Crosby hated to lose, and he hated to pay off his bets even more. After the match he was complaining, and Montague, who was known to hustle a bet now and then, said, "Bing, I can handle you with a shovel, a bat, and a rake."

Crosby, a single-figure handicap, couldn't believe his ears and decided to play Montague for the money he had lost earlier, double or nothing.

Crosby hit the green in two, leaving himself a thirty-foot approach putt. Montague hit the ball with the bat twice, leaving his second shot in a greenside bunker. After Crosby hit his first putt three feet from the hole, Montague gave him the short putt and proceeded to scrape the ball out of the bunker with the shovel. Then, using the rake like a pool cue, he calmly ran in his putt.

Crosby then did the only logical thing he could think of. He shook his head and headed back to the clubhouse for a stiff drink.

On a vacation to Scotland, Crosby and Phil Harris happened to drive past a scotch distillery following a late round of golf.

"Look, Phil, they're making the stuff faster than you can drink it," Crosby said.

"Yeah, but I've got them working nights," Harris replied.

In the 1965 Crosby, an amateur named Matt Palacio hooked his drive on the 18th hole at Pebble Beach. As it headed toward the water he said to his fellow players, "Only God can save that one."

No sooner said than done. The waves receded and the ball caromed off the rocks and wound up back on the fairway.

"Thank you, God," said Palacio.

One year at Pebble Beach during his tournament, Bing Crosby and Bob Hope went to a party at a friend's house, accompanied by Crosby's thirteen-year-old son, Lindsay, and some other guests. Hope left the party around midnight. The next morning he saw young Lindsay at breakfast and asked what time he and his father had left the party.

"Around four o'clock," said Lindsay.

"My God, you didn't let your father drive, did you?" asked Hope, remembering Crosby's condition at midnight.

"We had to," said Lindsay. "He was the best we had."

One year Bing Crosby, tired of the unpredictable weather at Pebble Beach, asked a friend, Father Len Scannell, if he could put in a good word upstairs for some sunny weather.

"Sorry, Bing," said the priest. "I'm in sales, not management."

BERNARD DARWIN

"Golf is not a funeral, although both can be very sad affairs."
—BERNARD DARWIN

Bernard Darwin was the longtime golf columnist for the *Times* of London. A semifinalist in the British Amateur, he filled in as a last-minute replacement in the 1922 Walker Cup at the National Golf Links, winning his singles match. Darwin, unlike virtually every other writer, never saw much point in quoting players about their rounds. "My readers," he once noted, "are not interested in what the pros say. They want to know what I thought." Indeed, Harry Vardon once said, "I never know how well I have played until I read Mr. Darwin's verdict in the next day's *Times*." He covered every great player from Vardon to Nicklaus before his death in 1961.

Bernard Darwin was a gifted writer and a player accomplished enough to play on the 1922 British Walker Cup team.

Like many players in the days before Gene Sarazen's invention of the sand wedge, Darwin had a terrible time when he found himself in a bunker. It didn't help matters that he was given to fierce fits of temper on the course.

One day, after a particularly nasty stretch in the sand, Darwin let fly with a string of expletives that included the Lord's name in a variety of combinations. He closed his tirade by looking heavenward and shouting, "And don't send your son down. This is a man's work."

"I was at Muirfield for the 1959 Walker Cup matches, and as my teammate Ward Wettlaufer and I were leaving the clubhouse we ran into Bernard Darwin," recalls Jack Nicklaus. "Ward was wearing a striped shirt that, while very tame by today's standards, was pretty daring for those days. Mr. Darwin, who was in his eighties at that point, looked at Ward's shirt and said, 'Tell me, dear boy, are those your old school colors or are they of your own unfortunate choosing?'"

Bernard Darwin was the longtime golf columnist for the *Times* of London. The grandson of the author of *Origin of Species*, Charles Darwin, Bernard was a fine player in his own right, having made the semifinals of the British Amateur and serving admirably as a last-minute replacement on the 1922 British Walker Cup team. If Darwin knew the subtleties of the game, he was also well aware of the emotions it could stir in a player. In fact, Darwin's temper was legendary, particularly as a young man. In one match he fell to his knees, bit a chunk of turf out of the ground, spat it out, and then called to the heavens, "Oh, God, now are you satisfied?"

DEAR OLD DAD

After losing to Nick Faldo in a playoff for the 1989 Masters, a dejected Scott Hoch returned to the clubhouse with his family. As he entered the locker room, he slapped the top of the doorjamb.

"What happened, Daddy?" asked his five-year-old son, Cameron.

"I messed up," Hoch said.

"Again?" Cameron asked.

Greg Norman's loss to Larry Mize in the 1986 Masters was one of the most painful in a career marked by soaring triumphs and bitter disappointments. Norman, Mize, and Seve Ballesteros were tied after seventy-two holes. Ballesteros was eliminated after the first playoff hole, the par-4 10th. Both Norman and Mize missed the green on the dangerous 11th.

Mize was away—some 140 feet from the hole—and stunned the golf world by chipping in.

Norman, who figured to have the advantage if they tied the hole and went on to the par-5 13th, looked on in utter disbelief, then missed his own attempt.

After sitting through a press interview that could not have been easy for him, his daughter, Morgan-Leigh, gave him a hug and consoled him the way only a little girl can console her father.

"Daddy," she said, "even though you didn't win, can we still have a party anyway?"

JIMMY DEMARET

Jimmy Demaret's start in professional golf was hardly auspicious. He left his hometown, Houston, in 1935, with his clubs, his car, and $600 in cash fronted by a nightclub owner, a bandleader, and an oilman.

On his way through Juarez, he managed to get into a game of high-stakes pool.

First he lost the car.

Then he lost the clubs.

Then he lost the $600.

He did manage to hang on to his pawn ticket, which he sent to his brother, who retrieved the clubs and sent them west. The rest, as they say, is history.

A writer once asked Jimmy Demaret why he thought golf held such a fascination for so many people. If the writer was looking for a deeply cosmic explanation, he had come to the wrong guy.

"Golf and sex are the only two things you can enjoy without doing either of them very well," he explained.

One of Jimmy Demaret's best friends was Don Cherry. This was only natural, since Cherry was a Texan, a fine amateur golfer, and a popular singer. Demaret and Cherry had a lot in common. The difference was that Demaret got paid for his golf and Cherry got paid for his singing.

Cherry showed up at Demaret's club—the Champions Golf Club in Houston—during the 1967 Ryder Cup matches. He was shoot-

ing a movie at the time and had shaved his head and grown a beard for the part.

When Demaret saw Cherry, he couldn't help himself.

"Don," he said. "You look great, but your head is on upside down."

Jimmy Demaret was watching the telecast of the 1958 Masters in the clubhouse at Augusta National. When Arnold Palmer hit his tee shot to the back of the green on the par-3 16th, Demaret said, "There's no way he gets down in two from there."

Palmer chipped in.

"See, I told you," Demaret said, laughing.

Like many professional golfers, Jimmy Demaret enlisted in the armed services during World War II. But since he served in the Special Services, he was never in much danger of encountering enemy fire. In fact, a writer once asked him how he spent the war years.

"I never got out of Shermans," he replied.

"The tanks?" the writer asked.

"No, the bar in San Diego," Jimmy said with a laugh.

Jimmy Demaret was a player who was known to take a drink now and then. Or two. Or three if the company was good and there was no pressing business to attend to—although in the great scheme of things, there was seldom anything more important to Jimmy Demaret than spending time with his friends.

One morning he showed up at the first tee to meet his pro-am partners. Since the night before had been spent with an especially convivial group, he was more than a little worse for wear. Naturally, his partners were sympathetic, including one who told Jimmy that a particularly wicked hangover had convinced him to stop drinking ten years earlier.

"You mean when you wake up in the morning, that's as good as you're going to feel all day?" an incredulous Demaret asked.

Jimmy Demaret was paired with an unusually inept partner in a pro-am, and no matter what he suggested, it was clear the man just wasn't going to improve. Finally, in frustration and desperation, the man turned to Jimmy and asked: "Isn't there anything I can do to improve?"

"Sure, play shorter courses," Jimmy answered.

Jimmy Demaret and Gene Sarazen were cohosts of the old "Shell's Wonderful World of Golf" series that ran in the 1960s and early '70s. Demaret's quick wit was one reason for the show's success.

During one match, Demaret and Sarazen were interviewing Billy Casper's wife, Shirley. In answering a question, she became momentarily confused and called Demaret "Gene."

"You think I look like Gene?" said the younger Demaret. "We better get the makeup guy over here in a hurry."

"Jimmy Demaret was a great friend of Bob Hope's," recalled Dwayne Netland, a former senior editor at *Golf Digest* who coauthored a bestselling golf book with Hope. "Bob had almost a professional admiration for Demaret's sense of humor. One time they were playing in the Crosby. Bob hooked his tee shot on the first hole out-of-bounds. Demaret looked at him and said, 'That's okay, Bob, there's always next year.' Bob loved it."

Another year at the Crosby, Demaret was on the tee when Phil Harris, nursing a world-class hangover, whiffed not once but twice.

"Don't choke now, Phil," Demaret said. "You've got a no-hitter going."

On a visit to Barcelona for a match in the old "Shell's Wonderful World of Golf" series, local officials arranged an audience with the cardinal of Barcelona for Jimmy Demaret, Gene Sarazen, and the series' producer and director, Fred Raphael.

After the formalities, the cardinal offered a blessing and closed by making the sign of the cross.

"In the name of the Father," he said, looking at Sarazen, the oldest of the three.

"And of the Son," he said, looking at Raphael, the youngest of the three.

"And of the Holy Spirit," he said, looking at Demaret, who was easily the most spirited of the bunch.

Jimmy Demaret always claimed he got his sense of style from his father.

"My daddy had a wonderful sense of mixing and matching colors," Demaret once told a writer.

"Was your father in the clothing business?" the writer asked.

"No, he was a housepainter," Demaret said, laughing. "But he was the Michelangelo of housepainters."

One day a writer, who was perhaps taking himself and golf a little too seriously, asked Jimmy Demaret if he thought golf was like life.

"I'm not sure," Demaret said. "Except that the older you get the harder it is to score."

Make no mistake about it: for all his kidding around, Jimmy Demaret was a very tough competitor. After all, no one wins three Masters without having a certain fire burning from within. But he also had a very compassionate side to him, as the late Dave Marr once recalled.

"Jimmy finished the 1957 U.S. Open at Inverness at 283," Marr said. "He and I were in the locker room watching Dick Mayer play the 18th hole. Now, Jimmy was forty-seven at the time, so this was probably his last realistic chance to win the Open. Mayer had a putt to take the lead, and when he made it Jimmy said, 'I'm glad he made that putt. That young man really needs the money.' He really meant it, too. There was no one else around, and he certainly didn't have to try and impress me. That kind of epitomized the kind of guy Jimmy was."

One year Jimmy Demaret was working as a commentator for a telecast of the Bing Crosby National Pro-Am from Pebble Beach. Arnold Palmer hit his drive on the par-3 17th over the green and down the cliff onto the beach.

As millions looked on, Palmer seemed at a loss to decide what to do next. Demaret was asked to explain the options offered by the unplayable lie rule.

"He can lift and drop the ball behind a line not nearer the hole," said Jimmy. "In that case, his nearest point of relief would be Honolulu."

Demaret was playing in the Bing Crosby National Pro-Am one year. When he woke up on Sunday morning, he looked out the window and saw Pebble Beach covered with snow.

"I know I got drunk last night, but how'd I wind up at Squaw Valley?" he asked.

Demaret and Ben Hogan were together on a storm-wracked flight to Dallas. The plane bounced around as lightning flashed outside the windows. Hogan's expression never changed throughout the ordeal, but when Demaret shakily emerged from the plane, he said, "Man, I don't ever want to go through that again. Lindbergh got a ticker-tape parade for less than this."

Back in the 1930s, entering the U.S. Open wasn't nearly as formal a procedure as it is today. In fact, just a few months before the

1935 Open, the USGA received a letter at its New York City headquarters.

"Enter me, Jim," was all it read.

Of course, Jimmy Demaret wasn't taking any chances that it might not get to the USGA in time. He sent it by airmail—from a post office eleven blocks from the USGA's office.

Demaret was a fixture at the old Bing Crosby National Pro-Am, which he won in 1952. One of the reasons he loved the tournament so much was that it gave him a chance to hang around with celebrities, many of whom were his friends.

"One year Jimmy was with Phil Harris at the bar and Harris was telling us about this new kid, Dean Martin," remembers Dave Marr. "Phil was in awe of how much he could drink.

" 'Hell, Phil, you could drink him under the table with one lip tied behind your back,' Jimmy said.

"Another time he told Phil that his face had enough wrinkles to hold a three-day rain," adds Marr.

"People talk about the great rounds of golf, but no one ever mentions Jimmy Demaret's first round in the 1952 Crosby," Cary Middlecoff began in one of those late-night sessions. "He shot a 74 under conditions that were just unplayable. Period. He might have been the best wind player I ever saw. The harder it blew, the better he played. It just rained all day and it was bitterly cold. Chunks of ice were being blown down the fairways. I was playing at Cypress Point, and by the time I reached the 16th green I'd had enough. My foursome marked our balls and headed in. Along the way I met Peter Hay, the pro at Pebble Beach. He was a Scot and a real stickler on the rules. I told him the wind was blowing so hard that I couldn't get the ball to stay on the tee. He just sort of glared at me and said, 'Show me where it says in the rule book that the ball has to be played from a tee.'

"Anyway, there was a big conference between Bing and some of the rules officials about whether the round should be called off," Doc continued. "They finally decided we had to go back out. We got back out on Cypress, and just as I was about to play a shot, this really powerful gust tore off the ocean. I turned away, and out of the corner of my eye I caught a glimpse of the old western actor Grant Withers. He was actually hanging on to a tree as the wind tore his rain suit off him.

"I ran into Jimmy later at Pebble Beach and we were trading horror stories," Doc said. "He told me that when he played 17 at Cypress—which is usually a drive and a short iron—the wind was so bad he had to hit a driver, a fairway wood, and a 4-iron. He one-putted for a par and said it was the greatest par of his life."

A young man approached Jimmy Demaret and wondered if he could get some advice.

"Mr. Demaret, I drive the ball long and straight," he said nervously. "I'm a good iron player. I'm especially good with my 1-iron. All my friends say I'm a good putter. What should I do?"

Demaret looked at him, took a sip of his drink, and pondered the question for what seemed to the young man to be an eternity.

"Join the Tour before you find out how hard the game really is," Demaret joked.

When Jimmy Demaret died in 1983 at the age of seventy-three, many of his friends traveled to Houston for the services. His widow mentioned to one of them that she was a little concerned because she didn't know if Jimmy had left her any money.

"Are you kidding? Jimmy had money in every bank in Houston," the friend replied.

Later, someone asked why he spread his money all over town.

"He had to," the man said, laughing. "He was friends with every bank president in Houston. He didn't want to hurt anyone's feelings."

ROBERTO DE VICENZO

During a 1968 "Shell's Wonderful World of Golf" match with Sam Snead at Congressional, Roberto de Vicenzo birdied an especially difficult 450-yard par 4. After he putted out, Jimmy Demaret and Gene Sarazen congratulated him.

"Yes, this is a very difficult hole," de Vicenzo said. "In my country we have a name for holes like this: a par 5."

One year Jimmy Demaret approached the great Argentinian golfer Roberto de Vicenzo prior to the start of the Masters.

"Roberto," said Demaret, "play as good as you can. I'm betting on you to be low Mexican."

GARDNER DICKINSON

Gardner Dickinson won seven times on the Tour, on great courses like Doral and Colonial, and beat Jack Nicklaus in a playoff for his final win, the 1971 Atlanta Classic. He had a 9–1 record in Ryder Cup play—the best percentage in the history of the competition— and with a record of 5–0, he and Arnold Palmer were the most successful American team in the competition's history.

But for all his success, his failure to win more tournaments bothered Dickinson. One Sunday night, after another disappointing final round, he sat around drinking scotch with Palmer. As the evening wore on, he finally asked Palmer what was lacking in his game. What was the missing piece?

Palmer thought for a moment. His answer spoke volumes about his own success—and the mind-set of a champion.

"I win because I love to win, but I'm not afraid to lose," Palmer said. "You need to win. That's a big difference. You put too much pressure on yourself."

In 1957, Gardner Dickinson came to the 16th hole at Cypress Point and left his tee shot down on the beach below the steep cliffs. By the time he was through, he had taken a 9 and shot himself out of the tournament. Still, according to Dickinson, there have been players who have suffered worse indignities.

"Henry Ransom hit it down on the beach one day and tried to play it back up to the green," Dickinson said. "The ball smashed off the cliffs and hit him in the chest. He told his caddie to pick up the ball and walked in.

" 'When they start hitting back at you it's time to quit,' he said," Dickinson recalled.

DISASTERS

Marty Fleckman was a twenty-three-year-old from the University of Houston who shot a 67 in the first round of the 1967 U.S. Open at Baltusrol. While Fleckman was one of the country's top amateurs and a protégé of Byron Nelson, few people expected him to be a serious threat to win the Open. But Fleckman hung on and came back with rounds of 73 and 69. Suddenly, it appeared that an amateur might win the Open for the first time since Johnny Goodman won in 1933.

Alas, it wasn't to be. Fleckman skied to an 80 in the final round.

"I finally got back on my game," he told reporters who asked him what happened.

Roland Hancock was a young professional from North Carolina who found himself in a very unlikely position with just two holes left to play in the 1928 U.S. Open at Olympia Fields, outside Chicago: he was leading.

Not only was Roland Hancock leading the Open, but he could afford to bogey the last two holes and still win.

But as luck would have it, as he walked to the 17th tee, a fan yelled, "Stand back. Stand back. Make way for the next U.S. Open champion!"

Roland Hancock double-bogeyed the 17th hole.

Roland Hancock double-bogeyed the 18th hole.

Roland Hancock missed joining Johnny Farrell and Bob Jones in a playoff by one stroke.

After two rounds in the 1991 British Open at Royal Birkdale, Richard Boxall was in excellent position to challenge for the championship. After opening with a 71, he shot a second-round 69 that left him three strokes out of the lead. But when Boxall, then thirty, woke up Saturday morning his left shin ached.

The pain continued as he warmed up prior to his round and steadily worsened as he played the front nine. Still, he was only one over par through the first eight holes and was three strokes off the lead as he stood on the 9th tee.

Then disaster struck.

As he hit his drive, there was a loud crack as his left leg shattered. As the gallery, his wife, and his playing partner, Colin Montgomerie, looked on in horror, Boxall collapsed in horrible pain from the stress fracture and was rushed to a nearby hospital.

The fracture required him to wear a cast for almost five months, and it would be six months before he could take even his first, tentative swings. At least now, though, he can laugh about the whole business.

"I went out in 34 and came back in an ambulance," he jokes.

Bob Drum

Dan Jenkins called Bob Drum "The Man Who Invented Arnold Palmer."

Everyone else called him "the Drummer."

When Drum was in the army (the mind boggles at the thought), a sergeant took one look and said, "Drum. It's a perfect name for you. Big, loud, and empty."

But the Drummer was utterly unique. As a writer for the *Pittsburgh Press*, he covered Arnold Palmer during his glory years. In fact, he's sometimes given credit for inspiring Palmer's final-round 65 at Cherry Hills in Denver, when he won the 1960 U.S. Open.

One version of the story has Palmer talking to Drum and Dan Jenkins in the locker room before the afternoon's final round. Palmer asks what would happen if he drove the first green, eagled the hole, and went on to shoot, say, a 65.

"Nothing," says Drum. "You're too far back."

"The hell I am," says Palmer. "A 65 gives me 280, and that wins the Open."

"Yeah, when Hogan shoots it," Drum replies. "You got no chance."

Palmer, suitably riled, drives the first green, birdies the hole, shoots 65, and wins the Open.

That's one version, the one told by the Drummer. The other version is about the same, only Jenkins is the one goading Palmer. Either way, the fact of the matter is that both of them were around when golf history was being made—just as they've been for the past half century.

The Drummer enjoyed an all-too-brief career as a feature commentator for CBS Sports with his "Drummer's Beat." One night, while CBS's expense money was weighing down his pockets, he proved why he's one of the best hang-around guys in the game.

"I'll have a Count [Smirnoff] and a glass of milk," he said to the bartender at the Sawgrass Beach Club while ordering a round for all his friends. I asked him what the hell the milk was for.

"You've got to foam the runway," he said.

The Drummer bought a lot of drinks that night. "I have to," he said. "I got to take care of all the guys who took care of me before I was famous."

Once, during his glorious employ by the *Pittsburgh Press*, he asked to go to the British Open to cover Palmer, who was not yet the Arnie America would come to know and love. That being the case, and Pittsburgh being a long way from Scotland, his editor refused. This prompted the Drummer to do what he does best, which is just what he damn pleases, so off he went.

As luck would have it, Palmer played his way into contention, eventually winning.

His editor wired Drum: "Need a thousand words on Palmer at British Open." The Drummer wired back: "Hope you get it."

JIMMY DURANTE

Jimmy Durante played golf once—and that was one time too many. It wasn't just that he didn't break 100. He didn't even break 100 for the front nine. When the death march finally ended, he asked his caddie what he should give him.

"Why not do us both a favor?" the caddie said. "Give me your clubs."

Dwight D. Eisenhower

President Dwight D. Eisenhower was perhaps the most passionate golfer ever to serve as president and certainly one of the most influential figures in the growth of golf in the 1950s and early '60s.

As president, he was used to a certain deferential treatment from people, and most of the time that extended to the golf course. Mulligans were a given. And so were most short putts. The thought that somebody would play through the President's foursome—uninvited—was all but unthinkable. But it did happen, at least on one bizarre occasion.

One afternoon President Eisenhower and some friends were playing at Augusta National. As they were putting on the 5th green, a ball bounded in front of the green and ran up toward the hole. A few minutes later a man walked briskly onto the green, announced he was playing through, putted out, and left without saying another word—of either thanks or apology.

The man was Ty Cobb.

Like many presidents, Eisenhower was a member at Burning Tree, the exclusive club in the Maryland suburbs, and enjoyed getting out for a round to help ease the pressures of the presidency.

One day at Burning Tree, Ike struggled more than usual. The worse he played, the faster his swing became. His caddie tried to be helpful.

"Slow down, baldy," he said.

Things went from bad to worse.

"C'mon, baldy, just slow it down," his caddie implored.

Finally all this got to be too much for the president's playing companions. One of them motioned the caddie aside.

"See here, that's the President of the United States you're talking to," he said to the caddie.

The caddie tried to make up for the error of his ways on Ike's next good shot.

"That's the way to hit it, President Lincoln," he said.

JOE EZAR

Joe Ezar was a trick-shot artist whose skills could rival those of any of his contemporaries. He occasionally surfaced at tournaments but was temperamentally unsuited for the discipline that lifestyle required. To say that he liked a night on the town was putting it mildly. In fact, he could make more money hustling bets and doing exhibitions than he could have if he had gone straight.

Legend has it that Ezar could press a ball into the turf and then hit it 200 yards with a fairway wood. He could also cold-top a ball, popping it into the air and then hitting it down the fairway, baseball-style.

The greatest Joe Ezar story, however, stems from a hustle he pulled in 1936 when he and 1934 British Open champion Henry Cotton were traveling through Europe on an exhibition tour. They were in Sestriere, in the Italian mountains, and Ezar bet the president of Fiat that he could tie the course record, 66, the following day. The man agreed to pay Ezar 5,000 lira for a 66 but 10,000 lira for a 65. When the man offered to pay 40,000 lira for a 64, Ezar came alive.

"I'll tell you what I'll do," said Ezar. "I'll write down the score I'll make on each hole."

Having done all that, he repaired to a nearby bar for the rest of the afternoon and much of the evening. The next morning his caddie had to literally drag him, shaking from a hangover, out of bed.

Ezar matched his predicted scores over the first eight holes. On the 9th hole he made a 4 instead of a 3 but then followed it on the 10th with a 3 instead of a 4. For the next eight holes he matched his predictions, and he pocketed a well-deserved 40,000 lira.

Sadly—if somewhat predictably—Ezar disappeared from view in the late 1960s.

DAVID FEHERTY

Ireland's David Feherty brought a quick wit with him when he came to America to play on the PGA Tour. A writer once asked him if he played for the love of the game or just for the money.

"Neither, actually," he said. "I play the game because my sole ambition is to do well enough to give it up."

One year Feherty came to Massachusetts to play in the New England Classic, not far from Boston—arguably the most Irish city in America. He was asked if he enjoyed playing in the tournament.

"Very much so," he said. "It's like playing in the Irish Open, except there are more Irish people in the galleries here."

When word spread that his marriage was in trouble, a friend approached Feherty and asked him if he'd lost weight.

"Yes, 150 pounds . . . 135 of them being my wife," he said. "I call it my Divorce Diet."

Feherty had a run-in with America's politically correct in 1997. This time he managed to offend animal-rights activists.

During a CBS telecast, play was delayed when a gaggle of geese took their time wandering across a green.

"It's funny how you never seem to have a shotgun when you really need one," Feherty said.

The activists were not amused. Feherty apologized—after a fashion.

"I assure you I've never shot anything but par," he said. And I haven't done that very often lately."

Maurice Flitcroft

If you have never heard of Maurice Flitcroft, don't feel too bad. He was never a great golfer. He was never even remotely mediocre. Still, he was one of the biggest stories of the 1976 British Open.

Flitcroft, a crane driver from Barrow-in-Furness, claimed he was a professional and, given the less-than-rigorous standards of the day, was given a spot in the Open qualifying at Formby, where he promptly fired an immaculate 121. Given Flitcroft's training in the game, which was limited to knocking balls around a local beach, this should not have been surprising.

The plucky Flitcroft got off to a shaky start, going 11-12 on the opening holes, scores attributed as much to his scorer's generosity of spirit as his particular skills.

"At the start I was trying too hard," he explained. "By the end of the round I felt I was finally beginning to put it all together."

As indeed he was. His card read 61-60.

His remarkable display triggered a frenzy among the British press, which tracked down Flitcroft's dear mother.

"I've called about Maurice and the Open championship," stated one reporter.

"Oh my, yes," she replied. "Has he won?"

When told the sad truth, she remained loyal if not upbeat.

"Well, the boy has got to start somewhere, hasn't he?" she replied, as only a mother could.

Moving along, some fourteen years later the amazing Flitcroft—after attempts at entering as an American named Gene Pacecky and as Switzerland's Gerald Hoppy—surfaced at the Open qualifying at Ormskirk, Lancashire, in 1990 and, alas, did not fare very much better. Entering as one James Beau Jolley from France, Flitcroft, now well into his sixties and disguised with dyed hair, a green balaclava, and a moustache, opened with a double bogey and a bogey and, given the contortions of his swing, was soon escorted from the course by an official.

Still, despite the indignity of it all, Flitcroft was not apologetic in the least: "I have always believed in my potential, but I was not warmed up properly," he explained.

Foreign Affairs

Australia's Peter Thomson is probably best known as the winner of five British Opens, but he was also instrumental in the growth of golf across the Pacific. As such, he's seen some things on the golf course that are . . . well, unusual.

"I was playing in Malaysia, and the tournament was plagued with terrible rain problems," he said. "It looked like the rains would never stop, so they hired a bumoo to come in and work his particular form of magic. The man sat under a tree in the midst of the golf course, working with a handful of bones. He built a small fire, roasted some garlic, and waved the smoke around. Then, before you knew it, the rains cleared. Bumoos are very good at their craft—and quite inexpensive as well."

For much of his life, Sam Snead was an avid sportsman who loved to hunt and fish almost as much as he loved to play golf. He traveled to Africa several times on safari, and on one of these trips he was talked into playing in a tournament in Nairobi. At the very least, he figured, it would be an easy way to pick up a few thousand dollars.

You can imagine his surprise when he won the tournament and was presented with the first prize: three leopard skins.

When Americans think of Canada, they don't really think of it as a foreign country. Still, it's not like going across town for a tournament. Just ask Jackie Burke, Jr.

Burke traveled north for the Canadian Open one year. After a long drive, he checked into his hotel in Toronto. After a good night's sleep, he came down to the lobby and asked for directions to the golf course. The directions must have been very complicated.

The Canadian Open was being played in Montreal that year.

One of the charms of international events such as the World Cup or the World Amateur Team Championship is that they draw players from small countries that don't have a chance in the world of winning—indeed, many don't have a chance of breaking 80—but come for the sheer sportsmanship of it all. Take the case of Switzerland's Hans Schweizer, who played in the 1960 World Amateur Team Championship at Merion.

Teeing off on the first day, he was visibly nervous. After his round, writers asked him if it was disconcerting to play in front of a crowd.

"Oh, yes," he said. "Before today only cows had seen me play."

One year the Wilson Sporting Goods Company, which Sarazen represented for most of his career, sent him to Japan to help convince golf professionals to buy up the overstock of aluminum-shafted clubs that were filling Wilson's warehouses.

Sarazen was successful, but when he returned to Japan a year later, he found that aluminum shafts weren't any more popular in Japan than they had been in the States.

"You say aluminum shafts here to stay," one Japanese professional told Sarazen. "You right. Nobody buy. Aluminum shafts sure to stay—in pro shop."

In 1950, Argentina's Roberto de Vicenzo received his first invitation to play in the Masters tournament. Unfortunately, something was lost in the translation.

Literally.

When his reply was received at Augusta National, it read that he was delighted to accept the invitation to play in "the Annual Teachers Competition."

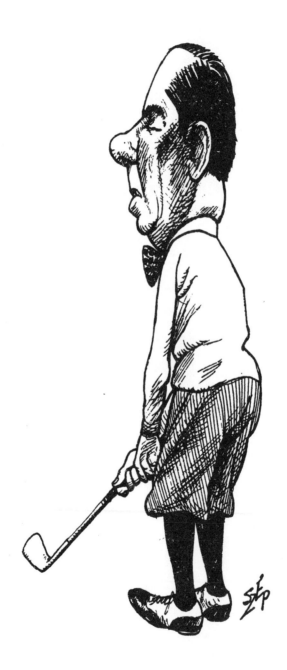

WALTER HAGEN

Walter Hagen began his professional career as an assistant pro at the Country Club of Rochester. The professional was a transplanted Scotsman named Andrew Christy, who helped Hagen develop his game to the point where Hagen soon became confident he could beat him.

Bad idea.

One day Hagen strode into the pro shop and issued his boss a challenge.

"C'mon, Mr. Christy," Hagen said. "Let's go out and see if you can beat me."

There was dead silence in the shop. Christy glared at Hagen, his face turning red with anger. The other people in the shop carefully studied their shoes. It was several moments before he spoke.

"Sonny, when I want to play golf with you I'll do the asking, not you," he said, then turned and walked out of the shop.

There was more than a touch of the showman in Walter Hagen, and he used this to particularly good effect in match-play situations.

In one tournament, he came to the final hole with the match all square. He pushed his drive into the rough, with a stand of trees between his ball and the green. His opponent's drive landed in the heart of the fairway.

Things clearly looked bad for Hagen. He paced around, dramatically studying all his options. Finally, he pulled a lofted club from his bag and motioned the gallery away, indicating that his only play was to pitch the ball back to the fairway. He addressed and was about to hit his shot, when he suddenly backed away and looked at the trees blocking his path to the green. As the crowd roared its approval, he put the club back in the bag, took another, and played a beautiful punch shot through the trees and onto the green. Flustered, his opponent played a poor second shot and lost the hole. Later, a friend praised Hagen for playing such a brave shot.

"Brave?" Hagen said. "Christ, I could have driven a truck through those trees."

In 1942, during the darkest days of World War II, golf impresario Fred Corcoran learned that he had to travel to London on business. His friend, Walter Hagen, told him to go to the Savoy Hotel and introduce himself to the hotel manager, Karl Hefflin.

Corcoran arrived at the hotel, went to the front desk, and asked to speak with Mr. Hefflin, telling the clerk that he was Hagen's friend. A few minutes later, Hefflin arrived, looking very grim. When he saw Corcoran, a look of relief swept over his face.

"The boy misunderstood," Hefflin explained. "He said Walter Hagen was here. We'd been bombed by the Nazis three times in the past month. I was just wondering how I was supposed to cope with the blitz and Walter Hagen, too."

Practice, as we know it today, was almost unheard of in Walter Hagen's day. For that reason, or perhaps because he was an uncommonly gifted athlete in the first place, he never understood why players would stand on a practice tee hitting balls hour after hour.

"I don't get it," he said to a friend one day as they stood by a practice tee during a tournament. "These guys already know how to hit the ball. It's a waste of time. I'd be afraid to practice like that. I might find out a way to do something wrong. These guys aren't getting any better. They're just punishing themselves."

On the eve of the PGA finals in 1926 a friend ran into Hagen at a party around midnight.

"My God, Walter, what are you doing up?" he asked. "Leo [Diegel, his opponent] has been in bed since eight o'clock."

"Yes," said Hagen, "but he hasn't been sleeping."

Sure enough, in the next day's match, Hagen made a point of giving Diegel—a mediocre putter at best—every early short putt. Then at a crucial point in the match he dropped the other shoe. Diegel, faced with a short putt for a tie, looked to Hagen to see if he would give him the putt. Hagen looked Diegel straight in the eyes and said nothing. Diegel's putt never came close to the hole. And he was never again in the match.

Walter Hagen loved to travel and was a goodwill ambassador for the United States as he barnstormed his way around the world. That is, at least, most of the time.

On one trip to Japan, the United States ambassador arranged for Hagen to play golf with a person of royal lineage, who was, by all accounts, quite mad about golf in general and Walter Hagen in particular.

The appointed hour came—and passed. The embarrassed ambassador assured the prince that Hagen would indeed be right along. And he was, in about an hour or so.

The match went off swimmingly. The prince had a wonderful time. When it was over, the ambassador lectured Hagen on the importance of being on time, especially when it comes to royalty.

"Why, he didn't have anyplace else to go, did he?" Hagen said. "It's not like he had to go back to work and punch a time clock."

Hagen was one of the first true worldwide golf celebrities. Like most players of his era, he realized that the money he won in tournaments paled in comparison to the money he could make playing exhibitions.

On one trip through Asia, he decided to be fitted for a custom-made suit. He arranged for the tailor to come to his room late one afternoon, following a luncheon in his honor.

As luck would have it, the luncheon ran longer than Hagen had planned, and the liquor was better—or at least stronger—than he had expected. One shooter led to another, and when he returned to his room he decided to lie down and take a brief nap—which lasted for several hours.

He naturally assumed that the tailor had arrived and, finding the snoozing Haig, had quietly left. But a few days later, as he was about to leave, the suit was delivered to his hotel.

"How's the suit?" asked his friend, the trick-shot artist Joe Kirkwood.

"It's beautiful, but it only fits right when I'm lying down," Hagen said. "I guess I'll save it for my funeral."

To say that Hagen was a confident, even cocky, player is a huge understatement. As captain of the 1929 Ryder Cup team, he paired himself against the captain of the British/Irish team, George Duncan, then forty-five.

"Boys, there's a point for our side," he told his team.

Duncan went on to win, 10 and 8, the most lopsided victory in Ryder Cup history.

Hagen was the nonplaying captain of the American team in the 1937 Ryder Cup matches in Southport, England. Anxious to praise all the appropriate figures, he had made extensive notes but unfortunately lost them before he reached the presentation ceremonies. Nevertheless, he persevered.

"You have no idea how honored I am to captain the first American Ryder Cup team to win on home soil . . ."

Several people in the crowd corrected him, pointing out that he meant to say "foreign soil."

"An honest mistake," he said. "You can't blame me for feeling so completely at home over here, now can you?"

Hagen loved the British, but he had a field day tweaking the noses of their institutions.

Once, while playing a celebrated round with the Prince of Wales (who would go on to be best known for giving up the British throne for American divorcée Wallis Simpson), he asked, "Eddie, hold the flagstick while I putt this one, will you?"

On another occasion he arrived at the 1920 British Open in a magnificent Austro-Daimler limousine. When he tried to enter the clubhouse, he was informed that professionals were restricted to the professional's shop. Hagen would do no such thing. He ordered his chauffeur to park the limo in front of the clubhouse, in full view of the members, where he was served a full lunch, including expensive wines, each day by his footman.

When in 1922 he won the British Open at Royal St. George's, he made a grand gesture of turning over his winner's check of 50 British pounds directly to his caddie, who, it is said, never recovered from such generosity and drank himself into an early oblivion.

The 1929 PGA Championship was played at Los Angeles's Hillcrest Country Club, a club whose membership included numerous members of the Hollywood community. That being the case, it doesn't come as a surprise that the club arranged to have Fay Wray, King Kong's love interest, act as the first tee announcer. Everything went along just fine until she introduced Walter Hagen as "The Opium Champion of the World."

When Leo Diegel died in 1951, Hagen and Joe Kirkwood traveled to their old friend's funeral. They initially went to the wrong church and caught up with the funeral party at the cemetery. After most of the people had left, Hagen and Kirkwood approached the casket.

"Are you in there, Leo?" Hagen asked. Then remembering Diegel's unorthodox, elbows-out putting stance, he asked, "How'd they ever get you in there, Leo?"

In the 1940 PGA Championship at Hershey (Pennsylvania) Country Club, Hagen, now past his prime, was scheduled to play Vic Ghezzi, a fine player who would go on to win the championship the following year.

When Hagen arrived at the course—late, as usual—it was raining and the course was muddy. Hagen stood on the first tee, took a couple of nips from a flask of scotch, and told Ghezzi to start without him.

"I told him I'd spot him the first two holes and join him on the third," said Hagen. "He was so mad he was going to win them anyway, so what the hell?"

Hagen gave Ghezzi the first two holes and beat him anyway, 2 and 1.

"I was paired with Walter one year in the old Inverness Four-Ball, and even though he was in his fifties then and well past his prime, I was still excited about playing with him because he had been my idol as a boy," remembers Byron Nelson. "We finished the front nine, and as we headed for the 10th tee Hagen turned for the clubhouse.

" 'Play hard, Byron,' he said. 'I'll see you on 14.'

"I'd like to say it didn't matter and that I played good enough for both of us, but the truth is we finished dead last," said Byron.

In 1933, after his glory days were over, Walter Hagen decided to play in the U.S. Open, more as a lark and a chance to see old friends than anything else.

On the eve of the Open, Gene Sarazen wrote a newspaper column suggesting that it was a mistake for his old friend and rival to risk damaging his reputation by playing in the Open. Sarazen suggested that Hagen should "sit back in an easy chair and enjoy the Open."

Surprisingly—or maybe not surprisingly, considering it was Walter Hagen—he played pretty well and in the final round even turned in a 66.

As Hagen relaxed over a drink in the clubhouse following his round, word came from the course that Sarazen was struggling and had played his way out of contention. Hagen summoned a member of the clubhouse staff, gave him a handful of dollar bills, and sent him on his way.

A short while later, the man met Sarazen on the course, placed an armchair next to him on the tee, and said, "Your easy chair, sir, from Mr. Hagen."

Hagen's love of life clearly extended to women. As Lady Bird Johnson once said about her husband, the late president, "Lyndon loved people, and half the people in the world just happen to be women." So it was with Hagen.

One evening, at a formal dinner in New York, he was introduced to Ernestine Schumann-Heink, a famous contralto with the Metropolitan Opera. Her notoriety did not impress him nearly as much as her figure.

"My dear," he said, gazing down at her low-cut evening gown, "did you ever stop and think what a wonderful bunker you would make?"

Being Mrs. Walter Hagen could not have been easy. He was hardly ever around, and as they say, even when he was around, he wasn't.

One night, he returned home late after another taxing day of being Walter Hagen. As he undressed for bed, his wife mentioned that he wasn't wearing the undershorts he'd put on that morning.

"Jesus Christ!" he exclaimed. "I've been robbed."

Hagen was a generous, if distant, father. Once he bought his son an expensive Austin roadster for his birthday. It was the perfect gift . . . for another birthday. Junior was only fourteen at the time.

Hagen's penchant for making—and spending—money was a big part of his legend. Indeed, his earnings from exhibitions and endorsements were all but unprecedented in his time. Naturally, Hagen being Hagen, his earnings were exceeded only by his expenses.

The late Charlie Price, a gifted writer who knew Hagen well, once summed up Hagen's finances this way:

"In his prime, Hagen made more money than Babe Ruth. But, of course, he also spent more than the entire Yankee outfield."

Like most players of his era, Hagen realized early that most of his earnings would come not from tournament purses but from exhibitions. Hagen played an extensive schedule, some 125 a year, usually with Australian trick-shot artist Joe Kirkwood. The men were paid in cash, which was carried around in suitcases. When the suitcases were full, the money was deposited in local banks—and often forgotten.

It was this utter disregard for money that often got Hagen into trouble, occasionally with the law. Prior to sailing for the 1928 British Open, Hagen learned that police were staking out the ship, the SS *Aquitania*, preparing to arrest him for failure to make alimony payments. Hagen, by this time the winner of five PGA Championships, two U.S. Opens, and two British Opens, sneaked aboard through a cargo door and got safely out of the country.

CLAUDE HARMON

Claude Harmon, who won the 1948 Masters, was one of those rare individuals who are great players and great teachers as well—witness all the years he was the professional at Winged Foot and Seminole. His sons went on to become fine teachers as well, with Butch receiving a lot of notoriety for working with players like Greg Norman and Tiger Woods. Still, Claude wasn't all that impressed by his son's high-profile pupils.

"Hell, Butch," he told his son once. "Anybody can teach Greg Norman. He's already the best player in the world. The real challenge is teaching a bunch of your members who can barely get the ball in the air. And let me tell you something. That's where the fun is, too."

None of Harmon's four sons was spared their father's considerable wit or his ability to deliver the needle.

At the 1980 PGA Championship at Oak Hill, Harmon's son Craig, the host pro, qualified for the championship but shot an opening-round 89.

"You cost me money," Claude said. "I bet everyone you wouldn't break 90."

Claude Harmon's win in the 1948 Masters (after not playing in a tournament for six months) is proof enough that he was an outstanding player, but if further evidence is needed, consider some of the rounds he played on some of America's most formidable courses. While he was the professional at Winged Foot, he once broke 70 for fifty-six straight rounds on both the East and West Courses. He also shot 61s on both courses, as well as on neighboring Quaker Ridge, another outstanding A. W. Tillinghast design. Harmon was also the professional at Seminole, the Donald Ross masterpiece in Florida, where he once shot an almost unbelievable 60—a remarkable feat he made sure wasn't lost on his son Dick, a professional and a fine player in his own right.

"When you take your sixtieth stroke, walk in," Harmon said to his son, as Dick headed out to play Seminole. "And let me know what hole you come in from."

Even when they became successful professionals in their own right, Claude Harmon's sons sought and respected their father's opinions on the game.

One day, Butch and Dick Harmon were discussing sports psychologists and what an impact they could have on improving a player's confidence. Claude listened patiently, at least for a while, but like most pros of his generation, he strongly believed that the best players were self-made. In fact, he had a pretty good example in mind.

"Whatever happened to a square clubface?" he asked. "That's what Hogan used to work on. He'd practice keeping the clubface square through the hitting area. You know, watching those balls fly long and straight down the fairway gave Ben all the confidence he needed."

Dutch Harrison

Dutch Harrison was another one of those characters who never won the number of tournaments he might have, mostly because he spent so much of his time—and made so much of his money—hustling people from coast to coast, using his skills and whatever scam was necessary.

One of his favorites was to set up some unsuspecting rubes over the course of a few pleasant afternoons and then announce that he was playing so well that he'd "take that caddie over there for a partner and still beat you." And usually for double or triple the usual bet. One of his favorite caddies for this was a quiet, unassuming fellow named Herman Keiser.

On one occasion Dutch used a spin-off of his usual routine. On the given morning, he arrived at the club with a sad expression on his face.

"I wanted to give you fellas a chance to win your money back, but my regular partner's come up lame," said Dutch. "I feel real bad, 'cause I have to leave town this afternoon. I'll tell you what, I'll take that old boy over in the caddie pen. The one in the overalls. Hey, you! Boy, do you play golf?"

"Yes, sir, but just a little," said the caddie.

"Well, that's probably good enough," said Dutch. "We'll get you some clubs from the trunk of my car. I've got a spare set."

Herman Kaiser, who would go on to win the 1946 Masters, did the best he could. Since his best was a 67, that was more than good enough.

"I'll tell you what, Dutch," said one of his opponents as he paid off his bet, "that's the best goddamned caddie I've ever seen."

CLAYTON HEAFNER

Clayton Heafner was playing in the second round of a tournament in which he had opened with a 66. Ordinarily, this would have kept him on an even keel, but for some reason he was in an unusually foul humor. Playing badly on the 15th hole, he threw down his club and announced that he was going to pick up.

"Oh, dear, you can't do that," said a woman in the gallery. "My husband and I have you in the Calcutta."

"OK, fine, I won't," he said, turning to his caddie. "You go pick it up." With that, he stormed off the course.

Ben Hogan

Take a look at some of the courses where Ben Hogan won his major championships—places like Augusta National, Merion, Carnoustie, Oakland Hills, Oakmont, and Riviera—and it becomes clear that like all great players, the tougher the course, the better he liked it. One day he was playing in a tournament. As he prepared to tee off on the first hole, he looked at a leader board and saw that two players he'd barely heard of were leading with impossibly low scores.

"What am I doing playing a tournament on a course where two guys like this can shoot scores like that?" he asked a friend.

One of the most famous photographs in sports is Hy Peskin's classic shot of Hogan hitting his approach to the 18th hole in the final round of the 1950 U.S. Open at Merion. Galleries lined the fairways and surrounded the green, looking on as Hogan rifled a 1-iron from just over 200 yards. The ball ended up some forty feet from the hole. Hogan got down in two and the next day beat George Fazio and Lloyd Mangrum in a playoff. It was his first win in a major championship following his near-fatal automobile accident.

Later, a writer asked Hogan how he was able to pull off such a difficult shot under such incredible pressure.

"I've been practicing that shot since I was twelve years old," Hogan said.

When Hogan won the 1950 U.S. Open at Merion, he did it without a 7-iron in his bag for the four rounds of regulation play. When reporters asked him why, he gave an answer that spoke volumes about his mastery of course management.

"There isn't a 7-iron shot at Merion," he said.

Coming to the 72nd hole of regulation play, Hogan laced a magnificent 1-iron approach that Cary Middlecoff called the "purest stroke I've ever seen," then went on to make his par.

At some point following his round, the 1-iron was stolen, and Hogan replaced it with his 7-iron. Some thirty years later, a collector found a 1-iron bearing Hogan's name and a worn area about the size of a dime on the clubface, perilously close to the hosel. He figured, rightly, that it had to be the missing 1-iron. He sent it to Hogan, who confirmed that it was and then gave it to the U.S. Golf Association for their collection of his memorabilia.

Don January grew up in Texas and, naturally, was a great admirer of Ben Hogan. And since he was one of the state's finest amateurs, Hogan was familiar with January as well.

January joined the PGA Tour in 1956 and promptly won the Dallas Centennial Open, establishing himself as one of the top young players. One day in his rookie year he happened to be practicing next to Ben Hogan. Summoning what must have been considerable nerve, he asked what Hogan thought of his swing.

There was silence as Hogan—as was his nature—carefully considered his answer.

"Something wrong with your elbow?" Hogan finally answered, then turned and walked away.

Armed—so to speak—with this revelation, January set out to correct the position of his left arm at address. He practiced and practiced and practiced. He read Hogan's books and instruction articles in the magazines. Then he practiced some more.

It wasn't until years later that he finally figured it out.

Hogan was talking about his right elbow.

Paul Harney, who won seven times on the PGA Tour, idolized Ben Hogan. So you can imagine how unnerved he was when, on his first trip to the Colonial, Hogan approached him on the putting green and invited Harney to join him for a practice round.

"I was so nervous I almost said, 'No, thanks.' But instead I went out and parred the first hole," Harney recalled years later. "That was the only par I made all day. By the time we finished I felt like dirt. I just felt awful. The next morning, I was eating breakfast in the clubhouse when Ben walked by and asked me if I wanted to play another practice round. I did, and parred the first hole. I didn't make another par until the 18th. As we walked off the final green, Ben said, 'Well, son, at least you improved.' "

On another occasion, Hogan invited a young player to join him for a practice round. After several holes, he noticed the rookie was paying close attention to Hogan's club selection. Finally, when they reached a par 3, Hogan gave him a bit of advice—and a lesson.

"Son, don't ever go by someone else's club selection out here," he said. "It's too easy to get fooled. I'll show you."

With that, he pulled out a 6-iron and hit it pin high. He took a second ball from his caddie and hit the 6-iron over the green, ten yards past his first ball. Then he took a third ball and dead-handed it, leaving it ten yards short of the first ball. Three seemingly identical swings. Three different distances.

After his final round at the 1951 Open, Hogan was congratulated by Ione Jones, the wife of architect Robert Trent Jones, who had made numerous controversial revisions to the course prior to the Open. Hogan thanked her and then let her know his opinion of her husband's work.

"If your husband had to play his courses for a living, you'd be in a breadline," he said.

Ben Hogan was a man of his word—a quality he admired in others.

"By 1958, I had won ten tournaments on the Tour," remembers Ken Venturi. "I was playing MacGregor Byron Nelson irons and Titleist balls. Ben knew I wouldn't switch irons, but he said that if I ever decided to switch balls he'd like a shot at offering me a ball deal. At that time, U.S. Rubber was making both the Royal ball and the Hogan ball, and John Sproul, who was the head of U.S. Rubber, came out to San Francisco and offered me a contract to play the Royal ball. It was worth five times what Ben could offer, plus bonuses.

"I told John I'd play his ball but I needed to call Ben before I signed the contract. I called Fort Worth, but Ben was out of town until the next day. John said he had to catch a flight. He wanted me to sign the contract and call Ben later. I told him I'd given Ben my word and that was that. He got pretty upset and said I was going to blow the deal. I didn't care. Ben had been awfully good to me when I came out on tour, and if keeping my word meant blowing the deal, so be it.

"Anyway, the next day we called Ben. I told him what the offer was and he said he couldn't match it. He thanked me for calling and was about to hang up when John told him what had happened the day before. Ben asked John to put me back on the phone.

" 'Ken,' he said. 'If there's ever anything you want or need, call me. I won't forget this.' And he never did."

Golf Digest once assigned Pulitzer prize–winning columnist Dave Anderson of the *New York Times* to ask a wide variety of golfers

a simple question: "If you could play just one course for the rest of your life, which course would it be?"

Naturally, one of Dave's first calls went to Ben Hogan. Dave explained the question to Mr. Hogan's secretary, and she suggested that Dave call back in a couple of days. When he did, he got a simple answer:

"Seminole," she said.

"Did Mr. Hogan happen to say why he picked Seminole?" Dave asked, politely.

"No, Mr. Anderson, and I think you're lucky to get as much as you did," she replied.

A few days later Hogan relented and explained that the variety of wind conditions on the seaside course in Palm Beach made the course play differently every day.

"I used to go there for a month before the Masters and play the course every day," Hogan told Anderson. "I was just as excited about playing it on the last day as I was on the day I arrived."

Hogan loved to play at Seminole and in fact was a member of the club. He particularly enjoyed playing in the annual pro-am tournament that the club hosted for many years.

One year a small controversy broke out when a young pro criticized the course in a local newspaper. Hogan took the man aside and sternly gave him a piece of advice.

"You listen to me," he said, his blue eyes flashing with anger. "You are a guest at every single course you play. You need them more than they need you, so you should count your blessings. If you can't bring yourself to say something nice about a course, just say, 'It's the best course of its type I've ever seen' and leave it at that. You won't be lying, and you'll be long gone before anyone tries to figure out exactly what you meant."

People who saw Hogan in his prime say that when he hit the ball it sounded different from everyone else's shots. They used terms like "crisper" and "sharper."

One day Jay Hebert and Jimmy Demaret were in the locker room changing into their spikes. Through an open window Hebert could hear balls being struck on the nearby practice tee.

"They all sounded pretty much the same," Hebert recalled. "But every thirty seconds or so there'd be a *pow*. I looked at Jimmy and he said, 'Ben's out there early today.'"

"Everyone talks about how Ben loved to practice, and that was true," Dave Marr once remembered. "But he loved to experiment. He'd hit all kinds of weird shots in practice rounds, just in case a situation came up in a tournament that might demand just that shot. One year we were playing a practice round at Augusta. We both hit good drives and good second shots on the [par-5] 13th. I started walking toward the hole, and Ben stopped and dropped another ball. Now he's got this ugly downhill lie to a green fronted by water. He took his 4-wood, choked down, and hit a low hook. The ball barely cleared the water, but instead of coming in hot like you might expect, it landed softly and rolled to a stop about fifteen feet from the flag. I heard him call me.

" 'David,' he said. 'That might be the best shot you'll ever see.' "

There's a temptation to see Ben Hogan as some sort of superhuman, ball-striking machine who could win at will. And while he certainly was a formidable competitor, he was also as human as the next guy—on occasion.

The 18th hole at San Francisco's Olympic Club is a short but tight par 4. Just the kind of hole you'd figure a player like Ben Hogan should own. But in the playoff with Jack Fleck for the 1955 U.S. Open, Hogan proved just how human he could be.

Fleck held a one-shot lead, and Hogan realized he needed to make a birdie. He hooked his tee shot badly, up onto the steep heavily roughed hillside that runs along the left side of the hole. He struggled to get the ball back to the fairway and wound up making a difficult putt for a double bogey 6.

Hogan indicated that his right foot had slipped on the downswing. Tommy Armour wasn't buying it.

"Hogan's human after all," Armour said. "His heart slipped, that's what slipped."

When Ken Venturi joined the Tour in 1957, he quickly caught Ben Hogan's attention and the two often played practice rounds together. Indeed, until he was injured in a car accident, many people predicted Venturi would become the game's dominant player in the post-Hogan era.

Over the years, many people have speculated on the true nature of Hogan's "secret." Some people say he changed his grip. Others say he changed his swing. Still others think it was just a matter of confidence—success breeding success. Venturi has his own theory.

"Ben just intimidated people," Venturi explains. "First of all, he'd outwork you. Then he'd outthink you. Then, when you arrived on the first tee, he'd look you dead in the eye. That was his way of letting you know that he owned you. You could be his best friend, but when they said 'play away' he wanted to beat you into the ground. And you know what? That's how you have to be if you're going to be a champion."

In 1967, Dave Stockton opened the Colonial National Invitational with a 65 that broke Ben Hogan's tournament record and gave him the first-round lead. When he followed it with a 66, he took a ten-stroke lead that seemed insurmountable.

"I walked into the clubhouse feeling pretty good about myself and saw Ben Hogan," Stockton recalls. "I kind of thought he'd say something to me, but he never even acknowledged we were in the locker room together. To tell you the truth, it kind of bothered me."

Stockton went out the next day and skied to an 81 that put him into a tie with Tom Weiskopf. Dejected, he sat in front of his locker and tried to figure out what went wrong. As he sat there, he heard Hogan ask an attendant where Stockton's locker was. Moments later, Hogan came around the corner.

" 'I know you expected me to congratulate you yesterday, but I didn't think it would mean that much to you because everyone else was congratulating you,' " Stockton quoted Hogan years later. " 'You played two fine rounds of golf and you got your bad round out of the way today. Don't get down on yourself. You can still win this tournament.' "

Sure enough, Stockton went out and edged Charles Coody by two strokes for his first PGA Tour victory.

Ben Hogan's association with Colonial Country Club stemmed in no small part from his long friendship with the late Marvin Leonard.

Leonard was a successful Fort Worth businessman who made his fortune in department stores and oil. The two met when the young Hogan was working as a caddie, and from that time on, Leonard supported and encouraged Hogan's interest in golf.

When Hogan first tried his hand on the Tour, he struggled and, by his own admission, went broke at least three times. But Leonard never lost faith in Hogan and, when things got rough, always came through with some money to help the Hogans out.

At one point in the late 1930s, the Hogans were driving to California for the start of the West Coast swing. When Leonard learned that they were down to their last few dollars, he sent them $200. When Hogan finally won some money, he contacted Leonard and tried to repay him.

"Ben, it's enough for me just to know that you want to pay me back," Leonard said. "I don't need your money, but I treasure your friendship."

Jules Alexander, the photographer who snapped the remarkable collection of photos that were published in *The Hogan Mystique*, is a student of Ben Hogan and his career.

"When Hogan was practicing, he'd often hit shots with a cigarette between his lips," Alexander recalled. "When we were looking at the photos with Ken Venturi, he made a remarkable observation: Hogan hit three shots in a row without removing the cigarette. With each shot, the ash on the cigarette grew longer but it never fell off. That's how smooth his swing was. It's almost impossible to do that."

According to Jules Alexander, Hogan once offered this description of a perfectly struck shot: "It goes from the ball, up the club's shaft, right to your heart."

The 1960 U.S. Open at Cherry Hills in Denver was notable for any number of reasons.

For starters, Arnold Palmer shot his dramatic, final-round 65 to win his only U.S. Open.

But for golf historians, Ben Hogan—remarkably, in contention in the Open at age forty-eight—was paired with a twenty-year-old amateur, Jack Nicklaus.

At the close of the tournament, in which Nicklaus finished second, two strokes back, Hogan famously remarked that "I played with a kid today who should have won the Open by 10 shots."

Nicklaus, in a tribute to Hogan's still-considerable ball-striking skills, responded that "if I had putted for Ben, he'd have won by 10."

Ben Hogan was a man of few words, to put it mildly. But like so many other parts of his life, there was a certain irrefutable logic to his silence.

"People who talk all the time never learn anything," Hogan once told a friend. "There's another advantage to choosing your words carefully: if you keep quiet, people may suspect you're not very smart, but it will be harder for them to prove it."

Ben Hogan had a keen, analytical mind, and he applied that intelligence to his pursuit of excellence.

"At one point, Ben noticed that late in a round he'd have trouble hitting his 4-wood just the way he wanted," his protégé, the late Gardner Dickinson, once recalled. "To figure out why, he waited until the end of his practice sessions, when he'd be tired, to work on his fairway woods. That's just how meticulous Ben was."

"Ben was playing with Claude Harmon in the Masters one year," recalls Sam Snead. "They came to the par-3 12th, which is one of the toughest holes in the world. Claude made a hole in one, and the crowd went crazy. Ben made a two, and as they walked off the green he said to Claude, 'You know, Claude, I can't remember the last time I made a two there. What did you make?'

" 'Why, Ben, I made an ace,' said Claude.

" 'Oh, well, that's great, Claude,' he said, as he headed off to the next tee.

"That was just Ben's way. He didn't mean anything by it. He just got into his own world out there, and that was that. I always liked to play with Ben. He played his game and let you play yours."

Hogan does have a fine sense of humor, but it is rarely displayed to those he doesn't know well. Tommy Bolt was a good friend and credited him with helping develop his game. They played together often. On one occasion, they came to the difficult 176-yard, par-3 16th at Colonial Country Club in Hogan's hometown, Fort Worth.

"We got into a friendly argument about which was the right club. I said it was a 5-iron, Ben insisted it was a 4. We put a little wager down, and I hit first, putting it in there about twenty feet. Ben took his damned 4-iron and put it inside me.

" 'See, Tommy, it was a 4,' Ben said.

" 'But you hit it fat, Ben,' I said.

" 'Yes, but the shot called for a fat 4,' he said."

As is their regular practice during the Colonial Invitational, CBS's Frank Chirkinian and Ken Venturi arranged to meet Ben Hogan for lunch at his club, Shady Oaks. Gary McCord, a CBS announcer and tour player, asked if he could stop by and meet Hogan.

When he arrived, he was introduced to Hogan, who pondered the name.

"McCord, McCord," he puzzled. "What did you do before you were an announcer?"

"Well, Mr. Hogan, I've played the Tour for fifteen years," said McCord.

"What did you ever win?" Hogan asked.

"Nothing, Mr. Hogan," said McCord.

"Well, why are you still out there?" Hogan asked.

"I don't know," answered McCord.

"I don't know either," said Hogan. "Would you like a drink?"

One year Hogan was paired with a talented young player in the Colonial Invitational. On the first hole, the young player hit his approach inside Hogan.

"You're away, I believe, Mr. Hogan," the player said.

The same thing happened on the second hole. On the fourth hole, a 226-yard par 3, the player hit a good drive. Hogan selected his club, made a good swing, and just after impact—without even looking at the flight of the ball—said, "You're away."

Ben Hogan has a subtle sense of humor. Sometimes it's extremely subtle. Once, when I was working on a profile of Hogan's protégé, Gardner Dickinson, I asked Hogan why he thought it was that so few successful playing professionals are able to make the transition and become great teachers. As always, there was a pause as Hogan considered the question.

"I wasn't aware that he was either," Hogan finally replied.

Several seconds went by as I tried to figure out how to carefully phrase my next question.

"I'm just kidding, of course," he added, with perfect timing.

In 1967 Hogan traveled to Augusta for the Masters. He was almost fifty-five years old and had been winding down his playing career to focus on his equipment company. A well-meaning fan approached him and said, "I suppose you come to Augusta now just to see your friends."

"I see my friends in Fort Worth," Hogan replied firmly.

Hogan went on to finish tenth after shooting a record 30 on the back nine in the third round, and a 77 in the final round.

Few players have ever been able to read a golf course and manage their game accordingly as well as Ben Hogan did. In fact, many people believe that the only rival he ever had in this regard is Jack Nicklaus.

A good example occurred one year at the Masters. Hogan had finished his round when a young amateur approached him.

"Mr. Hogan," he said, "I was wondering why you didn't try to reach the green on [the par-5] 13. You hit a good drive, and you could have easily reached the green."

Hogan looked at him for a moment and then answered tersely, "I didn't need a 3."

Prior to, say, the mid-1960s, very few golfers played by yardage. They played by sight, instinctively judging the distance, visualizing the shot it required, and then pulling a club from the bag. Hogan certainly played that way, believing that his eyesight and experience were more trustworthy than yardage books and markers.

Fred Raphael, who produced the old "Shell's Wonderful World of Golf" series, remembers a legendary match between Hogan and Sam Snead at Houston Country Club.

"There was a par 3 that we had listed as 152 yards," Raphael recalls. "When Ben came through in a practice round he looked at the green, then at the yardage. He said we were wrong, that the hole played 148 yards to the center of the green. After he played the hole, we paced it off. Sure enough, he was right."

One time Hogan and Tony Penna were partners in a four-ball match. On the first tee Hogan said that Penna would be the captain and would decide which putts should be given. On the 4th hole Penna gave a short putt to Willie Goggin. "That's it," said Hogan as they walked to the next tee. "You're not captain anymore. We can't be giving away putts like that."

For a long time, people—including some sportswriters who should have known better—insisted that golfers weren't really athletes. But if strength and eye-hand coordination count for anything, Ben Hogan in his prime was the very definition of an athlete.

When Hogan won the Hitchcock Belt as America's top athlete in 1953, he was introduced to former heavyweight champion Gene Tunney, who came away impressed.

"My God," Tunney said. "I shook Hogan's hand and it feels like five bands of steel."

During the years that he struggled to make it on tour, Hogan returned to Fort Worth many times with scarcely a cent to his name. In order to make ends meet, he worked dealing cards at night—one of the few jobs that would allow him to practice his game during the day.

"Ben could deal cards so they came out of his hand in a blur," remembers Paul Runyan. "His hands were remarkably quick. We used to have contests where we'd all sit around a table with a coin placed in the center. Someone would snap their fingers and we'd all try to cover the coin. Nobody could ever beat Ben. He was just too quick."

Ben Hogan's comeback from an almost-fatal car crash to enjoy his greatest success is the stuff of legends—and as such, it naturally attracted Hollywood's interest. The movie *Follow the Sun* starred Glenn Ford, and it doesn't take Siskel and Ebert to realize that the film left a lot to be desired.

As you'd expect, Hogan was on-site as a technical adviser and reportedly hit all the golf shots. He was determined to make the film as accurate as possible—which led to an early battle with the studio.

Hogan arrived at Riviera Country Club, where much of the film was shot, and noticed that the irons being used were not the same year and model he'd actually used. Hogan insisted that filming stop until the correct irons were located.

The producer and director argued that no one would notice.

"I noticed," Hogan said.

They told him that the delay would cost them $100,000.

Hogan didn't care.

Filming stopped until the correct clubs could be found.

Following the automobile accident, few expected him to play golf again, let alone win on tour. But when he won the U.S. Open in 1950 at Merion, Tommy Bolt quipped, "Ben, we're all proud of you. You've started a trend. We're all going to go out tonight and see if we can get hit by a bus."

Dave Marr, paired with Ben Hogan at Colonial one year, watched as Hogan made a double bogey on the first hole. As they walked to the next tee, Marr tried to console Hogan.

"Geez, Ben," he said, "tough start."

"Dave, that's why there are eighteen holes," said Hogan.

Ben Hogan was the captain of the 1967 Ryder Cup team that faced Great Britain and Ireland at Champions Golf Club in Houston. As is traditional, the captains introduced their teams at an opening dinner.

Dai Rees, the captain of the Great Britain/Ireland team, went on at length about his team's remarkable individual accomplishments, which in this era consisted largely of assorted East Sussex Four-Ball Championships and the like. These remarks were met with polite applause.

When Hogan rose to speak, he got right to the point:

"Ladies and gentlemen, it's my honor to present the United States Ryder Cup team—the greatest golfers in the world."

The fiercely partisan audience roared in approval.

They may not have been the greatest, but they were good enough to win, 23½ to 8½.

At one U.S. Open, Hogan led by a shot going into the final round. In his postround interview a writer asked him whether he'd "rather be ahead by a shot or behind by a shot" going into the final round.

Hogan looked at the writer in disbelief.

"Would you rather be rich or poor?" Hogan asked.

Ben Hogan's last tournament appearance came in 1971 at the Champion's Tournament in Houston. It was a brutally hot and humid day, debilitating for everyone in the field but particularly so for a man on the verge of his fifty-ninth birthday.

Standing on the 4th tee in the first round, he faced a carry of 175 yards over a ravine on the par 3. He pulled a 3-iron, but hit three balls into the ravine before making a 9 on the hole. He shot a 44 on the front, then went double bogey, bogey on the 10th and 11th. On the 12th he hit a good drive and put his approach on the green. Then he sent his caddie ahead to the green to pick up the ball and summoned a cart to take him to the clubhouse.

"I'm sorry, fellas," he said to his playing partners. "Don't ever get old."

With that, Ben Hogan ended one of the greatest playing careers in golf history.

Lanny Wadkins often played with Ben Hogan when he first came out on tour. In fact, he still has an uncashed check that Hogan wrote to settle up after one match. While Hogan enjoyed playing with younger players, there was never a lot of joking around on the course.

"I remember one match when I was kidding around with the other players in the foursome," Wadkins said. "Hogan looked over at me and said, 'I don't play jolly golf.' That was the end of the jolly golf for the day."

Hogan was at his best in medal-play championships, when he could pick a number to shoot at and then plan his strategy accordingly. Still, he had a fine Ryder Cup record and won two PGA Championships at match play. In the semifinals of the 1946 PGA Championship he beat his good friend Jimmy Demaret, 10 and 9. When the match was over, reporters asked Demaret if Hogan had said anything to him during the round.

"Sure," Demaret laughed. "You're away."

Hogan was paired with an awestruck young player late in his career. Beginning with his drive on the first hole, the young man could scarcely contain his admiration. Every time Hogan hit a shot, the young man told him, "Great shot, Mr. Hogan." Finally, Hogan had heard enough.

"Please don't say that," he said politely. "I'm the only one who knows if it was a great shot."

Unlike some other great players who went on to establish reputations as skilled teachers—most notably Byron Nelson—Ben Hogan never cared much for working with other players. He would teach by example, and if anyone was willing to pay attention, then so much the better for them. His work ethic was there for all to see, and his advice was simple:

"The answer is in the dirt. Go dig it out," he always said.

Still, on occasion, he would be moved to offer advice.

Jan Stephenson used to practice at Shady Oaks, Hogan's home course in Fort Worth. When Hogan was practicing she would watch him from a discreet distance, never daring to ask questions or even make small talk with him. One day, after she had just lost a tournament by skying to a 77 in the final round, he invited her to come over to his spot on the practice tee.

"Hit some," he said.

Stephenson—by her own admission "choking like a rat"—began working her way through her bag.

"I had studied his practice routine and I did everything exactly the same way he did," she recalled. "I kept waiting for him to say something. Finally, I couldn't take it anymore, and I asked him what he thought."

"How the hell can you ever shoot a 77 with that swing?" he said as he got in his cart and drove away.

Nick Faldo came to Fort Worth to visit Ben Hogan. They met for lunch at Hogan's club, Shady Oaks, and Hogan happily autographed a copy of his book, *Five Lessons of Modern Golf*, for Faldo.

In the course of lunch, Faldo asked Hogan what he needed to do to win the U.S. Open.

"Shoot the lowest score, Nick," said Hogan.

As they finished their meals, Faldo asked Hogan if he'd come out to the practice tee and watch Faldo hit some balls.

"Well, Nick, you're a fine player," said Hogan. "I might tell you something that would only confuse you. I've always believed you're better off working it out by yourself."

Faldo thanked Hogan and headed for the practice tee. Several minutes later, an employee of the Hogan company asked Ben if he wanted to go out and watch Faldo practice.

Hogan thought for a moment.

"Does Nick play our clubs?" Hogan asked.

"No," the man replied.

"Then I think I'll just sit here and finish my wine," said Hogan.

As Ben Hogan aged into his seventies and eighties, old friends would occasionally meet him for lunch at his club, Shady Oaks. The visits no doubt meant as much to Hogan as they did to his friends. One afternoon Dave Marr was in Forth Worth and met Hogan for lunch.

"We had a wonderful time, talking about old times and mutual friends," Marr remembered. "At the end of the lunch, Ben sat there, very quietly, carefully shining the silverware with his napkin. Finally, he looked up at me with tears in his eyes and said, 'Dave, do you know what I really miss? God, I miss tournament golf.'

"It made the hair stand up on the back of my neck."

In his later years, Hogan enjoyed eating lunch at his club in Fort Worth, Shady Oaks. A table was always reserved for him with a view overlooking the golf course. Occasionally, he would offer advice to his fellow members.

One day he ran into a friend in the locker room. Hogan asked the man how he was playing.

"Just awful," the man said. "I can't seem to figure out what's wrong. I'm so frustrated."

"I know," Hogan said. "I've been watching you, and it's painful. If you don't mind, I could give you a tip."

Naturally, the man was delighted, and for a good half hour Hogan broke down the man's swing and told him what corrections he had to make. Later, another friend asked the man if the advice had worked.

"Yes and no," the man said. "He cured my slice. The problem is, it took me a month to get rid of my new hook."

Even well into his seventies, Hogan had a remarkable ability to hit golf shots on demand. So he agreed to travel to Riviera Country Club to shoot a series of commercials for his equipment company. At the start of the shoot, he positioned himself in the center of a fairway and waited patiently for the crew to get in position. When everything was ready, the director told him to go ahead and hit the ball to the green.

"What would you like it to do when it gets there?" Hogan asked. "Bounce left, right, or back up?"

During this shoot, he also demonstrated his innate sense of fairness and his sense of humor.

Club officials had offered to close the course, or at least the holes Hogan was using, to member play. But Hogan wouldn't hear of it, protesting that it was the members' course and he was just a guest. Of course, he did take a certain pleasure in watching the members' reactions when they had to try to play through Ben Hogan.

At a recent Masters, several players were complaining about the severity of some of the pin placements. Hord Hardin, then chairman of Augusta National, listened to the comments and then dismissed them with an answer that spoke volumes about the respect people in the game still hold for Ben Hogan.

"We believe Ben Hogan would have found a way to play them," Hardin said.

Late in his playing career, Ben Hogan was paired with a young player, who was very much in awe of the Great Man. While understandably nervous, he was encouraged by his good play. When Hogan praised him following the round, it gave him just enough courage to ask Hogan a question about the golf swing.

"The answer is out there—in the dirt," Hogan said, pointing to the practice tee. "You've got to dig it out yourself."

Ken Venturi carries in his wallet a quote from Ben Hogan: "For every day I miss practicing it takes me two days to get back to where I was."

Several years ago, in an interview for CBS Sports, Venturi asked Hogan why he practiced so long and so hard.

"I had to," Hogan said. "My swing was so bad."

"Is that the only reason?" Venturi asked, sensing the answer beforehand.

"No, I loved it. There's nothing I loved more than waking up in the morning and knowing I could head for the course to practice. I always got the most pleasure out of improving."

Ben Hogan was once asked which of his accomplishments gave him the greatest satisfaction. Was it his record in the major championships? His return from a near-fatal accident to dominate the game? His uncompromising standard of play? None of the above.

"I get the greatest satisfaction knowing that I went dead broke out on tour more than once and still came back and made it on my third try," he said.

Ben Hogan existed in the rarefied air of the greatest champions. But in expressing his feelings for golf, he spoke for everyone who loves the game.

"The prospect that there was going to be golf in my day made me feel privileged and happy, and I couldn't wait for the sun to come up the next morning so that I could get out on the course again."

Ben Hogan was asked how he'd like to be remembered.

"I'd like to be known as a gentleman first, and then as a golfer. That's all."

After Ben Hogan died, his wife, Valerie, looked back on their life together and captured the pure essence of the man:

"I had the great honor of being with Ben in both the best of times and the worst of times, and he never disappointed me. Not once."

IRELAND

I once had a limousine driver in Chicago who offered a unique version of golf history. His name was Desmond, and he was a native of Ireland who'd come to America during World War II to work on the Manhattan Project, the top-secret effort to develop the atomic bomb.

Desmond was in his seventies and could have passed for the twin brother of Barry Fitzgerald, the actor who played the matchmaker in the greatest movie ever made, *The Quiet Man*, which also featured the most beautiful actress who ever lived, Maureen O'Hara.

All that aside, Desmond was a treasure who didn't need the money but drove his limo simply because it gave him a chance to meet new people. Honestly. Anyway, his story went something like this:

"Well, I suppose being a golf writer and all, you think that the game began with the Scots. That's not true, at all. The Irish invented it, we did. Back in the days when the great kings ruled Ireland they established what we called 'Common Grounds' for the use of all the people, you know, for gardens and the like. Now, since we Irish are a naturally caring people one of the uses of these common grounds were as places where the least fortunate mentally among us could gather and amuse themselves without being a bother to the rest of the people. I don't like to use the word *retarded* because God Himself wouldn't care for it, but let's just say they had a special grace from our Father and leave it at that.

"Anyway, one day it came to pass one of the elders in the village watched some of these people hitting stones around with sticks and thought it might be more fun for them if they had a goal to their hitting. So he dug a wee hole in the ground and then showed them how to hockey the stones into it.

"Well, of course this was a perfect game for them and it kept them occupied for hours on end. Now, about this time the Irish

began doing a fair amount of commerce by sea, and one of their favorite ports was St. Andrews in Scotland. When Irish ships began arriving in that godforsaken place they demonstrated their game to the Scots as a joke, you see. Naturally, the damned fools took it seriously. It's like their Presbyterianism—that religion of theirs. Christly dour, it is.

"Of course, they did the same thing with bagpipes. We gave them something that produces the softest, most lilting music you ever heard and they turned it into the most dreadful screeching imaginable. They use it to march to war and that's all it's fit for, really. Well, that's the Scots for you. British once removed, they are."

That's Desmond's story, and he's sticking to it.

The American Ireland Fund is a wonderful and very worthy organization that raises money in America to help fund charities and scholarships in Ireland, as well as promote political reconciliation and economic development in the six counties. As you might imagine, the fund is supported by Irish-American leaders in the political, business, and cultural communities—people who gather at a series of fund-raising dinners in cities across the country every year.

At a dinner in Boston, a speaker told the story about a hugely successful Texas rancher who traveled to Ireland to visit his ancestral home and play a little golf.

In the course of his round at Portmarnock, his caddie asked him about Texas—a place that had always captured his imagination.

"Boy, I get in my car when the sun comes up and I start driving," the Texan boasted. "By the time the sun sets in the west, I still haven't reached the end of my property."

The caddie wrapped a sympathetic arm across the Texan's shoulder.

"Don't feel badly, sir," he said. "I had a car like that once myself."

"Arnold Palmer and I played in the 1960 Canada [now World] Cup at Portmarnock in Ireland, which was quite a big deal at the time," Sam Snead recalls. "All the politicians and whatnot came out, and there were a lot of speeches. The weather was unusually good, very bright and sunny with hardly any wind. Well, this old bird—I think he was the prime minister or something—says, 'I want to personally welcome all of you American visitors to Ireland. As you can see, we are being blessed with typical Irish summer weather. In fact, this is the first typical Irish summer weather we've had in the past decade.' "

BOBBY JONES

Like many talented young players, Jones had a fierce temper on the golf course.

In the 1916 U.S. Amateur at Merion, Jones, then just fourteen, met the 1906 champion, Eben Byers, in an early match. The clubs flew early and often. Finally, at one point, Byers became so incensed that he fired a club into the woods and refused to let his caddie retrieve it. Later, Jones laughed about his victory.

"I only won because Eben ran out of clubs," he said.

Five years later, Jones traveled to St. Andrews for the British Open. The course baffled him, and in the final round he lost his composure. After making double bogeys on both the 10th and 11th, he tore up his scorecard and threw it into the wind. The British press, which would come to adore him, was merciless.

Early in his career, Bobby Jones was paired with Harry Vardon. The young Jones was understandably nervous and played badly. Vardon gave him a piece of advice: "Don't give up. Just keep hitting it. Something good might come of it." It was advice Jones never forgot.

In the 1925 U.S. Open at Worcester (Massachusetts) Country Club, Jones called a penalty upon himself, stating that his ball had moved when he addressed it. Nobody but Jones had seen the ball move, and the ensuing one-stroke penalty put him into a playoff with Willie MacFarlane, who beat him the next day.

Later, when Jones was praised for his sportsmanship, he bristled.

"There's only one way to play the game," he said. "You might as

well praise a man for not robbing a bank as to praise him for playing by the rules."

Perhaps no player is more closely associated with St. Andrews than Bob Jones. He won both the British Open and Amateur there and, upon his retirement from competitive golf, returned unannounced for a quiet round with friends that resulted in the entire town turning out to watch him play the Old Course one last time.

Like many players, Jones did not love the Old Course at first sight. In fact, his first visit—in the 1921 Open—resulted in a most uncharacteristic display of temper. Playing poorly in the third round, he took a 6 on the par-3 11th and tore up his scorecard in disgust.

But in time he came to understand the intricacies of the course and its considerable charm, as he explained when he returned to St. Andrews to be named an Honorary Burgess of the city—the first American to receive the honor since Benjamin Franklin.

"The more I studied the Old Course the more I loved it, and the more I loved it the more I studied it, so that I came to feel that it was for me the most favorable meeting ground possible for an important contest. I felt that my knowledge of the course enabled me to play it with patience and restraint until she might exact her toll from my adversary, who might treat her with less respect and understanding."

Jones faced a close friend, Watts Gunn, in the finals of the 1925 U.S. Amateur at Oakmont Country Club. Gunn and Jones were members at East Lake Country Club in Atlanta, and when they played at home, Jones—who carried a plus-four handicap—would give Gunn three shots a side.

When they met on the first tee prior to the finals, Gunn asked Jones if he was "going to give me three a side today."

"No," Jones said. "I'm going to give you hell today."

And he did, beating him 8 and 7.

In 1926, Bobby Jones was already the best player in the world, but when he went across the Atlantic for the British Open, he had been struggling with his game. No matter how often he changed clubs, he couldn't seem to find a driver he liked.

When he came to Sunningdale, outside London, for his qualifying round, he was still searching for a club that looked good to his eye. Jack White, the professional, showed him a driver he was particularly fond of—so fond, in fact, he had named it "Jeanie Deans" after the beloved Scottish heroine.

Before he hit even one ball, Jones sensed that this was the club he'd been looking for. In the first qualifying round, he shot a 4-under-par 66 that many believe is still the closest thing to a perfect competitive round. He went around in 33-33—66, taking just 33 putts. He hit every fairway and missed just one green.

When he holed his final putt, the gallery, according to a newspaper account at the time, "gave a reverential cheer and then dispersed awestruck, realizing they had seen something they had never seen before and would never see again."

After his round, Jones said, "I wish I could take this course home with me."

Indeed, so dominant and impeccable was his play that London's oddsmakers immediately made him a 3-1 favorite to win the Open at Royal Lytham—the shortest odds in British Open history. They knew what they were doing. Jones finished two shots clear of Al Watrous, to capture his first of three British Open titles. He would win ten of his thirteen major championships with "Jeanie Deans" in his hands.

When Jones retired from competitive golf after winning the 1930 British and U.S. Opens and Amateurs, many people were astonished. After all, he was only twenty-eight and the dominant player in the world. Still, those who knew him best knew the fierce toll that championship play took on him. British writer Bernard Darwin remembers seeing Jones following his final round in the 1930 British Open at Hoylake.

"I happened to be writing in the room where Bobby was waiting to see if he'd won," Darwin told a friend. "He was utterly spent, exhausted. He had to hold his glass with both hands, lest the good liquor spill. All he could say was that he would never, never do it again."

Jones completed the Grand Slam by winning the U.S. Amateur at Merion. He beat Gene Homans, 8 and 7, and as they shook hands he told him, "Gene, if you want to play again you'll have to come to East Lake for a Saturday-morning game. I'm through."

One of Bobby Jones's closest friends was O. B. Keeler, the Atlanta newspaperman who chronicled Jones's career. Keeler knew better than most the effects the pressures of championship competition had on Jones. He knew that after winning the British Amateur and Open and the U.S. Open in 1930, the twenty-eight-year-old Jones was contemplating his retirement from competition.

In the locker room after winning the U.S. Open at Interlachen, Jones was asked by a writer what he'd do when he retired.

"You'd better tell them, O.B.," Jones said to his friend.

Keeler climbed upon a bench and quoted the English poet Hilaire Belloc:

"If I ever become a rich man
Or if I ever grow to be old,
I will build a house with a deep thatch
To shelter me from the cold,
I will hold my house in the high woods
Within a walk of the sea,
And the men that were boys when I was a boy
Shall sit and drink with me."

Like many golfers, Bobby Jones was something of a loner. While he accepted being a celebrity, he very much treasured his privacy. One day a friend asked him if he liked people.

"Yes, I do," Jones replied. "But I like most people in small doses."

One year at the Masters, some players were complaining about how difficult it was to make birdies on certain of the holes.

"I don't agree with that and, frankly, don't understand it," Jones confided to a friend. "If you apply the proper imagination and strike the ball properly, you might get close enough to reasonably expect to make a birdie. That is all the course owes you."

Bobby Jones was very close to his father, the Colonel. The elder Jones wasn't all that much of a golfer, but he had a deep love for the game and a fine sense of humor.

In one of the early Masters, his son asked him to serve as a rules official. A player hit his ball into what he believed was casual water. He motioned the Colonel over and asked for a ruling.

"How do you stand?" the Colonel asked.

"Eighteen over," the player responded.

"Well, what the hell does it matter?" the Colonel said. "Take a drop or tee it up on a peg, for all I care."

By all accounts, Jones had a delightful sense of humor. He could, in the proper company, share a bawdy story with the best of them, and his wit was dry and to the point.

One afternoon, he was sitting with friends on the porch of his cottage at Augusta National. One friend reported a conversation with a Scotsman who, while finding many things admirable about America, detested its heavily wooded courses, preferring the barren links of his homeland.

Jones paused for effect and studied the holes that stretched out before him—each framed by beautiful, towering pines.

"I agree," he said. "I don't see any need for trees on a golf course."

While he was universally known as "Bobby," Jones preferred to be called "Bob" by his friends. He felt it was a little demeaning for a grown man to be called "Bobby," and one day he received a letter from a youngster that proved his point.

"Dear Bobby—When I grow up, I want to be a train engineer. Do you know what you want to be when you grow up?"

Bob Jones was very close to his father, whom everyone called "the Colonel." By all accounts they had a wonderful relationship, even though their personalities were quite different.

"The Colonel was the most rambunctious, energetic man I've ever met, while Bob was very quiet and modest," remembers Charlie Yates. "Bob was known to curse every now and again, but the Colonel could say a hundred words and not use the same swearword twice. One time we had an interclub match, and the Colonel was going to play with a man who could match him swear for swear. We decided to have a little fun, so we told each man that the other fellow was a preacher and they had to be on their best behavior. Well, everything went along just fine for about the first fourteen or so holes. But on 15, the Colonel hit a horrible shot and couldn't contain himself any longer.

" 'Goddamn, son of a bitch,' the Colonel yelled, then immediately apologized. 'I'm sorry, preacher. That just slipped out.'

" 'Preacher?' the man said. 'I'm not a preacher. They told me you were a preacher.'

"From that moment on, the sky was blue with profanity," said Yates.

Bob Jones always said that his favorite playing companion was his father, "the Colonel," even though he wasn't nearly a match for his celebrated son.

One day they were playing at East Lake. The Colonel lashed at the ball and sent a huge slice off into the trees. In frustration, he made a practice swing and then turned to his son.

"There," he said. "Now tell me what's wrong with that swing."

"Nothing," said his son. "Why don't you try it on the ball sometime?"

After winning the Grand Slam, almost all of Jones's tournament play was in the Masters, but it was largely ceremonial. In 1937, he came to the par-3 4th hole and hit his drive some 100 yards into the woods, where it came to rest in a stand of shrubs.

"My God," said an astonished Jones. "That's about as bad as I've ever hit a shot. The only thing worse would have been a whiff."

One of Jones's favorite playing companions was his father, "the Colonel," who made up in enthusiasm what he lacked in skill.

One day in the early 1940s the two paired to play Charlie Yates, the 1938 British Amateur champion, and a local minister in a match at East Lake. The match remained close. On one of the final holes, with the Colonel getting a stroke, he put his approach into a green-side bunker. He took several swipes at the ball then compounded his misery by three-putting, after which he unleashed a torrent of obscenities.

The Jones team went on to win the match, and as the foursome was walking off the final green, the minister said to Yates, "Charlie, I should have known we'd never beat such a combination of proficiency and profanity."

Jones was stricken with syringomyelia, a degenerative nerve disease. His condition was particularly cruel because it wasted his body while leaving his mind intact. Eventually he was confined to a wheelchair, but he struggled to maintain as normal a life as possible.

One day Charlie Yates asked Jones if he was able to sign a few copies of his book.

"Yes, but not too many," said Jones, whose hands were so afflicted by the disease that he could only manage a scrawl by using a pen attached to a rubber ball. "My hands don't work so well anymore."

Yates, a dear friend of Jones, had assumed that Jones would have his secretary inscribe the books. He immediately apologized to Jones.

"Oh no, Charlie," he said. "It wouldn't be proper to have someone else sign them."

It is one of the ironies of golf history that following his competitive career, the game's greatest amateur was declared a "non-amateur" by the USGA. The game's governing body determined that since Jones was making money from his line of Spalding golf clubs and from his instructional movies, he was no longer pristine enough to meet the strict standards of pure amateurism.

But in 1962 Joseph C. Dey, the wise and judicious executive director of the USGA, sent Jones an application for reinstatement of his amateur status. The application contained a number of questions, which Jones answered with tongue firmly in cheek.

Occupation: "Assistant."

Employer: "Clifford Roberts."

Do you understand the Rules of Amateur Status? "No."

Without mental reservations, have you decided to permanently abandon all activities contrary to the Rules of Amateur Status? "I have no mental reservations about anything."

Bob Jones played his last round of golf in 1948 at East Lake. One of his playing partners was Tommy Barnes, a fine amateur.

"We started on the back nine," Barnes remembers. "We came to the 8th hole—our 17th—and Bob was two-under. Bob hit a smothered hook. It was the worst drive I'd ever seen him hit. He made a double bogey and finished the round at even par. He didn't make any excuses, but he said later that he'd been having back and neck pains and some numbness. He felt like he was just losing strength. At the time, no one thought that we'd seen Bob's last round. No one could have imagined what the future held for Bob. Not in their worst nightmares."

Jones went to the hospital, where three growths were discovered on his cervical vertebrae. Two operations did nothing to ease the pain. Finally, in 1955, at age fifty-three, he was diagnosed with syringomyelia, a rare disease of the nervous system, which gradually wasted his body and resulted in his death twenty-two years later. News of his illness devastated his friends, as did the degeneration of his body over time.

Jones was reluctant to discuss the state of his health, and his friends rarely asked him directly, being acutely aware of how closely he'd always guarded his privacy, even at the height of his fame. But on one occasion a friend asked just what the extent of the disease truly was.

"There are two types of this disease, ascending and descending," Jones explained patiently. "In my case, the paralysis is from my waist down, so I still have my heart, lungs, and so-called brain."

Clearly, Jones knew better than most just how intense the pressures of competitive golf truly are. And he knew how much work it took to reach the top levels of the game. For those reasons, and because he knew how difficult it would be for his son to live up to his reputation, he was reluctant to see young Bob take up the game. But when the boy persisted, he arranged for him to get his first lessons from Stewart Maiden—the Scot who had molded Jones's game as a child at East Lake.

The practice session began early in the morning. At noon, young Bob laid down his club and headed for the clubhouse.

"Son, where are you going?" Maiden asked.

"To the clubhouse for lunch," he replied.

"I didn't say anything about lunch," Maiden said. "Come back here."

Practice—without a lunch break—lasted until twilight. Only then, with his hands sufficiently blistered and bloodied, could the boy return home.

With the possible exception of the galleries at the Masters, there are no galleries to equal those at St. Andrews. They are knowledgeable and respectful, as Bob Jones's son discovered the first time he played the Old Course.

A large gallery turned out to see how their beloved Bobby's son would fare. Young Bob hit a good drive and had just a short wedge shot onto the first green. Sadly, he shanked the ball into the Swilken Burn. When he dared to look up, he saw the gallery quietly walking away. Upon his return home he told his father what had happened.

"The galleries at St. Andrews expect excellence, but they will not stand by and gawk at a painful death," his father explained gently.

In 1958, Bob Jones traveled to St. Andrews to be presented with the Freedom of the Burgh. In the course of his remarks, Jones spoke movingly about friendship and his feelings about the people of St. Andrews. His words spoke volumes about the man himself:

"Friends are a man's priceless treasures, and a life rich in friendship is full indeed. When I say, with due regard for the meaning of the word, that I am your friend, I have pledged to you the ultimate in loyalty and devotion. In some respects, friendship may even transcend love, for in a true friendship there is no place for jealousy. When, without more, I say that you are my friends, it is possible that I am imposing upon you a greater burden than you are willing to assume. But when you have made me aware on countless occasions that you have a kindly feeling toward me, and when you have honored me by every means at your command, then when I call you friend, I am at once affirming my high regard and affection for you and declaring my complete faith in you and trust in the sincerity of your expressions."

When Jones died on December 18, 1971, word spread quickly around the golf world. At St. Andrews, players quit their rounds and silently walked off the course in Jones's honor.

For all his considerable success, Jones's modesty was reflected in his law office in Atlanta. It was smallish, and there wasn't any evidence of his remarkable accomplishments. In fact, there was scarcely any evidence of his great love for the game.

"Bob had a line drawing of the Old Course on one wall," recalls Charlie Yates. "There was another drawing, with Grantland Rice's wonderful reflection on athletic success—and life—that I thought summed up Bob's feelings so beautifully:

"For when the one Great Scorer comes,
To write against your name;
He writes not that you won or lost,
But how you played the game."

Jones died at home in the early evening of December 18, 1971, with his family by his side. Memorial services were private. In the spring of the following year, a Service of Thanksgiving and Commemoration was held at the parish church of the Holy Trinity in St. Andrews. Roger Wethered, whom Jones had beaten in the finals of the 1930 British Amateur, spoke for the millions who had been moved by the example of Jones's life.

"To have won through at golf after all those years when nothing would come quite right was an epic victory in itself, but the second victory—the one in which he was reduced to walking with a cane and, finally, to a wheelchair—was a victory of the spirit that will also live as long as his name is remembered."

As long as there are golfers, there will be a debate over who was the greatest player of all time. But at the time of his retirement from competitive play, there was no doubt how his contemporaries viewed Bobby Jones's place in history.

"I now come with faltering pen to write about the greatest of them all," wrote the legendary British golf writer Bernard Darwin.

Bobby Jones died in 1971, and a memorial service was held in May of the following year at the Holy Trinity Church in St. Andrews.

Jones, who was revered in Scotland, was remembered as a person who "never lost any of the values that make up the complete man: humanity, humor, consideration, and courtesy to all about him."

When Jones retired after winning the U.S. Amateur at Merion to complete his "Grand Slam," Keeler summed up his feelings for his friend:

"And now it was good-bye to golf. And I could still say what I said to people all over the world: that Bobby Jones was a much finer young man than he was a golfer. Wholly lacking in affectation, modest to the degree of shyness, generous and thoughtful of his opponents, it is not likely that his equal will come again."

When he heard of Jones's death, Ben Hogan issued a statement that was eloquent in its brevity.

"Bob Jones was sick for so long, and in fighting so hard to live he revealed his greatest strength to us. It was his strength of mind."

Just three days before his death in December 1971, Jones confided to a friend, "If I had known it would be this easy, I wouldn't have been so worried about it."

The *New York Times* once summed up his career—and life—by observing that "with dignity, he quit the memorable scene on which he nothing common did, or mean."

JOHN F. KENNEDY

President John F. Kennedy loved golf and was an accomplished player—far more so than he let on to the press and public, for fear he'd be compared to former President Eisenhower, whose passion for the game was well documented and sometimes criticized. In fact, when Kennedy moved into the Oval Office, one of his first discoveries—much to his amusement—were spike marks heading from the office to a putting green on the South Lawn.

In any event, Kennedy was determined to improve, and he hit upon a novel idea that made him sort of a forerunner of today's pros.

He arranged for his personal photographer, Cecil Naughten, to take home movies of the presidential swing. After each shot, Kennedy would signal whether the ball flew straight, left, or right. He planned to send them to Arnold Palmer—to whom he often likened his own style of play—to have Palmer critique them and offer advice.

Sadly, the tragedy of November 22 occurred before the films were sent.

Jack Kennedy may have been the most accomplished golfer to have ever lived in the White House. But since the Democrats had made such a big deal about President Dwight Eisenhower's passion for the game, he went to great pains to hide both his ability and love for the game.

One day, he took a break from campaigning for a round with his old friend, Red Fay. On one par 3, it looked as though Kennedy's tee shot would drop into the hole. Instead, it rolled past the hole, stopping just inches away.

"Tough break, Jack," Fay said.

"Are you kidding?" Kennedy quipped. "Do you have any idea how much it would have cost my old man to keep that quiet?"

JOE KIRKWOOD

One of Joe Kirkwood's most famous tricks was to hit balls using a club that had a lead shaft. One day he managed to hit himself in the head on his follow-through and spat out most of the teeth from the left side of his mouth. The crowd, thinking he was spitting out pieces of dried corn as part of his act, cheered wildly.

In 1930 Kirkwood returned to his native Australia for a series of exhibitions with Walter Hagen. Playing in Sydney, they were approached by an elderly lady.

"Joe, do you remember when you used to caddie for me?" she asked. "I'm so proud of you. My drawers are full of your accomplishments."

"I walked away and let Joe play his way out of that one," said Hagen.

Kirkwood and Hagen were staying in a hotel just off New York's Central Park. To entertain themselves they'd hit balls through a window into the park and then play their way back to the hotel, through the lobby, up the stairs, and into the room, finally holing out into a toilet.

"Walter and I were pretty evenly matched until we got to the bathroom," recalled Kirkwood. "Walter could never get the ball into the can. It drove him crazy."

TOM KITE

From his earliest days as a high school junior, through his years at the University of Texas, and throughout his successful professional career, Tom Kite had been particularly close to his longtime teacher and friend, Harvey Penick. Penick's influence on Tom has been profound and reaches far beyond his golf game.

At one point, when Tom began to enjoy some success as one of the country's top amateurs, word got back to Harvey Penick that success was starting to go to the young man's head. The soft-spoken Penick sought out Kite and sternly gave him a bit of wisdom.

"Tom, just remember one thing," he said. "You are who you are, not what you've done."

It was, Tom Kite would say later, one of the most important bits of advice he would ever receive.

In the final round of the 1978 Hall of Fame Tournament at Pinehurst's famed #2 course, Tom Kite was dueling Tom Watson. As he stood over his putt on the 5th green, Kite suddenly stepped back and announced that his ball had moved. While no one else had seen the ball move, he called a one-stroke penalty on himself. He wound up finishing in a tie for second, one shot behind Tom Watson, who won $50,000. Kite's check was for $19,333.33.

Later, writers asked Kite about the penalty.

"It was the only thing I could do," he explained. "When you break a rule, you suffer the consequences. I have to live with finishing second for a few days. I have to live with myself for the rest of my life."

In 1979, Tom Kite received the U.S. Golf Association's highest honor, the Bob Jones Award. And calling the penalty on himself at Pinehurst was only one example in a career filled with reasons why.

Tom Kite had agreed to play in an outing the day after his 1992 U.S. Open win. Certainly, people would have understood if he begged off, but Kite never gave a thought to not playing. Still, there was one thing that needed to be done.

That same day his wife, Christy, took the U.S. Open trophy to the Austin Country Club and presented it to Tom's longtime teacher, Harvey Penick.

"Here you go, Mr. Penick," she said. "Tom said this is for you."

A man came to the pro shop at the Austin (Texas) Country Club and introduced himself to the professional, Tinsley Penick, son of the much-revered teacher Harvey Penick.

"Tinsley," he said. "I'm forty-four years old and have all the money I'll ever need. I used to be a pretty good player, and I'd like to get back to working on my game. I'm thinking about the Senior Tour, and I figure if I dedicate the next six years to golf, I'll be good enough to do pretty well out there. How do you like my chances?"

Tinsley Penick took the man into the clubhouse.

"See that fellow over there having a sandwich?" said Tinsley. "He's forty-four, has all the money he'll ever need, and he thinks about the Senior Tour every now and then. Now how do you like your chances?"

The man having a sandwich was Tom Kite.

In the early 1990s, the members at Austin Country Club in Texas decided to commission a life-size bronze sculpture of the club's longtime professional, Harvey Penick, and one of his favorite pupils, Tom Kite.

When they approached Mr. Penick for his permission, he demurred, saying, "I've never done anything to deserve a statue."

When they approached Tom Kite, his reply was equally simple and to the point.

"I've never done anything to deserve being in a statue with Mr. Penick."

Nevertheless, the statue was erected on a spot near the clubhouse overlooking the golf course. Sadly, Mr. Penick couldn't attend the unveiling. Already quite frail, he was taken seriously ill and hovered near death, coming perilously close the evening before the ceremony.

"I can't die tonight," he said softly to his wife, Helen. "I want that ceremony to be joyous, not mournful."

Somehow, he held on that night and the next day until after the ceremony. Then he slipped quietly away from the people and the game he loved so deeply, and to whom he gave so much.

During the unveiling, Tom Kite fought back tears when he recalled being asked what was the best break he ever got in golf. He said it was when the Internal Revenue Service transferred his father from Dallas to Austin when Tom was thirteen years old.

"That's when I met Mr. Penick and Ben Crenshaw," he explained. "Even in my wildest dreams I couldn't have imagined a finer teacher or stronger competition."

KY LAFFOON

Ky Laffoon was another of those talented and colorful players whose skills were overshadowed by reports—true and otherwise—of his antics.

He came to the attention of the notorious golf hustler Titanic Thompson at a young age. Together the two kindred spirits perfected one of the greatest hustles in the game.

Thompson would wheel into town looking for a friendly game. At his side would be his trusty—if shabby—caddie. After a few days of easy pickings, Titanic would shake his head and announce, "Hell, my caddie can beat you guys. In fact, I'll give you a chance to win your money back. You can play him double or nothing for your losses."

True to the rule "once a sucker always a sucker," Thompson and Laffoon would leave town considerably richer for their efforts.

"Ky wasn't a fool or anything like that," remembers Jimmy Demaret. "He was just one of those people that things seemed to happen to.

"One year he was playing in a tournament down in Arkansas. He tossed a club into a tree and it got stuck. He threw up another to get it down, and that one got stuck. He threw a third up there and, wouldn't you know it, that one got stuck. He finally had to quit trying to get them down because he was running out of clubs to finish his round with. He went back the next morning to get them, but it had rained overnight and the hickory shafts were too warped to play with.

"The other thing about Ky was that he'd cost himself a fortune on the greens. He'd work real hard over a putt, miss it, then hockey the ball all around, getting madder and madder by the minute. He was a beauty."

During a friendly match one afternoon at a course in Florida, Ky's putter had been particularly useless. After missing yet another short putt on the final hole, he finally lost it. He stormed off the green and over to the nearby parking lot where he opened the trunk of his car and pulled out a pistol. He returned to the course with a wild look in his eyes. His playing partners were frozen, as much by his fury as by his pistol.

When he reached the green he shot his putter three times, put the pistol into his pocket, and then ceremoniously buried the shattered club in a nearby bunker.

There is at least one recorded incidence of Ky Laffoon's temper working in his favor. He arrived at the final hole of a tournament needing to make a par to win. He hit a good drive, and an excellent approach left him just three feet from the hole. When his first putt missed the hole by three inches, Laffoon went ballistic. He slammed his putter to the ground but hit the ball by mistake. The ball popped two feet into the air and dropped into the hole for a par.

"People have heard stories about Ky punishing his clubs and can't believe they are true, but they truly are," recalls Paul Runyan. "In those days we drove from tournament to tournament, and Ky would get in these dark moods after a poor round. It wasn't unusual for him to tie his putter to the rear bumper of his car and drag it along the road to punish it. He'd also open a door and drag a club along the pavement for a few miles, with sparks shooting up all over the place. Of course, in fairness to Ky, he occasionally did that to grind off some of the sole or sharpen the leading edge."

JACK LEMMON

Few golfers bring as much enthusiasm to the game as Jack Lemmon. The annual telecast of the AT&T is an exercise in high drama because of Lemmon's attempts (almost certainly in vain) to play well enough to be around for Sunday's final round. Still, what he lacks in skill he more than makes up in his sheer love of the game.

One year, in yet another one of his valiant efforts to get his team into contention, he suffered perhaps the ultimate indignity.

"There I was, pretty much out of it again, but I knew the cameras were on me, so I wanted to make a decent showing coming in," Lemmon recalls. "I had a putt for—I don't know—a double or triple bogey, and as I was lining it up I turned to my caddie and asked him how he thought it would break.

" 'Who cares?' " he answered.

"I couldn't really get mad," says Lemmon. "He had a good point."

199

Another year at the Crosby, Lemmon stood on a tee preparing to hit his drive. Just as he was about to swing, a dog burst through the gallery and ran right between Lemmon's legs. Lemmon never flinched. In fact, he hit one of his best drives of the day.

After his round he ran into a friend, who marveled that the dog hadn't upset his concentration.

"You mean that was a real dog?" Lemmon exclaimed.

LAWSON LITTLE

Lawson Little won the U.S. and British Amateur championships in 1934 and 1935 and went on to win the 1940 U.S. Open at Canterbury in a playoff with Gene Sarazen. But Little's win was not without its trying moments—moments that provide a valuable lesson for those who would forget that the golf swing is an athletic movement and not the second coming of the lunar lander.

Lawson took the early lead in their playoff, but on the 5th hole a fan approached and politely wondered if he might ask Little a question. Little, an outgoing and affable man, told him to go right ahead.

"I was just wondering whether you inhale or exhale on your backswing?" he asked.

"Are you serious?" Little asked.

"Oh, quite," said the man. "For myself, I think I inhale, but I'm not sure."

Hook, hook, hook was Little's reply as his swing broke down under the enormous weight of trying to figure out his breathing patterns.

BOBBY LOCKE

South African Bobby Locke, who won four British Opens, was not a person who minced words or worried excessively about other people's feelings. In fact, as Australian Peter Thomson once observed, Locke seemed "to take a particular joy in irritating people."

Locke was a remarkable talent. Sam Snead called him the best putter he ever saw. And although every one of his shots seemed to be a big, sweeping hook, he was a remarkably effective shotmaker.

One day Lloyd Mangrum, who shared Locke's approach to winning friends and influencing people, offered a bit of golf advice.

"Bobby, you've got too much right hand on that club," he said.

"I save the left hand for checks," Locke replied icily.

HENRY LONGHURST

The late Henry Longhurst enjoyed a long and distinguished career as a golf writer and commentator. His writing appeared around the world, and he worked, at one time or another, for the BBC, CBS, and ABC.

He made his CBS debut at a tournament played at Pleasant Valley Country Club in Massachusetts. As the fates would have it, play was delayed by torrential rains, leaving Longhurst with time on his hands and wet clothing on his back. Finally, he'd had enough and called to producer/director Frank Chirkinian on his microphone.

"I say, Frank," he said. "Do you suppose I might go to the clubhouse and get as wet on the inside as I am on the outside?"

Henry Longhurst was broadcasting the British Open championship from St. Andrews one year. At one point in the tournament, he summed up the plight of an American player who was struggling with the mysteries of the Old Course.

"And there now is the 3:25 train from Dundee," he intoned. "I can see clearly her numbers—3-3-4-4-3—and if our American friend had started that way it should have been damned less boring this afternoon."

Nancy Lopez

In 1979, Nancy Lopez had a season that put the LPGA on the map. She won nine tournaments that year, including a record five in a row. She was the darling of the press and the galleries, and it was a mutual love affair. She clearly adored the attention, even when it drew the spotlight to her private life.

When her first marriage failed, she took it very hard. A writer friend told her not to worry.

"Look at marriage as a golf tournament," he said. "That marriage was just a practice round."

She thought about it for a moment.

"Okay," she said. "But if I get married again, will that be a pro-am?"

Nancy Lopez learned to play from her father, Domingo, who ran an auto body shop in Roswell, New Mexico. From the earliest days of her career, her parents reinforced her belief that she was special. One day she volunteered to help with the dishes.

"No, Nancy," said her father. "Those hands are meant for golf, not dishes."

The fact that Nancy Lopez's first golf instructor was her father led the venerable golf writer Herb Graffis to wryly observe that Nancy "proves that golf isn't a difficult game to learn. Her old man could fix a fender in the morning and teach her how to play golf in the afternoon."

Like everyone else who has ever played this game, eventually Nancy Lopez did come face-to-face with some formal golf instruction. In her case it threatened to do more harm than good.

"I got into sort of a mini-slump at one point, and I was talking to my father about it," she remembers. "I told him I thought the problem was with my follow-through. He looked at me with this funny look on his face and said, 'Nancy, it doesn't make any difference to the ball what you do after you hit it.'"

Like most competitive kids, Nancy Lopez had a bit of a temper and wasn't always shy about displaying it on the course.

"One day I hit an awful shot and I slammed the club onto the ground," she remembers. "My father came over, looked me squarely in the eye, and said that if I ever did that again, he'd hit me with the club and that would be the end of my golf. I knew he'd never hit me, but I didn't doubt for a second that it would be the end of my golf for a long, long time."

Nancy Lopez's mother was an enthusiastic, if not necessarily good, golfer. But her contributions to her daughter's golf game were invaluable.

"We didn't have a lot of money when I was growing up," she remembers. "Dad would give my mother a little money each week for herself, and she'd save as much as she could, and then, when I was leaving to play in a tournament, she'd buy me a little golf outfit. Mom didn't understand that much about golf, but she understood love and little girls."

After a fine junior career, Nancy Lopez accepted a golf scholarship to the University of Tulsa, where she led her team to the NCAA championship. But college would prove to be just a brief stop on her road to the LPGA.

"I started out as an engineering major but switched to business administration," she says. "I finally dropped out of school after my sophomore year and turned pro. I had to. Tulsa didn't offer a degree in basket weaving, and that was about the only thing I could have passed at that point."

Nancy Lopez got her start in golf by playing with her parents. Her father, Domingo, was her first teacher, and even now, when she has a problem with her game, he can usually solve it—with common sense and without a lot of cosmic theories and psychobabble.

At one point in her career, she was mired in a slump and her frustration was obvious. After one round, she returned to her hotel room and got a phone call from her father.

"Nancy, I know what the problem is," he said. "You're not happy. You can't play this game if you're not a happy person. If you smile, the good scores will return."

Sure enough, he was right. Again.

It's often been said that no top athlete ever suffered fools more gladly than did Arnold Palmer, and that may well be true. But Nancy Lopez surely comes a close second.

One day she was on a flight when a man approached and introduced himself as one of her biggest fans. Then he asked if she ever watched *Star Trek*.

When she said that she'd seen it a few times, he pressed his hand gently to her face and held it there for a few seconds.

"It's a Vulcan Mind Meld," he explained. "I'm transferring your golf energy to me. I hope it helps."

Then he thanked her and walked away.

Los Angeles Country Club

From the very first, the Los Angeles Country Club has discouraged the membership of people in the show business community. When Robert Stack, who spent his boyhood at the club, became a professional actor, he quietly resigned his membership at the club.

Years later, after he had retired from acting and become a successful businessman, Randolph Scott joined the club—following one request from the board.

"Randolph," said a member, "we'd appreciate it if you'd do what you can to keep your old movies off television."

JOE LOUIS

When his remarkable boxing career ended, heavyweight champion Joe Louis turned his attention to golf. As you might expect, he had enormous power, but his short game left something to be desired. He was a low-handicapper—unfortunately, not as low as he thought. Louis was an easy mark for hustlers, and one who particularly enjoyed playing with him was the notorious Smiley Quick, who was every bit as skilled at plucking pigeons as was the legendary Titanic Thompson.

"It was painful to watch Smiley hustle Joe," remembers Paul Runyan. "He didn't just take his money; he reveled in picking him clean. I've heard that Smiley bought two condominium complexes with the money he took just from Joe alone, and I believe it to be absolutely true."

DAVIS LOVE, JR.

Davis Love, Jr., the father of PGA Tour star Davis Love III, was one of America's top teaching professionals before he died in a plane crash in 1988. He had the wisdom and patience to work with poor players, but at the same time he had the playing experience that made him a valuable teacher for even the best players in the game—many of whom traveled to Sea Island for lessons and advice. He was by nature a quiet, gentle man, but he also had a fine sense of humor.

Davis taught for many years in the Golf Digest Schools and was every bit as highly regarded as Bob Toski, Peter Kostis, Jim Flick, or any of the other top teachers. For much of that time the schools were run by an administrator named Paul Menneg, who, it can be fairly said, had a healthy respect for a dollar.

One time Davis sent in an expense report that included the cost of an umbrella. Menneg sent it back to Davis saying that the schools wouldn't pay for such an extravagance. Davis was incredulous and appealed to Menneg, to no avail.

A few days later Davis sent in a revised expense report with a note: "Paul, there's an umbrella in here someplace. See if you can find it."

"After I had played the Tour for a while I decided it was no life if I was going to raise a family, so I decided the time had come to become serious about teaching," said Davis Love, Jr. "I had always had a huge amount of respect for Harvey Penick, both as a man and a teacher, so I went to see him for some advice.

" 'Davis, have you ever played a musical instrument?' he asked me, and when I told him I hadn't he said the first thing I had to do was go out and sign up for some lessons. I didn't understand what the connection was between me wanting to learn to teach and playing an instrument, but if Mr. Penick said to do it, I wasn't going to question him. I went out and rented a clarinet and arranged to take lessons from a very nice lady who lived nearby. I set off driving to her house, and the closer I got the more nervous I became. By the time I reached her house I was actually sweating. I didn't know the first thing about playing the clarinet. I didn't know how to hold it. I didn't have a clue about reading music. And then when I actually sat down with her and realized how ignorant I was, I just about froze.

"Just about at that point, I understood what Harvey was up to. He wanted me to understand what it was like for a beginner to come for a lesson—and like so many of Harvey's lessons, it was one I never forgot."

Coming into the 1997 PGA Championship, Davis Love III had carried the burden as the "best player who hasn't won a major" for an uncomfortably long time. He looked as if he might shed it at the 1996 U.S. Open at Oakland Hills, but bogeys on the last two holes kept him out of a playoff with the winner, Steve Jones.

But Winged Foot would be different. Maybe it was because he loved the course. Maybe it was because the PGA Championship had a special meaning for the son of a golf professional whose life was tragically cut short.

Love opened with a 66, then went 71-66 to set the stage for a duel with his friend Justin Leonard, who had won the British Open just a few weeks earlier. The thirty-three-year-old Love began Sunday's round with a two-stroke lead and, by the fourth hole, had stretched his lead to three. After giving a stroke back at number 7, Love's birdie on 8, combined with Leonard's bogey, gave him a four-stroke lead.

But Leonard, who had come from three strokes behind to win the British Open, fought back with birdies on numbers 10 and 12. When Love bogeyed 12, it looked like shades of Oakland Hills all over again.

As the two played 15, heavy showers began to pound the course. While Love had a comfortable lead coming to 18, his victory was never completely assured until he hit the fairway with a 3-wood and then hit a 5-iron approach fifteen feet to the right of the hole.

As he and Leonard approached the green, the rains stopped and a rainbow appeared over the course. The symbolism wasn't lost on anyone. Not Love nor Leonard, Davis's wife and his mother, nor the members of the gallery.

"Look at the rainbow, Davis," people began to yell.

Love couldn't look. He could barely fight back the tears long enough to finish the hole. When he putted out, he finally looked toward the heavens.

The journey, which he had begun as a youngster with his dad, had finally come full circle.

George Low

George Low, who died in April 1995, was one of the legendary hang-around guys in golf. Dan Jenkins called him "America's Guest," and Low never saw any reason to disagree.

Low could usually be found in or near the clubhouse at a tournament, leisurely taking in whatever was going on around him. It was usually a good bet that a drink and a cigarette were not far away.

"George was born retired," the late Jimmy Demaret once said.

When Low wasn't at a tournament, he could usually be found at the home of a friend—usually a wealthy friend.

"I tend to favor places where a rich guy's got an extra bed and a kind heart," he used to say.

"I wish I just had your energy," Billy Maxwell once told Low as Low lounged around the clubhouse during a tournament.

"I wish I had a rock in each hand," Low replied.

When Low was diagnosed with cancer in 1994, doctors told him he had only six months to live.

"I'm playing extra holes," he told a friend.

Low was cremated. His ashes were buried at Cog Hill, the sprawling public golf facility outside Chicago.

At one tournament in the 1940s, Tony Penna checked into a hotel that was run by a friend of his. When he got to his room there was a large supply of free whiskey.

Word of Penna's good fortune soon spread, and it wasn't long before George Low and a friend showed up at Penna's door. Naturally, Penna denied knowing anything about any free booze. And naturally, Low and his friend didn't believe him.

The more Penna denied he had anything stashed away, the more convinced Low was that he was lying, and to find out Low and his friend took desperate actions. They opened a window, grabbed Penna, and hung him out the window some twenty stories above the street.

"It's in the trunk!" Penna yelled. When they had brought Penna back in, all three men sat down to some serious drinking.

In his role as one of the greatest hang-around guys in golf history, George Low spent an inordinate amount of time watching scoreboards. One afternoon he was doing just that when Arnold Palmer posted scores of 9-7-5.

"Pay him," said George. That's '21.' "

"George is a wonderful man, but if you loan him money you might as well write it off as a gift," says Dave Marr with a laugh. "In the winter of 1948, George was tapped out and he talked Claude Harmon into loaning him a couple hundred dollars. The loan went unpaid for several months. In April, Claude won the Masters. As he was walking to the awards ceremony to get his Green Jacket, George approached him and tried to hand him the $200.

" 'Oh, that's OK, George,' Claude said. 'Forget it.'

"George always did have a great sense of timing."

Many years ago George found himself in a match with the Duke of Windsor and one Robert R. Young, a railroad Tycoon, at Seminole.

Despite all the golf he played, the duke wasn't much of a threat on the course, and George won easily. As they strolled to the club-house, George kept waiting for the duke to reach into the royal pockets and cover his losses. The duke never made a move, and George, being the impatient type, began to nervously clear his throat. Finally Young took George aside and discreetly explained the realities of life among the royals.

"George, perhaps I should have mentioned this sooner, but the duke never pays off his wagers," he said.

"He don't what?" George asked, stunned that he had just wasted a good four hours on a stiff.

"His Royal Highness feels that it's rather an honor to play in his company and, therefore, he shouldn't consider paying," said Young.

"Mr. Young," said George, "from now on, you take care of your railroads and I'll take care of my dukes."

Al Besselink was a generous man, probably far too generous for his own good. But he drew the line at lending money to George Low, knowing all too well that it was money headed down a one-way street.

"George, lending you money is like sending lettuce by rabbit," he told Low.

LUCKY BREAKS

In 1966, Jim Ferree finished his final round at a tournament in Akron, Ohio. He was supposed to join a fellow player on a short flight to Chicago, where they were scheduled to play an exhibition. Ferree had played well in Akron, and as he cleaned out his locker, he decided to skip the exhibition and head for the next tour stop.

It was a lucky, even fateful, decision. The plane Ferree was supposed to catch crashed, killing Ferree's friend, 1964 British Open champion Tony Lema.

SANDY LYLE

Sandy Lyle won both the 1985 British Open and the 1987 Players Championship. When he was asked in the pressroom if there was a difference in winning the two, he said, "Yes, about a hundred years."

Sandy Lyle has something of a reputation for being a little on the spacey side. It didn't improve his reputation any when he took a hand in designing his new house and designed a room for his snooker table that was too small for the table.

In the 1992 Los Angeles Open, a lot of press attention surrounded the play of Tiger Woods, a local teenager who was the U.S. Junior Amateur champion. A reporter approached Sandy and asked what he thought of Tiger Woods. Sandy paused and looked puzzled.

"You know, the amateur who is playing this week," said the reporter.

"Oh, I thought it was a new golf course," said Sandy.

ROGER MALTBIE

Roger Maltbie is best known today as a member of NBC's golf team, where his insights are generously colored by his sense of humor. But he is also a fine player, who won five PGA Tour events despite twice undergoing shoulder surgery.

One of the high points of his career came in 1987, when he led the Masters going into the final round.

"I was as nervous going into that final round as I've ever been," Maltbie remembers. "Finally, my wife suggested I call my father. I did, and he told me, 'Son, it doesn't really matter what you do out there today. Your mom and I will still be very proud of you, win or lose.'

"I hung up the phone and cried for about twenty minutes," Maltbie continued. "It just purged the nervousness."

After nine winless years, Roger Maltbie won twice in 1985, and *Golf Digest* named him the magazine's Most Improved Player. He did an article for the magazine in which he described a drill he used to help him make a better turn on the backswing.

A few months later the magazine received a letter from a woman from Maine who had read the article on a flight to Hawaii, where she had been planning to take a golf vacation. The woman explained that she also had a problem making a good turn and tried Maltbie's drill when she got to the golf course. She promptly wrenched her back, making it impossible for her to play golf for the rest of the trip.

Ever since he took up the game as a kid, Roger Maltbie has been a huge Ken Venturi fan. In fact, he went to an exhibition Venturi held early in 1964 and asked him for an autographed ball.

Does he still have it?

"No, I was going to play in a junior tournament and I didn't have any decent balls, so I took the one Ken gave me, wiped his name off, and played with it in the tournament. A couple weeks later, he won the Open. Shows you how smart I am."

LLOYD MANGRUM

Talk with the players who knew him, and they'll tell you that Lloyd Mangrum, the winner of the 1946 U.S. Open, was a tremendous player who never got the recognition he deserved. The winner of two Purple Hearts for his service as an infantryman in World War II, he was also one tough guy.

"You wouldn't say Lloyd went looking for fights, but he sure didn't look the other way if he saw one coming," Sam Snead recalls. "One time, when he first came out on tour, he was playing a practice round in the group in front of Gene Sarazen. Now, Gene liked to play fast, and he wasn't afraid to hit into the group ahead of him if he thought they were playing too slow. He did this to Lloyd, and finally after about the third time, Lloyd picked up Gene's ball, walked back down the fairway, handed it to him, and told him the next time he'd jam it down his throat. And he would have, too."

One afternoon, as a favor to a friend, Lloyd Mangrum agreed to go over to Hillcrest Country Club and play a round with George Burns. After they finished playing, they were sitting around having a drink, when Mangrum offered his assessment of Burns's game.

"George," he said. "You're wearing a beautiful cashmere sweater, gorgeous slacks, and a great-looking shirt. You look just like a pro. It's too bad you play like a comedian."

Lloyd Mangrum was, by any measure, a tough guy. He was decorated for bravery in World War II after serving as an infantryman in Europe. His pencil-thin mustache and cold, dark eyes made him seem especially menacing.

One year, at a player's meeting, the Tour's policymakers announced that there would be substantial fines for players who used obscenities on the course.

"Listen to me you little ****," he said. "You **** can't **** tell me how the **** I **** want to **** talk. If you want to **** fine me, do it now."

DAVE MARR

Dave Marr, who won the 1965 PGA Championship and went on to a long and successful career as a golf analyst for ABC Sports, NBC Sports, and the British Broadcasting Corporation, is a person of uncommon wit and intelligence.

In 1986, the U.S. Open came to the exclusive Shinnecock Hills Golf Club on Long Island. The championship opened on a stormy Thursday, with the wind howling off the Atlantic. As Marr stood near the first tee watching the early players go off, a member of the gallery, who had just bought some food, dropped some dollar bills, and the wind carried the money racing along the ground.

"Welcome to Shinnecock," Dave said. "The only club in America where they overseed with pictures of dead presidents."

"When I was just starting to play in some tournaments outside of Houston, I entered the state junior championship. After the qualifying round, I found out I was supposed to play Don January in the first round of the second flight. He was like a legend in the state at that time. I went up and introduced myself.

" 'Don, I'm Dave Marr from Houston, and we're going to be playing tomorrow in the first round of the second flight,' I said.

" 'Listen, pipsqueak,' he said, 'I'm not playing in the second flight of anything.' That was how I met Don January."

As an amateur growing up in Houston, Marr played a lot of money matches with Tommy Bolt. He never had much money then, but he never had a problem covering his losses, either.

"Back then you'd win all kinds of stuff in amateur tournaments," Marr remembers. "I had outboard motors, clocks, radios—you name it. One time I won a shotgun and figured that would be something Tommy would like. I lost a match to him one day, went out to the car, and got the shotgun out of the trunk and brought it back into the clubhouse. Tommy took one look at me coming through the door with a shotgun and almost died on the spot."

In the 1969 U.S. Open at Champions Golf Club in his hometown of Houston, Dave Marr had a difficult approach to the 18th green. Looking up at the green, he saw the familiar, white-capped figure of Ben Hogan in the gallery. Marr pulled a 4-wood from his bag and cut the ball in within a few feet of the hole.

Later, in the clubhouse, he asked a friend if Hogan had said anything about his shot.

"Yeah, Ben said you hit too much club," said his friend.

Over the years, the late Dave Marr was occasionally criticized by writers for not being more critical of the players he covered, first on ABC and then NBC. The truth is, he wasn't afraid of calling a bad shot a bad shot. It's just that he had the ability to soften the criticism with his considerable sense of humor.

In one telecast, he watched as a player shot at a pin cut to the side of a green closely guarded by a pond.

"If that wasn't a pull, he's the bravest guy since John Wayne," Marr quipped.

If Marr was occasionally reluctant to be overly critical of players—especially struggling young players—it was because he never forgot what it was like to try to make it on tour when every dollar counted.

"I remember being in contention one year and I hit my approach shot into the water on one of the closing holes," Marr once said. "I thought, 'Well, David, you just drowned the mortgage payment.'"

Throughout his career, Dave Marr played in thousands of pro-ams and corporate outings. He always made it a rule to tell the amateurs not to be nervous.

"Trust me, there isn't a shot you can hit that I haven't seen before," he'd tell them.

Well, not quite.

In one pro-am, everything was going along nicely until they came to a par 3, and one of the players hit about as bad a shot as you can possibly hit. He laid the divot right over the ball.

"I take it back," Marr said. "That's a shot I've never seen before."

Dave Marr died in 1997 after a long and terrible battle with cancer. Although he was suffering and knew that death was near, he never lost his remarkable sense of humor. Shortly before he died, his daughter, Elizabeth, came to visit him in the hospital. Soon, she was overcome with emotion and began to cry.

"Dad, it's so sad," she said.

"Honey, you should see it from my point of view," Marr said.

BILLY MARTIN

In 1974, when Billy Martin was managing the Texas Rangers base-ball team, the club's owner, Bradford G. Corbett, arranged for Mar-tin to join Shady Oaks Country Club.

People who knew Martin were sure Corbett had lost his mind. They might have been right.

It wasn't long before Martin committed about as bad a mistake as you could make at Shady Oaks: he, along with his best friend, Mickey Mantle, ran afoul of the club's most revered member—Ben Hogan—and Martin was asked to leave the club.

A month or so later, he was going through his mail in the Rangers' clubhouse when he got his final bar bill from Shady Oaks.

"How do they expect me to pay this?" Martin asked a friend.

"Do you need some money?" the friend asked.

"Hell no," Martin laughed. "But they won't let me back on the grounds."

GARY MCCORD

Gary McCord based his successful television career on the short-comings of his golf game. He happily told anyone who would listen—which included millions of viewers on CBS Sports—that he played the PGA Tour for twenty-five years without ever winning. It worked like a charm, although sometimes people took him a little too seriously.

Playing in the Kemper Open one year, he was hitting balls on the practice tee when he overheard two women talking nearby.

"Look at that," one woman said. "He gets the ball into the air every time."

McCord couldn't help himself.

"Ma'am," he said. "See my name there on the side of my bag? That means I'm a pro. They won't put your name on your bag unless you can get the ball into the air. It's a Tour rule."

In the mid-1980s, *Golf Digest* sent a writer to California to do a profile on Gary McCord. The writer and McCord decided to fit in a little golf along with the interview. Since the writer didn't have any clubs, they drove to a rental warehouse where McCord was storing much of his worldly belongings—clubs, clothes, furniture, the works.

"You must not have much stuff left at home," the writer said.

"This *is* my home," said McCord.

MACHINEGUN JACK McGURN

Machinegun Jack McGurn was an excellent golfer, a player who took the label "shotmaker" to levels never seen before or since in the game's history. When not playing golf, McGurn allegedly worked as Chicago gangster Al Capone's chief executioner, a career that landed him a spot as one of the FBI's "Most Wanted."

McGurn entered the 1933 Western Open at Olympia Fields in Chicago, a tournament that attracted almost all the game's top players. McGurn entered under an assumed name, Vincent Gebhardi, which may have fooled tournament officials but had no effect on the local police, who were planning to arrest him under something called the Criminal Reputation Law—a law that would seem to have been written with Machinegun himself in mind.

Eight officers went out to Olympia Fields and caught up with McGurn on the 7th hole, where he was 1 under par and tied for the lead with Macdonald Smith. As McGurn and his playing partner, Howard Holtman, approached the 7th green, Lt. Frank McGillen confronted McGurn and read the warrant. McGurn asked if it would be all right if he finished his round. Since it was a lovely day for a walk, the police complied.

McGurn double-bogeyed the hole, which prompted his wife, Louise Rolfe (known as "the Blond Alibi"), to ask the police, "Whose brilliant idea is this?"

By this time, the press had been tipped off to the arrest. A photographer appeared and snapped photos of McGurn playing the 8th hole—a hole he finally finished with a 7-over-par 11. Walking off the green, he grabbed the photographer and said, "You've busted up my game, pal."

On the next hole, McGurn's twosome was joined by one Arthur Tilly, who had been playing in the previous twosome but whose playing partner had walked off the course. Tilly, a lawyer and former chairman of the Chicago Bar Association, didn't realize what he was getting himself into. Anyway, McGurn calmed down and finished with a 45-41-86 and was duly arrested.

"They say I broke the law, but what law did I break?" he protested. "I was out playing a game of golf. Why don't they go out and arrest all the punks pulling stickups and shooting cops? Me, I haven't done anything for a year. What are they gonna charge me with, carrying concealed ideas?"

233

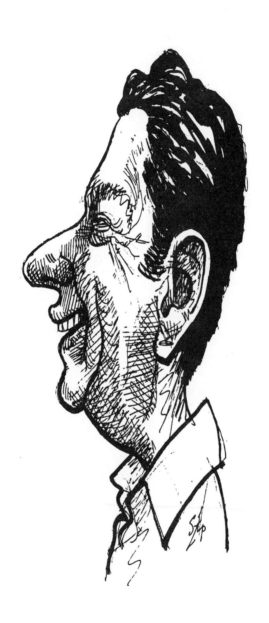

Dr. Cary Middlecoff

Sometimes even the best players have certain holes they just can't seem to play. No matter what they try, they just never seem comfortable. The 5th hole at Colonial, a 466-yard par 4 guarded down the right side by the Trinity River, was a hole that always gave Doc Middlecoff problems. Then one year he came in from a practice round and told the writers he'd figured out how to break the jinx the hole had on him.

"First I stand on the tee and throw two new balls into the river," said Doc. "Then I throw up. Then I hit a ball into the river. It's like a peace offering."

"The boys on tour used to kid Doc about being so slow," Sam Snead recalled fondly after Middlecoff's death. "They'd say he didn't give up being a dentist because he wanted to play golf, but because he couldn't find any patients who could keep their mouths open long enough for Doc to get the job done."

Like every good golfer, Doc occasionally succumbed to the pressure of competition and the sheer difficulty and innate unfairness of the game. The most celebrated case came in the 1953 U.S. Open at Oakmont in Pittsburgh.

"I just hated late starting times," he remembers. "I hated the waiting around and the spiked-up greens. At Oakmont I let that begin to eat at me. I played all right on the front side, but on 10 I hit my second shot into a bunker. Well, that just did it. I was never a good bunker player in the first place, and this just put me over the edge. I looked over there at the Pennsylvania Turnpike, which cuts through the course, and I said to myself, 'I don't have to take this any more.' With that, I just slashed the ball out of the bunker and sent it running down the turnpike. I motioned to my caddie and started in. One of the players asked me if it was in my pocket. 'No, my ball is on its way to Ohio, and I may just play Inverness tomorrow.'"

JOHNNY MILLER

On the Monday prior to the start of the 1973 U.S. Open, a woman approached Miller and introduced herself as a clairvoyant.

"You are going to win the Open," she said. "I am never wrong."

She did the same thing throughout the week, meeting Miller as he came off the final green after each round. Naturally Miller was more than a little skeptical. But after he opened with a round of 71 and followed it with a 69, he started to believe. When the woman didn't show up on Saturday and he shot a 76, he wasn't quite sure what to think.

Prior to his final round he received an unsigned telegram predicting victory for him. Clairvoyant or not, he shot a 63, passed twelve players, and won the championship.

In 1993, after six years without a victory, Johnny Miller won the AT&T National Pro-Am at Pebble Beach. It was a remarkable win that, among other things, ensured that Miller would be invited to play in that year's Masters, where he'd had three second-place finishes.

Even though he was talented and had a remarkable record, he was almost forty-seven years old, and nobody expected him to win at Augusta. But that's not to say there wasn't any pressure on him.

"My four sons are going to caddie one round each," Miller said. "That's a lot of pressure. If I miss the cut, two of them are going to get stiffed."

Alas, he missed the cut by a shot—and two of them did get stiffed.

WALTER MORGAN

Walter Morgan spent twenty years in the U.S. Army—including two tours in Vietnam—and developed into a fine player. After he left the military, he qualified for the Senior PGA Tour, becoming one of the few African-Americans on the Tour. While he has been successful and respected, he's still not as widely known as some of the more prominent players who had come from the regular Tour.

One day he was paired with Jack Nicklaus. The large gallery greeted him with polite applause when he approached his ball on the first tee.

"I'm Tiger Woods," he joked to the crowd, mimicking the Nike commercial.

YOUNG TOM MORRIS

The son of St. Andrews professional Old Tom Morris, Young Tom exists as a legendary—and tragic—figure in the game.

Born in 1851, he won the first of his four straight British Opens in 1868. His father also won four, beginning with the second British Open, in 1861 at Prestwick.

Young Tom dominated golf in Scotland in his short career, which ended with his tragic death in 1875 at the age of twenty-four.

In September, Young Tom and his father had traveled to North Berwick for a challenge match against Willie Park and his brother, Mungo. These matches were extremely popular and lucrative. Each player had wealthy financial backers. As much as hundreds of pounds could change hands, and the matches attracted large galleries.

The North Berwick match ended suddenly when word arrived that Young Tom's wife had become seriously ill following the birth of their child. Father and son raced for a ship waiting to take them across the Firth of Forth and home to St. Andrews.

Before the ship could sail, a second messenger arrived and told Old Tom the awful news: both mother and child had died. Old Tom waited until St. Andrews was in view before telling his son, who was inconsolable.

Three months later, on Christmas morning, Young Tom died. Some say it was from drink. Others insist it was a broken heart.

Today, a plaque commemorating his life can be found at the ancient St. Andrews Cathedral. On it is written:

"Deeply regretted by numerous friends and all golfers, he thrice in succession won the championship belt and held it without rivalry and yet without envy, his many amiable qualities being no less acknowledged than his golfing achievements."

Mother England

241

An older American couple were on a golf holiday through Scotland when they stopped in a small town near Balmoral, the Queen's country estate. As they wandered through the small shops, they spotted a distinguished woman, dressed in tweeds, who was looking at some of the goods. After a few moments, the American woman approached the lady.

"I must tell you that you look exactly like the Queen," the American said.

"How terribly reassuring," said the Queen, extending her hand.

In the years before World War I, British Prime Minister Lloyd-George divided his time between running the government and playing golf. He often did both from his beloved Walton Heath Golf

Club some twenty-five miles south of London. In fact, so many influential members of the government were members at Walton Heath that it was said the Empire was ruled from the Gentlemen's Card Room.

Alas, the fact that Lloyd-George lived near Walton Heath and spent so much time there wasn't lost on the country's women suffragettes. One group blew up his house, which earned its leader, Emily Pankhurst, three years in prison. A second group hid in Walton Heath's woods one day when the Prime Minister was out golfing with the boys. When he appeared, they charged out of the woods, knocked him to the ground, and tried to remove his pants.

And people think sexual politics is rough-and-tumble these days.

Edward, Duke of Windsor, is best known as the man who abdicated the British crown for Mrs. Wallis Simpson, the American divorcée whom he, as king, could neither marry, live without, nor keep tucked away as a mistress.

But Edward was a passionate golfer who, since he wasn't yet weighed down with either kingly duties or anything approaching a real job, had plenty of time to play. On a trip to Egypt in 1928, the prince decided that he must hit a drive from atop one of the pyramids. What a sport. With his collection of lackeys and hangers-on applauding madly, he climbed to the top and played away.

And to think, there are people who, to this day, wonder why the British lost their empire.

The Duke liked to spend time with the other swells in Palm Beach and enjoyed playing at Seminole with his friend Chris Dunphy.

One time Dunphy invited the Duke and Duchess to come for dinner. When they accepted, it presented an awkward problem for the Dunphys since they had houseguests—Mr. and Mrs. Ben Hogan. For some reason—it couldn't have been a very good one—the Hogans weren't invited to the dinner.

The Duke and Duchess arrived at the appointed hour, and after they had been introduced to the other guests, the Duke took Mr. Dunphy aside.

"Where's Ben?" the Duke asked. "I was hoping to talk about golf with him."

Great Britain may have been under siege by the Nazis during World War II, but it didn't stop the Brits from playing golf—with a few modifications. Witness these "Temporary Rules, 1941, of the Richmond Golf Club, London."

1. Players are asked to collect the bomb and shrapnel splinters to save these from causing damage to the mowing machines.

2. In competitions, during gunfire or while bombs are falling, players may take shelter without penalty or ceasing play.

3. The positions of known delayed action bombs are marked by red flags at a reasonable, but not guaranteed, safe distance therefrom.

4. Shrapnel and/or bomb splinters on the Fairways, or in Bunkers, within a club's length of a ball, may be moved without penalty, and no penalty shall be incurred if a ball is thereby caused to move accidentally.

5. A ball moved by enemy action may be replaced, or if lost, or destroyed, a ball may be dropped not nearer the hole without penalty.

6. A ball lying in a crater may be lifted and dropped not nearer the hole, preserving the line to the hole, without penalty.

7. A player whose stroke is affected by the simultaneous explosion of a bomb may play another ball. Penalty: one stroke.

During World War II, Luftwaffe pilots dropped heavy bombs on Sunningdale, the lovely parkland course near London. After the war, the membership debated what to do with the craters near the right side of the 18th green.

With classic British common sense they elected to do the obvious: they made them into a fearsome bunker.

Percy Belgrave "Laddie" Lucas was a British Walker Cup player and captain who distinguished himself as an often-decorated fighter pilot in the Royal Air Force during World War II.

On one mission, his plane was badly shot up in a battle over the English Channel. When he made it back over land, he began to look for a place to land his crippled Spitfire. Happily, he spotted a familiar site—Prince's—the course where Gene Sarazen won the 1932 British Open. He set the plane down on the first fairway but soon ran out of land and ended up in a swamp.

"I never could hit that fairway," said Lucas, who did the only logical—and typically British—thing after climbing out of the wreckage. He walked up to the clubhouse, introduced himself, apologized for any inconvenience he may have caused, and ordered a large gin.

The British are big on tradition, which is certainly admirable, especially when it comes to golf. Take the British Open, for example.

In 1946, Sam Snead arrived at St. Andrews for the British Open. He had never seen anything like the place, with its huge double greens, seemingly random bunkering, and somewhat unkempt conditions. On top of all that, he had a succession of caddies that could only be termed "colorful."

"I had this one old boy in my first practice round," Sam recalls. "We got to one of the greens, and he pointed to a spot and said that's where the pin would be on the last day. I asked him how he could be so sure. He gave me kind of a funny look and said, 'Because that's where it's been for the last fifty years.' And he was right, too."

Henry Cotton was one of England's greatest golfers. He won three British Opens—an accomplishment that served only to fuel his considerable ego.

After finishing a round in the British Open one year, he was approached by a gentleman dressed in clothes that were more than a little on the garish side.

"Henry, great playing, pal," said the man as he enthusiastically pumped Cotton's hand.

"Thank you," said Cotton, his voice dripping with sarcasm. "And you must be an American."

The 1959 Great Britain/Ireland Ryder Cup team was almost killed when their flight from Los Angeles to Palm Springs was caught in a massive electrical storm and went into a violent and frightening free fall over the mountains. So terrifying was the incident that the players insisted the plane return to Los Angeles, where they boarded a bus and were driven to Palm Springs.

The Americans prevailed in the Ryder Cup, 8½-3½, but even in defeat, the Great Britain/Ireland boys showed their class. After the matches, each member of the team received an elegant card inscribed with the following:

"Being a founding member of the club [of which only team members belonged], you have a high position to uphold. To avoid the risk of dropping low in the eyes of the other cofounders, you must raise your glass and toast each and every one of them at 5:30 A.M. on 20 October every year you are lucky to remain alive, which you are lucky to be at the moment."

October 20 is the anniversary of the team's brush with death.

246 After Nick Faldo decided to move to the United States and play the PGA Tour virtually full-time, a British writer asked him if there was anything he missed about living in England.

"A bit of rain now and again," Faldo replied.

Royal St. George's at Sandwich, England, is a regular site of the British Open, but like many clubs in both the United States and abroad, it had a policy of not admitting women. Actually, the club didn't even allow for the existence of women. This didn't mean they couldn't play the course. In fact, given an odd sort of logic, the discrimination worked in women's favor since what didn't exist couldn't be charged greens fees, so women happily played for free.

Nobody ever thought much about any possible ramifications until a young woman, one Fiona MacDonald, was named to the Cambridge University golf team, which plays an annual match against Royal St. George's.

What to do?

In a brilliant example of why there will always be an England, the club's membership sat down and, many brandies and cigars later, came up with an utterly practical solution.

On the eve of the match, the Royal St. George's Golf Club named Miss Fiona MacDonald an honorary man.

MUIRFIELD

Perhaps inspired by his friend Sam Snead's win in the 1946 Open at St. Andrews, Claude Harmon traveled to Muirfield to take a shot at the title. Harmon, the reigning Masters champion, learned on the first tee that his playing companion had withdrawn but would be replaced by a member, one Major W. H. Callender, who told the press that he'd "be delighted to give the old boy a game."

By the third hole, the major had seen enough of Harmon's game and took it upon himself to offer some advice. "One should grip down on the shaft and employ a short swing," said Callender as he demonstrated to a bemused Harmon. "It makes it so much easier to control the ball in the east wind."

JoAnne Carner, whose string of USGA championships is exceeded only by Jack Nicklaus and Bob Jones, was playing Muirfield with her husband, Don, and two friends. Before teeing off, Paddy Hamner issued a stern warning.

"I want you to get a bloody move on," he scolded them. "I want you out of here in less than four hours."

Suitably terrorized, the four raced around. When Carner hit her drive into the rough on the 17th, she elected to take a drop rather than hold up play. When they reached the clubhouse, Hamner asked what she had shot.

"I believe I had a 74," she said.

"No, it was a 76, Mrs. Carner," he said, gloating. "I saw you drop that ball in the rough on the 17th."

If Paddy Hamner was a piece of work, he had nothing on one of his predecessors, Colonel Brian Evans-Lombe, a retired cavalry officer who lorded over the place for seventeen years.

One Sunday morning Evans-Lombe spotted an unfamiliar figure sitting by himself in the smoking room. The colonel approached the man and inquired who he might be. Evans-Lombe was informed that the man was, in fact, a member of twenty years' good standing.

"In that case," the secretary sniffed, "you should come here more often so I might at least recognize you."

An unusual feature of Muirfield is its sod-faced bunkers, which became popular in Scotland toward the turn of the twentieth century as a means of giving definition to the holes. Building up the facings of the bunkers also makes them more penal. Just how punishing are the bunkers at Muirfield? In the 1987 Open, Arnold Palmer found himself taking five strokes to finally get out of one.

"I'm not saying God himself couldn't have gotten my first shot out, but He would have had to throw it out," said Palmer.

An earlier golfer found himself in one of Muirfield's deeper bunkers and lost track of the number of strokes it cost him.

"I went in a quarter after the hour and emerged thirty minutes later," he said. "I'll leave it to you for your best estimate."

THE NATIONAL GOLF LINKS

The National Golf Links in Southhampton was founded by Charles Blair MacDonald, a very wealthy and autocratic golf enthusiast, who patterned many of the holes after some of the more famous holes in Scotland.

MacDonald had a wonderful approach to members who had complaints or suggestions about the club. If he thought the ideas had merit, he would commission the job—billing the member for the work. In one case he overheard a member grumbling about the vast swarms of mosquitoes rising from a pond on the 14th hole. MacDonald ordered the pond drained and billed the startled member, who was advised to either pay up or leave.

MacDonald's nephew, Peter Grace, announced rather boldly, after playing the course with his uncle for the first time, that it was simply too easy. For example, he said, the first green could be driven with a good shot.

"Don't be ridiculous, Peter," C.B. shot back. "No one has ever come close to reaching the green. Nonsense."

With that, the two headed for the first tee, where Grace hit what could arguably have been the most expensive shot in golf history. His drive rocketed off the clubface, bore through the prevailing wind, bounced, and rolled onto the front edge of the green. His uncle, horrified, marched away without uttering a word. He didn't need to. That night he wrote his impetuous nephew out of his will—a decision that cost Peter Grace $1 million.

BYRON NELSON

In 1927 Walter Hagen traveled to Dallas in search of his fourth straight PGA Championship. Playing Joe Turnesa in the final, he came to a hole playing straight into the bright sun.

"I wish I had a hat," he said to nobody in particular.

In the gallery nearby was a young boy who had followed Hagen throughout the entire round. He shyly stepped forward and handed Hagen his little baseball cap. Much to the delight of the gallery, Hagen wore it for his tee shot.

That little boy was Byron Nelson.

Byron Nelson, Ben Hogan, and Sam Snead were all born in the same year and competed against each other hundreds of times. Here's one for the trivia books: how often did they finish 1-2-3?

"The peculiar thing is, as far as I know, it only happened once," Nelson recalls. "It was at Houston in 1946."

And for bonus points, what was the order of finish?

"I won, Ben was second, and Sam was third," says Nelson.

In 1945 Nelson won eighteen tournaments, including an astonishing eleven in a row. His ball-striking was so remarkable that he would actually become bored in the course of a round. But the streak began to take its toll on him. One morning as he was leaving for the course, he said to his wife, Louise, "I wish I would just blow up and get this over with."

When he returned from his round, Louise asked him if he had blown up.

"Yes, I did," he said. "I shot 66."

Back in the early days of the Masters, the old Bon Air Vanderbilt hotel hosted big pretournament Calcuttas where people would bid—often enormous sums—on individual players or, in some cases, pools of players.

In 1938 Byron Nelson, the defending champion, agreed to appear at the Calcutta as a favor to Masters officials, even though he had very real reservations about gambling. After waving to the crowd, he went to the back of the room to watch the action unfold. Bidding would begin at $100, and if no one bid on a player, he would be pooled with groups of other players.

When Ben Hogan's name was called, the room was silent. Feeling bad that his boyhood friend's feelings might be hurt, Nelson bought Hogan for $100—the only time he ever participated in a Calcutta.

"The next day Ben asked if he could buy half of himself back from me, and of course, I said that would be fine," Nelson remembers. "It took Ben a little time to scrape up the $50, but he finally did. We never made any money because Ben finished twenty-fifth, but I'd like to think it gave him a little boost of confidence."

A few years after the death of his first wife, Louise, Byron remarried. His wife, Peggy, is a writer, and the two are totally devoted to one another. In 1995, fifty years after he won eleven tournaments in a row on tour, a writer asked Byron if he could play just one last

round of golf with any three players, who would the players be. The first person he named was Peggy.

"One day I was working on a piece of furniture in my workshop when the phone rang," Byron remembers. "I picked it up at the same time Peggy answered it in the house, but I didn't say anything. The caller was from an advertising agency in Dallas that wanted to pay me $25,000 to do an ad for a whiskey—Old Grand Dad, I think. Well, Peggy said to the man, 'You must not know Byron very well. He's never taken a drink in his life, and he'd never endorse something he doesn't believe in.' She thanked him for his interest, and that was that. A couple of minutes later, she came out to the workshop.

" 'Well, I see you cost me $25,000,' I joked."

"Byron was very influential in my career," remembers Miller Bar- ber, who won eleven tournaments on the regular Tour and twenty-four times on the Senior Tour. "I used to caddie for him and shag his practice sessions when he was the pro in Texarkana. We'd play matches for a dime, but what I remember most is watching him practice. I've never seen anyone hit the ball so consistently straight. I think the real reason I went bald so fast is that he kept bouncing balls off my head."

Byron Nelson was playing in the 1945 Tam O'Shanter tournament in Chicago, which at the time offered the biggest purse in golf. The tournament organizer was George S. May, a promotional genius.

In one round, when Nelson made the turn in 34, May was there to meet him on the green. In front of a huge gallery, he bet Byron that he couldn't shoot another 34 on the back.

He was right. Byron shot a 32 and collected $100.

Byron Nelson is very soft-spoken and a gentleman in the truest and best sense of the word. But anyone who believes he isn't competitive to the core is mistaken. One person who learned this the hard way was Frank Stranahan.

Stranahan was the heir to a healthy fortune who went on to win the British Amateur in 1948 and 1950 and lost in the finals of the U.S. Amateur in 1950. By most accounts, Stranahan could be difficult at times and was perfectly capable of trying the patience of a . . . well, a Byron Nelson.

Nelson was the professional at Inverness, where Stranahan's family had a membership. Stranahan's father insisted that Nelson give his son lessons, but the younger Stranahan proved intractable, insisting on doing things his way—Nelson's playing record and reputation as a teacher notwithstanding. Finally, Byron just gave up.

One day Stranahan came into Nelson's pro shop with two friends and challenged Nelson to a match. Nelson declined at first, but there was something about Stranahan's attitude that lit up Nelson's competitive fires.

"I'll tell you what, Frank," Nelson said. "Not only will I play you, but bring along your two friends, too. I'll play your best ball."

Nelson went out and shot a record 63 on a course good enough to have hosted three U.S. Opens and a PGA Championship.

Byron Nelson has led an exemplary life. A devoutly religious man, he has always stressed that people in the public eye, especially athletes, have a responsibility to set a good example. That's why, when asked if he ever did anything he regrets, he points to a decision he made in 1936 that bothers him to this day.

"I was approached by a cigarette manufacturer who offered me $500 to endorse a brand called 20 Grand," he recalls. "Now, of course, that was quite a bit of money in those days, and I didn't think it through. I didn't realize the consequences and how many people something like that could influence, so I agreed to endorse the cigarettes, even though I never smoked. Well, as soon as those ads appeared I started to get the most painful letters from teachers and Sunday-school teachers asking me how I could do something so terrible. I must have gotten five hundred or more letters, all asking me why I would stoop so low just to chase the almighty dollar. And they were right, of course.

"Well, I just felt terrible about the whole thing, and I went to the company and tried to give them their money back if they would just cancel the ads," he went on. "They wouldn't and I still regret it. I've prayed about it often and I made a promise to the Good Lord, and said that for as long as I lived I'd never again do anything to influence people in the wrong way."

It's a promise Byron Nelson has kept for almost sixty years.

People will always debate who was the greatest player in history. But when you ask who best personified the term "gentleman," Byron's name is always at the top of the list.

"When I was still an amateur, Byron and I played a series of exhibitions around California," recalls Ken Venturi, who, like Tom Watson, was a protégé of Nelson. "I learned a lot during that time. After we played he'd go over my round, asking me why I played a certain shot or hit a certain club. He was trying to refine my playing. But one thing I'll always remember from those exhibitions is that when we arrived at a course Byron would quietly find out what was the course record and who held it. If it was held by the local pro or amateur, he'd never try to break it. He knew that record meant more to them than it would to him. That's a perfect example of the kind of man he is."

JACK NICKLAUS

Jack Nicklaus took his first golf lesson in the summer of 1951 and shot a 51 for his first nine holes of golf. A few months later he shot a 91, and a short while after that, he won his first tournament—the Scioto Country Club Junior Championship.

"I threw a 121 at the field and they folded," Nicklaus recalled later, laughing.

Jack Nicklaus idolized Bobby Jones. When Nicklaus qualified for the 1955 U.S. Amateur as a fifteen-year-old, it took on a special importance because 1955 marked the silver anniversary of Jones's win in the 1930 Amateur at Merion, when he completed the Grand Slam. Jones was scheduled to address the annual contestants' dinner.

During the championship, Nicklaus reached the green on a 560-yard hole in two, which no one else in the field had been able to do. After his round, Jones sought out Nicklaus.

"Young man, I've heard that you're a very fine golfer," said Jones. "I'd like to come out and watch you play a few holes tomorrow."

The following day Nicklaus came to the 11th hole 1-up on his opponent. When he saw Jones in the gallery he fell apart, bogeying the next hole and then taking a double bogey on 12 after slicing his drive deep into the woods.

Jones, sensing that he was making Nicklaus nervous, quietly left. Nicklaus went on to lose the match on the final hole. But Jones knew talent when he saw it and passed a note to Jack through Jack's father. It said:

"I believe I was a fairly good young golfer, but I didn't become what I would consider to be a really good golfer until I had been competing for a number of seasons. When I first started to play in the bigger tournaments, I would run home to Stewart Maiden, our professional at East Lake, as soon as something went wrong. Finally,

I matured to the point where I understood my game well enough to make my own corrections during the course of a tournament, and that's when I'd say I became a good golfer."

They were words Nicklaus would never forget.

Playing in the finals of the 1959 U.S. Amateur at The Broadmoor, Nicklaus came to the 36th hole of his final-round match against Charlie Coe. The match was even, and after watching Coe's 8-iron approach run off the back of the green, Nicklaus punched a 9-iron to within eight feet of the hole. Coe hit an excellent chip, and the ball nearly dropped into the cup. Perhaps sensing the inevitable, Coe motioned to Nicklaus that his putt was good, conceding the hole, the match, and the championship.

"No thanks, Charlie," said Nicklaus. "That's not the way I want to win."

With that, Nicklaus calmly made the putt that would give him the first of his record twenty major championships.

Even as an amateur, Jack Nicklaus's talents were undeniable. Tom Weiskopf has always said that when he first met Jack at Ohio State, Nicklaus was "already the best golfer in the world."

Nicklaus was paired with Don January in his first year at the Masters, 1959. On the 465-yard, par-5 13th hole, January outdrove Nicklaus by forty yards. He assumed that Nicklaus would lay up short of Rae's Creek. So did Nicklaus's caddie, Willie Peterson.

"Lay up, son," said Peterson. "You can't get there today."

Nicklaus blistered a 3-wood, which easily carried the creek and left him with an eagle putt.

"That kid's gonna run us all off the Tour," January said to his caddie.

Jack Nicklaus came to the 1962 U.S. Open at Oakmont Country Club having turned pro earlier in the year. While he had yet to win as a pro, he was already established as one of the game's best players, and the Open was billed as a duel between the twenty-two-year-old Nicklaus and the thirty-two-year-old Arnold Palmer, then at the peak of his career and the Tour's most popular and dominant player. The location of the tournament only added to the drama. Oakmont, just outside of Pittsburgh, is near Palmer's hometown of Latrobe, and Palmer was very much the favorite.

The two tied at the end of four rounds, and as they prepared to tee off in the playoff, Palmer asked Nicklaus if he wanted to split the purse, a common practice in those days.

Nicklaus didn't give it a moment's thought.

"No, Arn," he said, "that wouldn't be fair to you. Besides, you don't really want to do that, do you?"

He then went out and won his first professional title, 71 to 74.

If there was ever any doubt about Jack Nicklaus's willpower, it should have been erased following his win in the 1962 U.S. Open at Oakmont in a playoff with Arnold Palmer. It wasn't just the win but something that happened afterward.

Nicklaus was watching a highlight film that showed him standing over a short putt with a cigarette dangling from his lips. At that moment, he resolved never to smoke on a golf course again because he felt it set a bad example for kids. And he hasn't since that day.

Mass interviews at golf tournaments, particularly the majors that attract a lot of writers who don't ordinarily cover the sport, don't exactly resemble "Meet the Press."

One year at the Masters, a reporter asked Nicklaus, "Jack, how did you find the course?"

"Well, I've been coming here a long time, and it's pretty well marked by road signs," he said with a laugh. "I really didn't have a problem."

Jack Nicklaus and Tom Weiskopf were paired in the 1973 Ryder Cup matches at Muirfield and faced England's Clive Clark and Ulsterman Eddie Pollard in the afternoon four-ball. Barbara Nicklaus, eight months pregnant at the time, had followed the morning match, but as she stood on the first tee in the afternoon, she told her husband that she didn't think she could follow the entire match.

"Don't worry," said Jack, loud enough for his opponents to hear. "It won't be a long walk."

On the first hole, he stunned everyone, including his partner.

"We came to the first green," remembers Weiskopf. "I had it about ten feet from the hole, and Jack was probably about twenty feet away. He told me to 'rack my cue.' I said, 'What do you mean?'

" 'Pick it up.'

" 'Oh, you mean mark it.'

" 'No,' said Nicklaus. 'Pick it up. There's no way in the world I'm going to miss this putt.'

"Of course, Jack being Jack, he made it—and we went on to win, 3 and 2."

Many golfers have superstitions. In Jack Nicklaus's case, it was very simple: he liked to have his caddie, Angelo Argea, hand him three white tees just prior to the round. On the way to the second tee, he wanted Angelo to wish him good luck.

One time, Angelo got the tee part of his job out of the way, but he managed to forget the second part of the assignment.

"Angelo, did you forget something?" Nicklaus asked as they stood on the second tee.

"No, boss," said Angelo.

"Are you sure?" asked Nicklaus, as his fellow players waited for him to tee off.

"I don't think so," said Angelo, after thinking for a moment.

"Well, think again," said Nicklaus.

"Oh, yeah," said Angelo. "Good luck, boss."

"Thanks," said Nicklaus, who could then finally go ahead and play the second hole.

After a brilliant amateur career, Jack Nicklaus turned pro in 1961. His first victory as a professional came at the 1962 U.S. Open at Oakmont, when he beat Arnold Palmer in a playoff. Still, for all his obvious talent, not all his fellow professionals were all that impressed in the beginning.

"Right after Jack won the Open, we went to Portland for the next tournament," remembers 1959 PGA champion Bob Rosburg. "I used to travel a lot with Fred Hawkins, and he said, 'Jack might be good, but I'd like to see how well he'd do if he lived like we do.' It got back to Jack, and he went out with us every night for a few drinks. I guess it didn't bother him too much. He won by four strokes, and that included a two-stroke penalty. After the tournament, I asked Fred what he thought. He said, 'I guess he can play.'"

"Jack has a good sense of humor and can really give you the needle," remembered the late Dave Marr. "Back in 1972, he lost the Tournament of Champions in a playoff to Bobby Mitchell. Bobby took some of his winnings and bought a toupee. About a month later he ran into Jack at a cocktail party. Jack took a look at the hairpiece and said, 'Bobby, I always knew winning was great, but I didn't know it could make your hair grow back.'"

Standing on the 18th tee in the final round of the 1967 U.S. Open, Jack Nicklaus seemed virtually certain to win his second Open. Even after he pushed his drive into the rough, his four-shot lead over Arnold Palmer looked insurmountable.

Studying his lie, he decided to play safe and pitch out short of the water. Maybe the shot was too easy or the lead too large. Whatever the reason, he stubbed the shot, barely advancing the ball.

Embarrassed, he said to Palmer, "What a dumb shot."

"You said it," Palmer replied. "I didn't."

In the 1970s, Jack Nicklaus developed an interest in wine and set out to learn all he could about the subject. One night at a PGA Tour dinner his knowledge was tested by veteran writer Dick Taylor, a longtime friend.

The evening's wine selections were brought to the Nicklaus-Taylor table wrapped in linen.

"All right, Jack, let's see how much you really know," Taylor said. "Let's see if you can identify what these wines are."

Nicklaus went through the elaborate ritual of swirling the wine in the glass, breathing the wine's bouquet, and tasting it. He puzzled over the wines momentarily, then identified them perfectly.

"I was astonished," Taylor recalls. "The next day I ran into [then-PGA Tour Commissioner] Deane Beman and told him how impressed I was that Jack was so knowledgeable about the wine."

"Well, he should have been, Dick," Beman said, laughing. "I asked him to pick out the wine for last night's dinner."

By every account, Jack and Barbara Nicklaus are superb parents. But being the child of a celebrity isn't always easy. So you can imagine Nan Nicklaus's reaction when a couple of girls in her dorm approached her on her first day at the University of Georgia.

"Hey, are you really Jack Nicholson's daughter?" one girl asked. "He was great in *The Shining*."

The Nicklaus household has always been crawling with kids: their five children, their children's friends, and now their growing number of grandchildren.

One evening Jack returned home after winning a Senior Tour event. He pointed out that he won with six new clubs in his bag.

"Were they all woods?" asked one of his son Gary's friends.

Playing in the 1991 Tradition, a Senior PGA Tour event, Nicklaus found himself trailing by twelve shots after the first two rounds. To

no one's real surprise, he went on to shoot rounds of 66 and 67 to win the tournament and the $120,000 first prize.

Later, a writer asked a fellow player, Frank Beard, if Nicklaus was really that good.

"No," said Beard. "He's been on a thirty-year lucky streak."

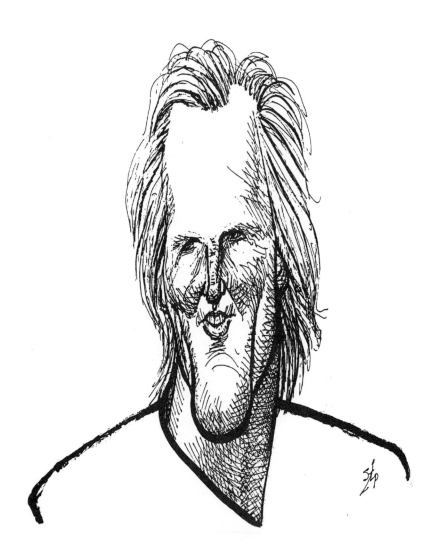

GREG NORMAN

Following his devastating loss in the 1996 Masters, Greg Norman decided to take a break from golf. He, Nick Price, their wives, and a few other friends boarded Norman's yacht, *Aussie Rules*, and cruised south. After a few days of fishing and relaxing, they discovered a nine-hole course on Cat Cay. Norman, his brother-in-law, and two crew members headed for the course. Days later, somebody asked Greg if he liked the course.

"It's hard to say," Norman said. "We had eighteen beers for eighteen holes. When the beer ran out, we quit."

From the time he turned pro in 1976, Greg Norman built his game around the idea that someday he'd be competing in the United States.

To that end, he worked to develop a swing that would allow him to hit the ball high and stop it quickly on the greens. To do this, he would go to a spot near the practice ground at Royal Queensland, where he was laboring as an assistant to professional Charlie Earp, and practice launching 5-irons up over the tree. In typical Norman fashion, he wasn't satisfied until he could move in as close as possible to the tree and still cut the ball up over the highest limbs.

"Greg," said Earp, one of Australia's most respected teaching pros. "It's fine to hit the ball high, but you've got to learn to get it down."

"I've got to hit it high in America," said Norman, rocketing another ball over the tree.

"Yeah," said Earp, "but you'll be playing in England before you'll be playing in the States, and if you hit that shot there, you'll be playing your next shot from Paris."

In the odd way it sometimes happens in both sports and life, people looked at Norman with a new respect and admiration for the way he took the loss. He answered all the questions candidly. The letters and telegrams poured in. The ovations that greeted him in the tournaments that followed were both louder and warmer than they had ever been before.

One person who was moved by Norman's actions was a man who knows something about winning—and losing—under pressure.

On a wall at Ted Williams's house, the great Red Sox hitter and outfielder hung photos of just two golfers: Bobby Jones, for the grace he showed in victory, and Greg Norman, for the courage he displayed in defeat.

Norman's final round that Sunday in 1996 was so devastating and painful that some people literally could not watch as it played out slowly over the afternoon. One of them was Ben Crenshaw, the two-time Masters champion.

Crenshaw was in Butler Cabin, working as an analyst for CBS Sports. At one point, after Norman's last chance died with a tee shot into the water on 16, Crenshaw quietly removed his microphone and walked outside onto a small patio. There, alone with his thoughts and his profound sense of history, he quietly shed a tear for Greg Norman.

Another was Norman's close friend, Nick Price. As Norman's nightmarish afternoon began to play out, Price was watching on television in the locker room at Augusta National. Before long, it became too painful to endure.

"I knew just how much the Masters means to Greg," said Price. "I could see what was happening not only to his game but to him as a person. I couldn't watch it."

So Price cleaned out his locker and left for the airport.

MOE NORMAN

"What am I going to do with another toaster? I've already won twenty-seven of them."

—MOE NORMAN, explaining why he tanked the last few holes of a tournament so he could win a radio (that he had already agreed to sell) instead of a toaster

If you've never heard of Moe Norman, you're not alone. He may be the best player Canada has ever produced. He certainly is the most—how should we say this?—unique. People rank him with the Hogans of the game for his ball-striking ability. Why didn't he win more tournaments? Read on. . . .

Playing in a tournament in Canada, Moe was told that all he had to do was par the final hole to set a course record.

"What is the hole?" he asked, and was told it was just a driver and a 9-iron. With that, he hit his 9-iron from the tee, followed it with a driver off the fairway, then sank the putt for a birdie and a course record.

In another tournament he came to the final green with a three-shot lead. Just to make things interesting, he chipped his ball off the green and into a bunker, and then got up and down for the win.

All good golfers seem to have outstanding eye-hand coordination, and that is certainly true of Moe Norman. Once, while waiting on a tee during a tournament, he began to idly bounce the ball off the

face of his driver. A spectator bet him $1 per bounce over and under 100 bounces. Moe was still going strong at 184 bounces when he deliberately stopped and collected his $84 from the ashen-faced man.

"I could have gone all afternoon, but I didn't want to hold up the tournament," he explained.

Moe Norman won the 1955 Canadian Amateur and earned an invitation to the Masters the following year. The invitation arrived one frigid winter's day at the Kitchener, Ontario, bowling alley where Norman was working as a pinsetter.

When spring arrived, Norman boarded a bus for Augusta. While he liked the course very much, he never felt comfortable among the top players or with the clubby atmosphere at Augusta National. Midway through the second round he left the club, got on another bus, and returned home.

Norman traveled to a tournament in Canada, but when he arrived he found the course blanketed by fog. An official asked him if he'd like to go to the range and hit some practice balls. Norman said that wouldn't be necessary—he'd just grab a handful of balls and hit them down the first fairway with his driver. A few minutes later, when a caddie went down the fairway to retrieve the balls, he found two of the balls touching each other and the other four within a ten-foot circle.

CHRISTY O'CONNOR, SR.

Himself, as Christy O'Connor was affectionately known, was one of the best golfers Europe produced in the post–World War II era. He was an enormous talent, posting a second in the 1965 British Open, along with several other high finishes. Happily, his love for the game was matched only by his love for life and whatever good times came along the way.

In the 1973 Ryder Cup matches at Muirfield, O'Connor lost to J. C. Snead in the morning matches of the final day. Disappointed, he told the Great Britain/Ireland captain, Bernard Hunt, that he wanted to be left out of the afternoon matches, preferring to follow the course of play from the comfort of the bar.

Upon reflection, Hunt decided that he wanted Himself to take on the formidable Tom Weiskopf in the afternoon and implored O'Connor's wife, Mary, to get the old boy out of his chair and onto the first tee in plenty of time.

"Ordinarily, a player with a few drinks under his belt wouldn't be of much use," said Hunt. "But Christy was capable of the most remarkable golf under these conditions. The problem was that if the effects of the drink began to wear off, Christy could lose his edge."

To guard against this calamity, Hunt pulled aside two of O'Connor's friends—one of whom happened to be a priest and, therefore, had the further attraction of bringing God into the fray—and gave them a job of immeasurable importance.

"Whatever you do," he told them, with more than a hint of conspiracy in his voice, "keep Himself topped off."

To that end, they agreed to meet Christy on every tee with a little liquid something, just in case of an emergency.

When O'Connor arrived on the first tee, he shook hands with Weiskopf, who thought there was something strange going on.

"I kind of took Bernard aside and asked him if Christy had been drinking," Weiskopf recalled. "He looked at me, smiled, and said, 'God yes, and if we can keep him that way you don't stand a chance.'"

As it turned out, Himself, suitably fortified, played Weiskopf to a tie, but in the end the United States prevailed, 19-13.

Ireland's Christy O'Connor, referred to reverentially by his countrymen simply as "Himself," was one of the purest players in the game's history. He was a member of ten Ryder Cup teams, winning almost forty percent of his singles matches and might have won more if he hadn't been so naturally caught up in the fellowship of such affairs—a temptation he faced in the 1963 World Cup matches at St. Nom la Bretèche near Paris.

Moments before he was due to tee off, he sat in the locker room nursing a hangover of unbearable proportions and pleading with a writer from a London paper to bring him some coffee. The writer begged off, pointing out to O'Connor how unseemly it would be to have Ireland's greatest champion stagger to the first tee armed with a jug of coffee.

"Fine, then," said O'Connor. "Get some coffee. Some very black coffee. Go down the first fairway to the 200-yard stake. From there march off sixty-five paces and wait in the woods for me."

"Yes," said the writer.

"With very black coffee and lots of the stuff," reminded O'Connor, not losing sight of the important details.

The writer, loaded with a steaming mug of the elixir, waited patiently deep in the woods. He heard the crack of the ball off O'Connor's drive and the telltale rustle of the ball crashing to earth through the canopy of leaves. He saw the ball land, very nearly at his feet, followed soon after by O'Connor, who had just hit one of the greatest tee shots of our time under unspeakable pressure.

The nephew of Ireland's legendary Christy O'Connor himself, Christy Jr. came to world attention when he beat Fred Couples in a crucial singles match on the final day of the 1989 Ryder Cup match at The Belfry in Sutton-Coldfield, England.

Once, back home in Ireland, O'Connor took an afternoon off to play a casual round of golf with a friend. The fine, soft mist they began in soon turned into a heavy, lashing rain that caused them to walk in and repair to the bar for a warming drink.

"You know, if this wasn't my living, I wouldn't do this if you paid me," O'Connor said.

Francis Ouimet

Golf has been blessed in that so many of the game's great champions have also been great sportsmen (and sportswomen). Certainly, Francis Ouimet, who won the 1913 U.S. Open as an amateur, would fall into that category.

Ouimet, who also won two U.S. Amateurs, played on eight Walker Cup teams, and served as team captain twice, was the first American honored as captain of the Royal and Ancient Golf Club of St. Andrews.

No less a figure than Bob Jones summed up Ouimet, the player and the man, when he wrote:

"As one who was first his awed admirer, later his fellow competitor, and now, as always, his staunch friend, I salute him with all possible fervor."

Francis Ouimet's win in the 1913 U.S. Open was easily one of the great upsets in all of sports. Ouimet was a twenty-year-old amateur facing the two great British professionals, Harry Vardon and Ted Ray, in a playoff at The Country Club in Brookline, Massachusetts—the course where Ouimet had learned the game as a caddie. To say that there wasn't a lot of conversation among the players that day is an understatement.

"When they congratulated me on the 18th green, it was the first time either had spoken to me all day," he recalled. "They didn't talk to me, and I was afraid to speak to them."

In 1963, the U.S. Open returned to The Country Club on the fiftieth anniversary of Ouimet's victory. On the eve of the championship, the club hosted a dinner for the presidents and professionals from Massachusetts clubs.

During the course of the evening, people were asked to guess what they thought would be the winning score. The guests, no doubt in awe of players like Arnold Palmer and Jack Nicklaus, suggested that the scores would be on the low side.

Most woefully underestimated the character and resolve of "The Old Lady of Clyde Street." One who didn't was Francis Ouimet.

"Gentlemen," Ouimet said. "I will remind you that this is a very subtle course."

Subtle indeed.

The low score at the end of four rounds was 293—nine over par and four over the highest guess of the evening. In all, par was broken just five times in regulation play and was never broken in the eighteen holes played on the final day.

Francis Ouimet and Gene Sarazen were great friends and competitors, and when Ouimet died, his family asked Sarazen to serve as a pallbearer.

"At the church the day of the funeral, I was thinking about Francis and how, just before the Open, he always said to me, 'Gene, make sure those greens are fast.' After the service, when it came time to say good-bye to Francis, I tapped on the coffin, bent down, and whispered, 'Francis, make sure those greens are fast up there.' "

SE RI PAK

Despite LPGA star Se Ri Pak's understandable reluctance to all but give her life over to golf as a child, her father would not be moved by her pleas or arguments or even her tears. He drove her relentlessly. They would work in wilting heat or in the winter when ice would form in her hair.

"He made me strong," she said later. "Many times I wanted him to give me a chance to rest or to spend time with my friends. But then I would tell myself to just show him that I could do what he wanted, that I could do anything I wanted. Finally, I got to the point where I wanted to do well because I loved the game and loved my parents and I wanted to prove that my father knew what he was doing. That he wasn't crazy."

For Joon Chul Pak, it wasn't enough that his daughter master the mechanics of the game. He would ensure that she was mentally tough as well. There may have well been madness in his method, but there's little doubt that it worked.

There was a cemetery near their home, and they would routinely pitch a tent amid the graves and spend the night. After a while, he began leaving her alone with her thoughts and fears.

"Don't be afraid," he would console her. "I won't let the ghosts get you."

Many people, including his wife, were more than a little skeptical about at least this part of the grand design. But one evening, when she was sixteen, he got the answer he had been awaiting for all those years.

"I was getting ready to leave her one night, and she said, 'I'm warm here now,' meaning she was finally strong enough to be comfortable," he said. "We never went back to the cemetery."

It didn't take long for Se Ri Pak to become well aware of the bitter realities of golf in South Korea. It was a game for the wealthy and privileged, with membership fees at private clubs running from $200,000 to over $1 million a year. While her parents had sacrificed so she could enjoy the benefits of a membership, there was never any feeling of being part of the country's golf elite. Indeed, the truth was far from it.

In her sophomore year in high school, Se Ri entered a prestigious tournament, the Golf Digest Cup. Her father, spotting a group of parents nearby, went over and tried to strike up a conversation.

What happened next wasn't pretty, to be sure, but without a doubt it left a strong impression on a young girl who worshiped her father.

"The parents completely ignored me," said her father. "They treated me like I wasn't even there because their social status was so much greater than ours. I called to Se Ri and told her to come over to where the trophy was being displayed. I picked up the trophy and handed it to her.

" 'This is yours,' I said. 'Go ahead and take it.'

"Se Ri took the trophy, and the parents looked at me as though I was a madman," he went on. "This greatly angered me, so I shouted to them, 'So what if I dare touch your trophy. My Se Ri is going to win it anyway.' "

Joon Chul Pak remembers his daughter's smile. He remembers the scorn reflected in the faces of the other parents. And he remembers that his daughter won the tournament and took the trophy home with her.

ARNOLD PALMER

When Arnold Palmer was twelve years old, he broke 80 for the first time. Naturally, he was very proud of this great accomplishment and couldn't help bragging just a bit.

Bragging was not something that sat well with his father.

"When you're good, you don't have to tell people what you can do," Deacon Palmer said. "Just show them."

Arnold Palmer's father, Deacon, was a club professional, and even when Arnold was a youngster there was little doubt that he would follow in his father's footsteps. He worshiped his father and loved the game passionately.

Still, Arnold's mother wasn't sure that a pro's life, especially a 285 Tour pro in the 1950s, was a life she wanted for her son. Even after he won the 1954 U.S. Amateur at the Country Club of Detroit, she had serious misgivings. And she didn't feel any better after talking to Richard Tufts, a friend of the Palmer family who would go on to become president of the United States Golf Association.

"Mr. Tufts, I'm worried about Arnold," Mrs. Palmer confided. "I think he's going to turn pro after the Amateur."

"I'm sorry to hear that," said Tufts. "With a swing like that, he'll never make it on tour."

Arnold Palmer came on tour at a time when Ben Hogan and Sam Snead were ending their domination of the professional game. Whereas the young Palmer was every bit a match for Snead's charisma, he couldn't begin to match Hogan's precision as a shot-

maker. In fact, he was just the opposite. Where Hogan would take apart a course with surgical precision, Palmer would attack with abandon, often saving pars from impossible spots.

In one tournament Palmer missed a green and found himself down in a ditch with no real shot at the pin. As he studied his options, he spotted a friend, the sportswriter Jim Murray, in the gallery.

"You're always writing about Ben Hogan," said Palmer. "What would he do in a spot like this?"

"He wouldn't be in a spot like this," said Murray.

Arnold Palmer won the 1954 U.S. Amateur, which qualified him for an invitation to the Masters the following spring. When he arrived at Augusta National, Jackie Burke, Jr., asked the twenty-four-year-old if he would like to join him and Ben Hogan for a practice round. Naturally, Palmer accepted the invitation, although he didn't exactly make an instant impression on Hogan.

On the first hole, Hogan hit the fairway and the green and made his par. Palmer hit his drive into the trees, scrambled around, and managed to sink a tough putt for his par. The next hole, a par 5, wasn't any better. Hogan hit the green in regulation and made his par. Palmer was in and out of the woods, and made another difficult putt to save par. Palmer hit another poor drive on the third hole, and as Hogan and Burke walked up the fairway to their balls, Hogan turned to Burke and asked a very logical question:

"How in hell did this guy get in the tournament?"

It's safe to say that Arnold Palmer is one of the most, if not *the* most, recognizable golfers in the game's history, in no small part because of the amount of advertising he's appeared in over the years.

One of his most widespread and successful ad campaigns was for Pennzoil, in which he was featured driving an old tractor around a golf course. The commercials were so successful that people would bring cans of Pennzoil to tournaments and ask Arnold to autograph them—which he did, happily.

Another commercial called for Arnold to hit shots to a green that had been cleared of snow. It wasn't a long shot, but Arnold's ability to hit ball after ball onto the green impressed a member of the film crew, who had no idea whom he was watching.

"This guy is good," the technician said. "He's wasting his time being an actor. He should turn pro."

"Arnold called me one day when I was working at the *Pittsburgh Press*," recalls Bob Drum. "He said he's got a guy who wanted to pay him two thousand bucks to write a golf book. He says we'll split it fifty-fifty. Well, Christ, I'm making $60 a week at the paper, so this was like dying and going to heaven.

"I asked him when we could get together, and he said that was the problem. The guy wanted the book in three months, and Arnold was going to be gone. I asked him what the hell I was supposed to do. I didn't know anything about golf. I was a baseball player. He says to me, 'All you have to know is two things: take the club away slow and hit it hard.'

"Well, I couldn't very well write a book with just that, so I went to the Pittsburgh Public Library and got out every book I could find on golf. I stole a chapter from each book, and that's how Arnold's first book got done. The only question was what we should call it: *Take It Away Slow* or *Hit It Hard*. We called it *Hit It Hard* 'cause *Take It Away Slow* sounded like a porno book.

"A few months after the book came out, I decided I should learn how to play this golf. I called Arnold and told him I wanted to come up to Latrobe and get a lesson from him. He said, 'You don't need to come up here. Everything I know is in the book, just read it.'

" 'Read it!' I yelled at him. 'I wrote the damned thing!' "

In one tournament early in his career, Palmer came to the final hole of a tournament leading by a shot. The hole was a reachable par 5 guarded by water in front of the green. As he stood in the fairway sizing up the shot, the gallery was calling for him to go for the green in two. Palmer studied the wind, took a drag on his cigarette, hitched up his slacks, and reached for a fairway wood. His caddie, Creamy, put his hands over the wood.

"Don't do it, boss," said Creamy, with visions of lost money passing in front of his eyes. "Just lay up."

Palmer looked at him quizzically.

"No, I want to go for it," he said, reaching again for the wood. "I can get there easily."

"Don't do it," said Creamy, pushing the wood back into the bag as the other players looked on, bemused.

"Creamy, it's my reputation," said Palmer. "Give me the wood."

Reluctantly, Creamy took off the headcover and handed the wood to Palmer, who promptly hit the ball into the water and lost the tournament by a shot.

In the 1967 Crosby National Pro-Am, Arnold Palmer came to the 14th hole at Pebble Beach trailing Jack Nicklaus by a shot in the final round. Trying to reach the green on the par 5 in two, he pulled out a 3-wood and gave it a rip. The ball hit a large tree and bounced out of bounds. Palmer dropped another ball and again hit

his 3-wood, and again his ball hit the tree and went out of bounds, ending his chances for a win.

That night the tree was hit by lightning and destroyed.

Jack Burke was on the practice green one afternoon when Arnold Palmer arrived with a golf bag full of putters.

"Arnold, that's a bag full of indecision," said Burke.

Arnold Palmer always enjoyed playing practice rounds for a little change, especially with young, aggressive players such as Lanny Wadkins, Curtis Strange, and Tom Weiskopf. And he hated—absolutely hated—losing.

"I really enjoyed the matches I played with Arnold and the other guys, and I know they made me a better player," remembers Tom Weiskopf. "One match that really stands out was at Harbour Town. Arnold and I were playing Lanny and Bert Yancey. I can't remember exactly what the match was, but we usually played $20 automatic one-downs—enough to get your attention but not enough to kill anyone.

"We finished the first eighteen around two o'clock and we were down. Arnold says he wants to go another nine to try to get back to even. So we go nine more and we're still down, and Lanny's giving us the needle pretty good, so Arnold says we're going nine more. It's about four-thirty or so and it's going to get dark pretty quick, but Arnold is so mad and so determined that he's not going to lose money that there's no way we're not going. We finished the last two or three holes in the dark and Arnold still lost money. He just couldn't believe it.

"You know, when I pretty much stopped playing the Tour in 1983, one of the things I missed most were those matches in the practice rounds."

There's a theory that holds that almost every golfer at some point suffers a loss so devastating that it effectively ends his or her career. Tom Weiskopf admits that, for him, it was losing to Jack Nicklaus in the 1975 Masters—his fourth and last second-place finish at Augusta.

People close to Ben Hogan say his game was never quite the same after he finished second to Dr. Cary Middlecoff at the 1956 U.S. Open at Oak Hill.

And people who follow the game believe that Arnold Palmer never recovered from blowing a seven-stroke lead with nine holes left to play at the 1966 U.S. Open at San Francisco's Olympic Club.

"It looks like second is the best I can do," said Palmer's playing companion, Billy Casper, as he made the turn on Sunday.

"I'll do everything I can do to help you," Palmer replied graciously.

He did more than anyone dreamed possible.

Hoping to set an Open record, Palmer attacked the back nine. He gave up a shot at 10 and another at 13. He gave back two more on 15 and two on 16. He lost another on 17 and barely managed to par 18 to force a Monday playoff, which he lost, 69-73.

"I've never seen anything like it," Casper said later. "I tried to talk to him after we putted out on Sunday, but he was in shock. Total shock. I've never seen anything like it."

In 1991, Arnold Palmer came to Royal Birkdale for the British Open and checked into what was the best suite in the best hotel in the area. There was just one problem: through an oversight he had been given the suite that a young couple had reserved for their honeymoon.

The groom was beside himself. Not only would this cast a pall on the Great Day, but it was hardly the best way to start a marriage. The hotel management could offer the groom little hope that the situation would be resolved to his satisfaction, so he appealed directly to Palmer.

Not only did Palmer give up his suite, but he also stopped by and toasted the couple with champagne following that day's round.

Thousands, indeed tens of thousands, of golfers idolized Arnold Palmer. One who went on to a successful professional career was Roger Maltbie, who won five tournaments in his first eighteen years on tour and is now an insightful golf commentator for NBC Sports.

Maltbie's first contact with Palmer came when he was eight years old. His parents had brought him to Pebble Beach for the Bing Crosby National Pro-Am.

When the Maltbies reached the second tee, Roger became separated from his parents and, lost in Palmer's enormous gallery, began to cry. Palmer heard him and walked over to the ropes, took him by the hand, and walked him down the middle of the fairway.

"Roger, get over here," called one of his parents from the gallery, certainly every bit as relieved as angry.

"Arnold has been my hero from that day on," says Maltbie.

When you've won as many tournaments as Arnold Palmer, it's easy to understand how a guy could sometimes make a simple mistake when it comes down to the small details.

Take the case of Royal Troon.

Palmer was playing a practice round prior to the start of the 1989 British Open at Royal Troon when a photographer approached and asked him to pose next to the plaque commemorating his historic win in 1961. Naturally Palmer, the most accommodating superstar in all of sports, agreed. The problem was, nobody seemed to know where the plaque was located. Finally, after several minutes, Palmer called over to his longtime caddie, Tip Anderson, and asked if he knew where the plaque was.

"Four hundred miles away," Anderson said. "We're on the wrong course."

Sure enough, there is a plaque honoring Palmer at Royal Birkdale, the site of his first British Open victory.

There's never been a golfer—or possibly any public figure—who has enjoyed a better relationship with the press than Arnold Palmer. He's always been fair and open to the writers, and they have responded in kind.

One year at Augusta, Palmer was in contention going into the final round and played horribly, shooting an 81 that included a missed four-inch putt.

Palmer went to the locker room following his round and was sitting dejectedly by his locker, sipping a beer, when a group of writers quietly approached.

"Arnold, we hate to bother you at a time like this . . ." said one of his friends.

Palmer looked up and smiled.

"Boys, we've talked when the times were good, and we'll talk when the times are bad," he said.

The U.S. Golf Association gave Arnold Palmer a special exemption from qualifying for the 1994 U.S. Open at Oakmont. Palmer had played in his first Open there, in his backyard, as a twenty-three-year-old amateur in 1953. The following year, he won the U.S. Amateur. Nine years later, in 1962, he again played in an Open at Oakmont, this time as the favorite. He lost in a playoff to Jack Nicklaus.

For Palmer, who won the Open in 1960 at Cherry Hills and finished second four times—three in playoffs—the emotion of the moment was heightened by the knowledge that the 1994 Open would be his last and that it would be played before thousands of his most loyal fans.

In an inspired pairing, Palmer played with Rocco Mediate, a thirty-one-year-old Tour pro who was born and raised near Pittsburgh and who idolized Palmer. As the two men came up the 18th hole at the close of the second round, it was clear that Palmer would miss the cut. The enormous gallery ringing the hole gave Palmer a standing ovation, and he responded by tipping his hat, smiling ruefully, and fighting back tears brought on by all the memories.

After putting out, Palmer and Mediate shook hands and embraced as the crowd's roar swelled again. At that moment Mediate, tears welling in his eyes, spoke for every one of his fellow players.

"You made all this possible," he said.

A few moments later, after signing his scorecard, Palmer was interviewed by ABC's Mark Rolfing. Rolfing was so choked up that he could barely ask his questions. Palmer could barely answer them.

What happened next is virtually unheard of in sports. Palmer was escorted into the interview area, which was jammed with writers, all of whom sensed they were witnessing an historic moment in golf. Many had known Palmer throughout his career and counted him as a friend. Some were mere infants when he won his first event on the regular Tour.

The room was still when Palmer began to speak.

"You all know pretty much how I feel. I have talked with most of you pretty much over the years . . ."

Finally, the emotion became too much. Tears filled Palmer's eyes and flowed down his face. He buried his face in a towel.

"I mean, it has been . . . well, you know, forty years of fun, work, and enjoyment. I haven't won that much . . . I've won a few tournaments . . . I've won some majors, but I suppose the most important thing is that . . . is that it has been as good as it has been to me."

He paused again to compose himself, and again put the towel to his face.

"I'm a little sun-whipped and tired, ready to take a rest. Hopefully there'll be a few more tournaments along the way. . . . That's about all I have to say. Thank you very much."

As Palmer got up to leave, the writers gave him a standing ovation. He made his way toward the exit, paused, and again covered his face with the towel, his back to the room. The ovation, which had ebbed, picked up and washed over Palmer again. Then he left, the most popular player in the history of the game. The most popular player who will ever play the game.

Rocco Mediate was right. He was the man who made it all possible.

Thirty years after his first visit to both St. Andrews and the British Open, Palmer returned for his final appearance. He and his wife, Winnie, stayed in the same room they always stayed in at Rusacks Hotel, and when he opened with rounds of 71 and 73, he seemed certain to make the cut.

But in the back of his mind, Palmer was concerned. After an emotional final trip across the Swilken Bridge on the 18th hole, Palmer left his birdie putt on 18 just inches short and had to settle for a par.

Finally, late in the day, Palmer got the bad news. The cut had been the lowest in the championship's history, and he'd missed it by a stroke.

When he received the news, Arnold Palmer sat in his room and cried freely.

Prior to the 1990 British Open at St. Andrews, Palmer announced that, barring any unforeseen circumstances, it would be his final British Open. At age sixty, he felt it was time to move off center stage.

Palmer played valiantly, getting from the galleries the thunderous applause and loving adulation that he, as much as anyone in the game's history, so deserved. It appeared certain that he would make the cut.

But golf is not always fair—or dramatic. When the scoring was finished on Friday, he had missed the cut by a single shot.

That evening Palmer was in the Jigger Inn with his longtime caddie, Tip Anderson, and some friends. Anderson was inconsolable.

"I should have done better," he said, as tears streamed down his weathered face.

"No," said Arnold, taking Tip's hand in both of his. "We should have done better, old friend."

Palmer traveled to St. Andrews for the 1995 British Open; he had announced it would be his last British Open as a player. He did promise to come back for the fall meeting of the R and A.

"I'm playing like a member now, so I might as well play in their tournament," he joked.

When it became obvious that he wasn't going to make the cut, a huge gallery turned out to watch Palmer play up 18. Billy Andrade, who attended Wake Forest on an Arnold Palmer scholarship, lingered on his way down the first fairway and gave Palmer a thumbs-up. As Palmer crossed the ancient stone bridge over the Swilken Burn—which every great player in history except Ben Hogan has walked across—he paused and waved to the crowd, which roared its appreciation.

Even England's Nick Faldo came out of the clubhouse to honor Palmer, though he insisted he had another reason:

"I just wanted to see a Scotsman cry," he joked. "I couldn't find one."

HARVEY PENICK

For much of his long and distinguished teaching career, Harvey Penick was the best-kept secret in golf. The longtime professional at the Austin Country Club, he taught players as diverse as Ben Crenshaw, Tom Kite, Betsy Rawls, Kathy Whitworth, and Sandra Palmer—as well as thousands of weekend players who benefited from his wisdom, insights, and friendship.

Throughout his career, he kept a little red notebook filled with his thoughts and impressions. In 1991 he showed it to writer Bud Shrake and asked him if he thought there might be a book in it. Shrake instantly realized that not only was there a book there but a classic. He approached Simon & Schuster, the publishing house, who offered a very healthy advance. Shrake reported the offer to Penick, who appeared crestfallen.

"I don't know, Bud," Penick said. "That's a lot of money, and I have a lot of medical bills to pay."

Shrake laughed and explained that S & S was going to pay *them* to write the book. Penick was stunned by the publisher's generosity, but it proved to be a wise investment: *Harvey Penick's Little Red Book* went on to become the biggest-selling sports book in history.

In 1994, NBC golf announcer Jim Lampley asked Harvey Penick if he would autograph a copy of his book for actor Jack Nicholson, Lampley's friend and golf partner. Lampley was somewhat taken aback when he realized that while Penick was more than happy to sign the book, he had no idea who Jack Nicholson was. When Penick was told that Nicholson was a highly acclaimed actor, he wrote: "Dear Jack—Congratulations: I understand you've had a good career. Harvey Penick."

Among the thousands of people who sought out Harvey Penick for lessons, one was Betsy Rawls. She first came to Mr. Penick as a student at the University of Texas, and the woman who would go on to win four U.S. Women's Opens was immediately impressed.

"Harvey changed my grip slightly and then charged me $3 for my first lesson," she says. "When I finished my second lesson, I asked how much I owed him. 'Nothing. I'm just telling you the same thing I told you the other day.' And he was absolutely serious. He wouldn't take a cent."

One morning Tom Kite brought a friend—a writer—to Austin Country Club for a round of golf. Tom's father joined them, and when they made the turn Harvey Penick arrived at the tee in his golf cart. Penick followed them for three holes. This must have inspired the writer, who made two birdies and a par.

"What do you think, Mr. Penick?" Tom asked. "Does he have any talent?"

"Your friend has all the talent in the world," Penick replied softly. "The question is, 'Does he believe?'"

Of all the great players Harvey Penick touched, he was especially close to Ben Crenshaw and Tom Kite. While Tom moved to Austin, Texas, as a twelve-year-old, Mr. Penick had known Ben since he was a youngster.

"My dad arranged for me to take lessons from Harvey beginning when I was about seven," remembers Crenshaw. "The first thing he did was put my hands on the club, which was an old mashie he found back in the storeroom and cut down for me. He never told me how I should hold it. He just very gently placed my hands on the club. After he was satisfied with my grip, he gave me a little putter and a ball and told me to chip the ball onto the practice green and then putt it into the hole. I think I said something like, 'Gosh, Mr. Penick, I want to play golf,' and he said, 'Ben, you are playing golf.'"

In the spring of 1995, Harvey Penick was near death. Both Kite and Crenshaw made special efforts to visit their old friend and teacher. On one visit—near the end—Penick asked Ben how he was playing. Crenshaw told him that, of all things, he wasn't putting very well. Penick asked Ben to get a putter and hit a few putts.

"Ben, I want you to trust yourself," he said weakly. "Just make two good practice strokes and then hit it—and don't let the putterhead pass your hands."

A few days later, Harvey Penick died. And a few days after that, Ben Crenshaw won his second Masters.

PINE VALLEY GOLF CLUB

Whenever people are asked to select the best course in the United States, Pine Valley in Clementon, New Jersey, invariably winds up near the top, if not at the top, of the list. It is a beautiful yet fearsome test of golf that inspires both awe and terror for golfers of all skill levels.

In the 1920s a fine British player, Eustace Storey, came to the punishing 2nd hole, paused, and said to his host: "I say, do you chaps actually try to play this hole or do you simply photograph it and go on?" he asked.

The opening stretch of holes at Pine Valley is as demanding as any in golf. Much to his own amazement, J. Wood Platt, a gifted amateur in the 1920s, found himself 4-under through four. As he reached the tee on the 226-yard, par-3 5th hole he simply headed for the adjacent clubhouse.

"I'm going in, gentlemen," he said to his playing companions. "It's got to go downhill from here, and I'm going to quit while I'm ahead."

British writer Bernard Darwin played the first seven holes in level par, hit a good drive on the short 8th hole, then took a 16. He retired to the clubhouse and announced, "It's all very well to punish a bad stroke, but the right of eternal punishment should be reserved for a higher tribunal than a greens committee."

Major Tom Fotheringham, the captain of the Royal and Ancient Golf Club of St. Andrews, made his first visit to Pine Valley with considerable expectations. He began his round on the 145-yard, par-3 10th, which he aced—without question the greatest start in the history of Pine Valley. When he finished his round he was warmly welcomed at the clubhouse.

"Of course, you will keep the ball as a memento of your majestic shot," a member said to him.

"Oh dear, no," said Fotheringham. "I'm afraid I hit it in the water on 16."

The Crump Cup is an invitational tournament that attracts some of the nation's top amateurs to Pine Valley annually. One year, a player making his first appearance opened with a respectable 79. The next day he followed up with a 98.

"What happened?" he was asked.

"I found out where the trouble is," he said.

The first segment of the old "Shell's Wonderful World of Golf" series was filmed at Pine Valley and featured Byron Nelson and Gene Littler. The match was close until the 226-yard, par-3 5th hole, when Littler missed the green to the right and made a 7.

"You have to understand that the 5th is a hole where only God can make a 3," said a consoling member.

Any listing of America's best golf courses invariably finds Pine Valley at or near the top, and with good reason: it is beautiful, demanding, surprisingly fair, and as visually intimidating as any course in the world.

So it was with considerable intimidation that Fred Raphael—the producer and director of the old "Shell's Wonderful World of Golf"—accepted an invitation to play his very first round of golf—ever—at Pine Valley, where the inaugural match would be played between Byron Nelson and Gene Littler.

"My old friend Gene Sarazen got a set of clubs for me from Wilson, and when he found out where I was playing he gave me six dozen of the smaller British golf balls," Raphael recalls. "I was playing with some members who worked for Shell. I think I shot about 150. About a month later, all the members got a letter from the club's president, Mr. John Arthur Brown, announcing that some twenty-nine illegal British balls had been found on the property, and if Mr. J. Arthur Brown found out who was using illegal balls, he would personally toss them out of the club. My friend from Shell asked me what I thought we should do. I told him to write Mr. 307 Brown and tell him to keep looking. There were four more balls out there somewhere."

The Walker Cup is the supreme example of sportsmanship in golf. The players lucky enough to be selected to represent their countries forge bonds of friendship—among both their teammates and opponents—that last through the years. Two opponents in the 1936 Walker Cup teamed to write a poem describing their mutual feelings about Pine Valley:

> We think that we shall never see
> A tougher course than Pine Valley;
> Trees and traps wherever we go
> And clumps of earth flying through the air.

This course was made for you and me
But only God can make a three.

Ed Sullivan, the newspaperman who went on to become one of the biggest stars in the early days of television, was a passionate golfer. As a boy he had learned the game as a caddie along with one of his best friends, Gene Sarazen.

One day Sullivan drove to Pine Valley for his first round at the celebrated course. When he finished and repaired to the clubhouse, he was asked what he thought of the course.

"I know why it's called the Shrine of American Golf," Sullivan said. "People come here to have their games buried."

GARY PLAYER

When the young Gary Player arrived at St. Andrews in 1955 for his first British Open, he was understandably nervous and excited.

"I stood on the first tee and hit a screaming hook," Player remembers. "I was paired with this old fellow, and he asked me what my handicap was. I told him I was a professional here to play in the Open championship. He thought for a second, looked at where I had hit my drive, and said, 'Well, you must be a very good chipper and putter.'"

When Gary Player joined the PGA Tour in 1957, he already idolized Ben Hogan and tried to mold his game in Hogan's image. Imagine his excitement, then, when after his first round with Hogan, the Great Man took him aside in the locker room.

"Gary, you're going to be a very good player," Hogan said. "Do you practice much?"

"All the time," Player said.

"Double it," Hogan said and walked away.

When Gary Player won the 1965 U.S. Open at Bellerive Country Club in St. Louis, he gave away his $25,000 first prize: $5,000 to help fight cancer and $20,000 to the U.S. Golf Association to help promote junior golf.

"That does it," said Bob Rosburg. "I always knew the USGA was tougher than cancer."

Throughout his career, Gary Player has seemingly willed himself to success by assuming the role of the underdog, even if that has meant inventing some reason why he was the underdog when no other reason appeared obvious—at least to anyone but him.

After two rounds at the 1974 British Open at Royal Lytham and St. Annes, he held a five-stroke lead over the field. Anyone else would have been ecstatic, but not Player. For him, this was a calamity of the first order.

"No man can possibly win with such a lead," he told the press. "You don't know whether to continue attacking the course or fall back and protect your lead. You're totally of two minds. No, I'm afraid I'm done for. I won't be able to play a shot tomorrow."

Naturally, facing such enormous odds, he somehow managed to hold on and win by a mere four strokes.

POLITICIANS

It's safe to say that the late, great Thomas P. "Tip" O'Neill had a cordial, but not exactly close, relationship with President Jimmy Carter.

Tip was the Speaker of the House. Jimmy Carter was a president who didn't exactly love wheeling and dealing with pols.

Tip was a Boston Irish Catholic who understood the weaknesses of the human spirit. Jimmy Carter was a Southern Baptist who tended to take a pretty stern view of the human condition.

Tip was known to take a drink now and then. Jimmy Carter? Well, no.

Tip loved golf. Jimmy Carter ran in road races and set the schedule for the White House tennis court.

And on and on and on . . .

One day Tip was playing in a pro-am to help raise money to fight heart disease. When he reached the 6th green, a cart pulled up and a young man from the pro shop staff breathlessly told the Speaker that the President wanted to speak with him.

"Is it important?" Tip asked.

"I don't know, sir," the kid said. "All I know is that it's the President."

"Tell him I'll call him at the turn," said Tip, who then went on to make his putt.

True to his word, when he putted out on the 9th hole, Tip went into the pro shop and called the White House, only to be told that the President was busy.

"Well," said the Speaker. "Tell him that unless there's a war, I'll talk to him after my round."

"One day I'm playing with Sammy Snead and a couple guys down at Pine Tree in Florida," O'Neill relates. "Now the most I ever play for is a few bucks, but we get into it, and I wind up losing a hundred or so, all fair and square, mind you. Off we go to the clubhouse for a pop and a little gin rummy. Now I'm a pretty good gin player. As a matter of fact, I'm one of the best. I got my hundred back plus a little extra.

"As Sammy gets up to leave he shakes my hand and says, 'O'Brien, you're a hell of a fella. What 'ya say you do for a living?'"

Former President Gerald Ford and the late, great Tip O'Neill were fierce political foes but the best of friends, in no small part because they shared a love of golf. Even after Ford had lost the presidency and Tip had retired as Speaker of the House, they still played a lot of golf together. Still, even though they were great pals, it didn't stop Tip from occasionally making a joke at his friend's expense.

"Geez, I love playing golf with Jerry Ford when we're in Palm Springs," Tip once said. "The problem is there's over fifty courses out there and I never know which one we're going to play 'til the President hits his first drive."

It's a pretty good bet that no professional has played with more prominent politicians than has Sam Snead. One afternoon he played with then–Vice President Richard Nixon, and he got a revealing glimpse into the man who would go on to become the only president to resign from office.

"Well, Nixon wasn't what you'd call a good athlete, but he was a plugger," Sam explained. "I always thought he took up the game because Ike played. One day we're playing and the Vice President hit it off into the boonies. If he'd had a hundred Secret Service men with him, he couldn't have found that ball. I told him just take a drop, but he said he wanted to have a look. He's in there thrashing around. He might have gotten eaten by a bear, as deep in the scrub as he was. The next think I know the ball came a-flyin' out of those trees. I told him it was a hell of a shot, but he couldn't have gotten that ball out of there with a bazooka."

THE PRESS

When the 1923 British Open was played at Troon, the professionals were not allowed to dine in the clubhouse. In fact, they weren't even allowed in the place. That didn't faze Walter Hagen, who had his limousine pull up in front and then had a lavish meal served at a portable table nearby, horrifying the members.

If the club members and championship officials seemed to hold the players in a certain low esteem, it paled in comparison to their attitude to the press. One year, when the championship was played at a particularly snooty club, the pressroom was in an old potting shed littered with beer bottles and broken pots—unacceptable even by the standards of the day. The writers lodged a complaint, and a committee of members and officials came by to investigate. When they arrived they spotted a lone writer finishing his report.

"Look," exclaimed a member. "There's one of them in there now."

Almost to a person, writers are great procrastinators. If we can find a way to put off writing a piece, we'll do it. Any excuse will do. None is too trivial. For some reason, this is especially true when it comes to books. Maybe the sheer volume of the work required is simply too daunting. Whatever the reason, it usually takes the magical combination of a deadline and a dwindling bank balance to produce the required inspiration.

That was certainly the case with the legendary Herb Graffis. In a business filled with colorful characters, Herb Graffis stepped— full-blown—from *Front Page*.

"I was doing a book with Sam Snead and we'd already blown the deadline," Graffis once explained. "The publishers were screaming about money and contracts and all that usual publisher's stuff, so I went down to the 1938 PGA Championship at Shawnee-on-Delaware. I talked to Sam a little bit, and then I went back to my room at the hotel. It was miserably hot and humid and there was no air-conditioning, so I did the only sane thing. I took off all my clothes, wrapped a towel around my waist, and sat down at the typewriter with a case of cold beer. When I woke up the next morning, the beer was gone and the book was done."

Herb Graffis once gave a young writer a valuable piece of advice.

"Son," he said. "Well-meaning people are always going to tell you to 'write about what you know.' That's nonsense. Do that and you'll starve. In this business, you've got to write what they'll pay you to write."

In the early 1950s, Bill Davis talked two friends, Howard Gill and Jack Barnett, into joining him in starting a new magazine, *Golf Digest*. Some twenty years later, they sold the magazine to The New York Times Company and Bill became a vice president with the company. But for all his other responsibilities, he always kept his hands on the magazine and in the game. In fact, one of his great joys came from meeting the new editors that came on board as the magazine grew into the largest golf magazine in the world.

Bill was frequently brilliant. He was always quirky. He was occasionally maddening, mostly because his mind raced along in a totally nonlinear way. In short, Bill could make you crazy without really trying.

One evening, as he neared his retirement from The New York Times Company, he attended a dinner for the editors of *Golf Digest* and its sister magazines. Bill got up to speak, and in the course of his sort of rambling speech, he stressed that every writer needs a good editor.

"Even Hemingway would have been a better writer if I had edited him," Bill said.

"Yeah," one editor said to the person next to him. "But he would have committed suicide ten years earlier."

For many years, Bill Davis played in a company golf tournament open to all employees. It was a match play event that was played out over the course of the summer. Davis loved to participate in it because as the magazine grew, it gave him a chance to get to know new employees.

One year he was scheduled to play Steve Szurlej, the magazine's senior staff photographer. Davis invited Szurlej to play at one of his clubs, Millbrook, in the wealthy New York City suburb of Greenwich, Connecticut.

There were no caddies available when Davis and Szurlej arrived, so Szurlej decided to carry his bag, while Davis pulled a cart.

They teed off the first hole and headed down the fairway. As Szurlej walked ahead to his ball, he heard a crash, and looked back to see Davis picking up his bag. A few minutes later, he heard another crash and saw Davis again picking up his clubs. When it happened a third time, Szurlej went back to see what the problem was. It didn't take long to figure out.

"Bill," he said. "I think you've got to pull the wheels out away from the cart."

It's no secret that not everyone who gets credit for writing a book actually sits down and does the typing. Bill Davis was no exception.

One year he came up with the idea for a coffee table–size book based on *Golf Digest*'s ranking of the "100 Greatest Golf Courses in America." It was an inspired idea.

Davis walked into the office of one of the magazine's senior editors, Ross Goodner, and gave him the good news.

"Ross, I'm going to do a book based on the '100 Greatest' and you're going to write it for me," he said, scarcely able to contain his enthusiasm.

Goodner, who had known Davis for years, saw his life pass before his eyes.

Nevertheless, the book somehow got done and was an instant success. A few months after its publication, Davis was playing at the Garden City Golf Club just outside New York City with another of his editors.

"Gee, do you know who designed this course?" he asked the editor as they walked toward the third green. "I should know, but I haven't read that part of my book yet."

One day in the late 1970s, *Golf Digest* held an advertiser outing at the Stanwich Club in the New York City suburb of Greenwich, Connecticut. It was a hot, humid day, and a combination of the weather and the generous amount of alcohol flowing from the open bars took a toll on some of the attendees—including one editor.

Following dinner Nick Seitz, who was then the magazine's editor, rose to give a short speech. As is usually the case at these sorts of outings, he praised the editorial staff, citing their unparalleled enthusiasm, energy, devotion to the game, and so on. Then he began to introduce his staff individually. His intentions were good, but his timing was not. Unknowingly, he picked just that moment to single out a senior editor who had just passed out in his chair and had unleashed a resounding snore.

It was the highlight of the outing.

One year Dick Taylor, the longtime editor of *Golf World* magazine, traveled to New Zealand to cover that country's Open championship. While he was there he was asked to serve as a television commentator, along with Australian Peter Thomson, a five-time British Open champion.

In a production meeting prior to the first day's telecast, the director told Dick that he would be responsible for profiling the foreign players.

"But I don't know any of the foreign players," he protested.

"No, Dick, you don't understand," said Thomson. "Over here, the Americans are the foreign players."

Peter Dobereiner, who died in 1996 at the age of seventy, was said to be the most widely read golf writer in the world, and there is no reason to doubt that. Dobers, as he was known, had been the golf correspondent for England's *Daily Mail*, *The Guardian*, and *The Observer*, and he also was a contributing editor and columnist for *Golf Digest*.

One of his friends was Renton Laidlaw, a Scotsman who reported on golf tournaments around the world for the British Broadcasting Corporation. Laidlaw would phone his reports from the pressroom, and to help silence the din, he would occasionally put a box over his head.

One day he was seated near Dobers, and in the course of his broadcast he reported that play has been postponed by rain. With that, Dobers went into action. He walked over and began tapping gently on the top of the box.

"Ah," said Laidlaw. "I think you can hear the rain coming down now."

Peter Dobereiner knew the ability of a well-aimed and slyly delivered barb to deflate even the largest and healthiest of egos. Take Jack Nicklaus, for example.

One evening Peter and some other writers were invited to join Jack at a dinner in St. Andrews. The waiter grandly announced that one of the evening's entrées would be a magnificent salmon caught that day by none other than that noted angler, Jack William Nicklaus, himself.

"It's just my luck," Dobereiner said, loud enough for Nicklaus to overhear. "I'll probably get the piece that contains the bullet."

Nicklaus took the bait—so to speak—and insisted that Dobereiner sit next to him at dinner.

For decades now, the Golf Writers Association of America has held a tournament in Myrtle Beach, South Carolina, on the weekend prior to the Masters. In 1965, they invited the executive secretary of the United States Golf Association, Joseph C. Dey, to compete in the tournament.

Dey, who began his career covering golf for a Philadelphia newspaper, accepted. Everything was fine until he attended a pretournament cocktail party that featured an auction of the field. This put Dey—a man of great rectitude—in an awkward position. The USGA had taken a strong stand against such auctions on the heels of a scandal surrounding a Calcutta at the Deepdale Country Club Invitational in the 1950s.

When Bob Drum, the association's president, began auctioning off teams, Dey voiced his concerns.

"Bob, this isn't a Calcutta, is it?" he asked.

"Nope, it's a Bombay," the Drummer replied.

The late Charlie Price was a stylish and gifted writer. He was a keen observer of the game and a friend to generations of players dating back to Bob Jones and Walter Hagen.

In the early 1960s he collaborated with Bobby Jones on a book, *Bobby Jones on Golf*. Their routine was to work in the morning and then break for lunch, usually hamburgers that were brought to Jones's office. Before lunch they would have a martini. Sometimes a couple of martinis.

"You know, Charlie," Jones said one day, "I shouldn't drink these things. They interfere with my medicine."

"I know, I shouldn't drink them either," Price said. "They make me drunk."

Every year at the Masters, the executives from Tokyo Broadcasting host an elaborate party. One of the great attractions is the elaborate and seemingly endless supply of Japanese food.

One year a writer arrived toward the end of the party and made his way into the kitchen, where he sat at a table with several waitresses who were having a late dinner. After helping himself to a heaping plate of sushi, he struck up a conversation with one of the women, who he assumed was from Japan.

"How . . . long . . . have . . . you . . . been . . . in . . . the . . . United . . . States?" he asked, speaking slowly, since he assumed the woman spoke little English.

"Why, I've lived here all my life," she answered with a southern drawl that would have done any true Daughter of the Confederacy proud.

Many people treat golf as though it's some kind of religion, but religion and golf don't always mix. Just ask Jim McKay, the veteran television journalist and longtime anchor of ABC's golf coverage.

On Good Friday, when he was fourteen years old, he and his cousin, Frank Callahan, decided to play a little golf at a course called Cobb Creek. On their way home, they passed their parish church, and naturally, since McKay is Irish to the depths of his soul, the guilt began to set in. They quietly went inside the church, leaned their golf bags against the rear wall, and slid into an empty pew.

Safely ensconced in the bosom of the church on one of the holiest days of the year, everything seemed in divine order.

That is, until both bags fell over with a shattering crash.

The good nuns have taken rulers to knuckles for less. A lot less, come to think of it.

George Kimball is a sports columnist for the *Boston Herald*. He's a great bear of a man, with curly red hair and a bushy beard to match. He's also something of a throwback to the days when sportswriters were often as well known for their exploits as the players they covered.

According to legend, one night George was in a bar with a friend. The friend excused himself and asked George to "keep an eye on my drink."

Big mistake.

George took him literally, took out his glass eye, and dropped it in the man's drink.

For many years, *Golf Digest* hosted a Senior PGA Tour event in Rhode Island at the Newport Country Club. One of the highlights was the press day, when writers from around New England would take advantage of a chance to play at the club—which hosted the first U.S. Open and U.S. Amateur—for free.

One year, as part of the fun and games, there was a Closest to the Pin contest on one of the par 3s. To make things a little more interesting, a small company that was building hickory-shafted replicas of old clubs agreed to supply clubs for the contest in hopes of getting a little free publicity from the writers.

As luck would have it, George Kimball was in the first group that day. When he came to the hole where the Closest to the Pin contest was being held, he got up and lashed into the ball.

Well, not exactly into the ball. He hit about four inches behind it. The ball barely moved, but the force did shatter the club.

"It must have been a bad shaft," said George, looking at the sorry remains of the club, still in his hands.

As a young man Charlie Price, the gifted writer, tried his hand on the Tour without—as he'll be the first to admit—much notable success. Finally he asked Clayton Heafner for some advice.

"Charlie," said Heafner, "did you notice that all the guys doing well out here are built like truck drivers, but they have the touch of hairdressers? Well, you're built like a hairdresser, and you have the touch of a truck driver."

Peter Thomson, the Australian who won five British Open championships, was playing in the 1957 St. Paul (Minnesota) Open. The course was laid out in such a manner that several holes were routed near a parking lot.

As Thomson, a man noted for a dry wit, was leaving one of the greens, he was approached by an eager young reporter covering his first tournament.

"Mr. Thomson, how was your round?" the reporter asked.

"Most satisfactory, considering I've only played two holes," Thomson said.

In 1971, the Golf Writers of America asked Argentina's Roberto de Vicenzo to present its Richardson Award, which he had won the year before, to longtime *New York Times* golf writer Lincoln Werden.

"I get this trophy, I think, because I signed the wrong scorecard a few years ago in the Masters. Mr. Werden, I think, gets this award for spelling my name wrong three times."

For many years a competition called "The Writer's Cup" was played between golf writers from the United States and those from Great Britain and Ireland. In the long and finest tradition of golf writers, it involved numerous freebies, very little journalism, and a great deal of partying, and golf at some wonderful courses. One year the outing was particularly noteworthy, as much for what happened before a single shot was even struck as for the (dubious) quality of the golf. Peter Dobereiner, a longtime British golf writer and observer of the game, remembers.

"Well, the calamity began several weeks before, when one of the American writers, Larry Dennis, was preparing for the competition by practicing his golf swing in the luxurious confines of his living room," Dobereiner recalls. "He was quite gung-ho to win all the points for America, and as his finely calibrated swing had been idled all winter, it was clear that he dare not wait until he arrived in Ireland for the matches. Unfortunately, the act of watching her husband swing a golf club bored his poor wife into a stupor and she fell asleep, only to be awakened when Larry hit her foursquare on her foot, breaking every bloody bone in her ankle. I suspect it was the most solid contact Larry had made in some time.

"At any rate, Mr. and Mrs. Dennis, broken leg and all, arrived in Dublin for the next stage of the journey, which would serve as testimony to the ingenious nature of the Irish. The matches were to be played in Ballybunion on Monday, but through an oversight the writers were in Dublin on Sunday with no flights scheduled for Shannon. The people from the Irish Tourist Board devised what was really quite a clever solution: they arranged for the writers to board a special Air Lingus flight filled with people making a pilgrimage to Lourdes.

"The flight was in the air for just a few minutes when the pilot announced that 'due to a small technical problem we shall have to set down in Shannon for just a few moments.' At the same time, the flight attendants went to all the writers and whispered that indeed the fix was in, and that when the plane arrived in Shannon, they should depart.

"The plane landed and the writers, including Mrs. Dennis, began to depart," Dobereiner recalls with a laugh. "One of the attendants, noticing the cast on her leg, pulled her aside and said quietly, 'Not you darling. We're not quite to Lourdes yet.' "

One of the British writers who regularly came to the Masters was Leonard Crawley, the golf correspondent of the *Daily Telegraph*. Crawley, an enormous man given to wearing red suits that matched his ruddy complexion and generous mustache, had been a Walker Cupper, a first-rank cricketer, and a superb marksman in his youth.

For all his skills, Crawley was completely incapable of dealing with even the most basic of modern conveniences, including the telephone and the typewriter—clearly a disadvantage for even the most talented journalist.

Still, such was Crawley's value that the *Telegraph* allowed him to hire a secretary to assist him wherever he went.

He arrived at Augusta to find that a lovely, young, shy—if conscientious—woman had been hired to assist him. Crawley was forthright in describing her responsibilities.

"Missy, your most important daily duty is to see that my cigar never goes out," he said, handing her a box of matches.

With that out of the way, Crawley set out for what he considered the most important part of a reporter's job—legwork—although in his case this was done largely in a sitting position in the convivial company of old friends.

After a particularly arduous afternoon of research and countless snifters of the club's finest brandies, Crawley fell into a much-deserved nap, his cigar clenched firmly between his teeth.

Well, this put his Missy in an awkward position. She wanted to do her job as instructed by the imperious Crawley, but were her nerves up to it? With trembling hands—as Crawley's fellow writers looked on in gleeful anticipation—she approached the cigar, flame in hand.

Alas, she missed the cigar and sent his brandy-sodden mustache into flames. Crawley awoke in a rage, and after he extinguished his face, sent Missy on her way, ending what might have been a most promising career in journalism.

No discussion of the golf press would be complete without a mention of "The Drummer." Bob Drum came to golf as a sportswriter for the *Pittsburgh Press*. He was primarily a baseball writer who was assigned to cover a kid from nearby Latrobe named Arnold Palmer.

"I went out to cover him in the Pennsylvania Junior and he lost in the first round," Drummer remembers. "If I had known he was going to grow up and become Arnold Palmer, I would have been nicer to the bum."

Be that as it may, Drummer's golf writing career took off when Palmer became the game's dominant player in the late 1950s and early 1960s. But in March 1961, with Palmer the defending champion at both the Masters and U.S. Open and the runner-up in the 1960 British Open, Drummer was diagnosed with cancer.

"The doctor told me this was a serious problem, and they wanted to cut me right away," says Drummer, now seventy-six. "I told him to forget it. I had to get down to Augusta. I told him we'd do it right after the Masters so I'd be fixed up in time for the Open at Oakland Hills in June.

"You'd think after all that I went through," says Drummer, "Arnold could have won at least one of them."

"When Dan Jenkins was writing for *Sports Illustrated*, he'd kind of take it personally if Palmer or Nicklaus or one of the heroes didn't win the tournament he was covering," remembers Bob Drum. "In 1970, when Dave Stockton won the PGA Championship at Southern Hills, Dan spent most of his story writing about who didn't win, which was basically Arnold or Jack. You couldn't blame him. I mean, Stockton was this short-hitting guy who could putt and who nobody had heard of before. What was Dan supposed to do?

"Anyway, a couple of weeks later I'm at a tournament and Stockton comes into the pressroom," says the Drummer. "He's all upset and he says, 'Where's Jenkins? I want to talk to him.'

"Whom should I say is calling?" I asked him.

Bill Brendle, who died in 1982, was a longtime public relations guy for CBS Sports who, unlike a lot of publicists, was actually a good and helpful source. He was also quick with his American Express card—which sometimes got him into a little jam with his expense reports. More than once the bill arrived and he had to ask the waiter to "do me a favor and date this thing tomorrow. I already used up today last night."

During the 1994 British Open, writers scrambled to learn more about Jesper Parnevik, the young Swede who finished second.

"What is your father's name?" a writer asked.

"Bo," answered Parnevik.

"How do you spell it?" the writer asked.

"B.O.," he replied.

A group of writers arranged to play at the Yale University Golf Course in New Haven. Their starting times were delayed by an NCAA women's tournament. As they waited, one of the writers noticed a woman driving by in a golf cart. He whistled and motioned her over.

"Are you the beer lady?" he asked.

"No, I'm the Yale coach," she replied as she drove away.

The Yale course is celebrated as a virtually pure example of architect Charles Blair MacDonald's work. Since it is an old course, it has a number of quirky characteristics, most notably blind drives and approaches.

After a round one glorious fall day, a friend asked Peter Andrews, the celebrated humorist and writer, what he thought of the course. Andrews had not had a particularly profitable day and glumly gave his assessment of MacDonald's work.

"Eighteen good reasons to send a young man to Harvard," he growled.

A golf writer was flying from Germany to London, and as the plane began its approach to Heathrow, suddenly the lights of the city went black. The plane was forced to circle while waiting for the lights to return. After a few minutes, the pilot came on the loud-speaker with what was supposed to be a comforting announcement.

"Ladies and gentlemen, this is your pilot speaking," he said in a clipped German accent. "You have nothing to be concerned about. There are no pilots in the world with more experience flying over a blacked-out London than the German pilots of Lufthansa."

Television golf commentators are not always picked for their jobs because of their vast knowledge of the game's intricacies. In fact, many have only a passing knowledge of—or interest in—the game. Sometimes this becomes apparent to even the most casual viewer.

One year CBS Sports tried out a new announcer at the Masters, of all places. The announcer was assigned to the 14th hole, and things went smoothly enough until Sunday afternoon, when Seve Ballesteros came to the hole. Ballesteros hit a magnificent drive, leaving himself just 100 yards to the hole.

Seve studied the shot, pulled a wedge from his bag, and set up over the ball. Just as he was about to play his shot, he was distracted. He looked over at the gallery and said, "Fore, please."

The announcer spoke up.

"Seve has decided to change clubs," he whispered. "He's asked his caddie for a 4-iron."

Unlike writers, who have editors and erasers, announcers live or die with their words as they are spoken. Occasionally, they aren't always the best choice of words, as another announcer for CBS Sports learned at the Masters.

Nick Price had settled over his ball and was preparing to play, when he noticed that the wind had changed direction.

"There was a gust of wind from Nick's rear just as he was about to play," the announcer said.

No sooner had the words left his mouth than CBS's veteran producer/director Frank Chirkinian barked a question into the announcer's headset.

"Did Nick have Mexican food last night?"

Lesley Visser, who currently does on-air work for ABC and ESPN, got her start at the *Boston Globe* in the mid-1970s. She was one of the first women to break into the old-boys' clubs that were the sports departments of major American newspapers. In Lesley's case, it didn't hurt that she combined a graceful writing skill with a world-class personality and sense of humor.

One time she and a friend were in a bar when a drunk came along and tried to pick her up. After a few minutes, Lesley had heard about all she could stand.

"You sure know a lot about sports," he told her.

"I work for the *Globe*," she answered. "And what do you do?"

"I work for a company that grinds optical lenses," he said.

"Oh, that must be why you're making a spectacle out of yourself," she said.

Perfect.

In 1970, the unions for Britain's newspapers went on strike and the publishers refused to send writers over to cover the U.S. Open at Hazeltine. The only British writer at the tournament was Leonard Crawley, the legendary golf correspondent for London's *Daily Telegraph*.

This would have been seen as a shrewd move by the British publishers were it not for the fact that England's Tony Jacklin won the championship, becoming the first British subject to win the U.S. Open since Tommy Armour, who was born in Scotland, won in 1927.

As Crawley prepared to call his story in to London, he paused to gleefully savor his incredible good fortune.

"At this moment, gentlemen," he rejoiced, "all of England lies prostrate at my feet."

Early in his newspaper career, Crawley was sent to the English Boys' Championship. Upon his return he submitted an expense report that included £25 for entertaining some of the players. Naturally, the paper's accountants questioned the expense, figuring that the only person Crawley was entertaining was himself. Crawley protested.

"It's remarkable how much lemonade the little tykes can drink," he said.

Crawley was an accomplished sportsman and quite a good golfer in his own right. He was a member of the 1932 Great Britain/Ireland Walker Cup team and played quite well at The Country Club just outside Boston. But going into the final day's singles match against George Voight, a box of matches exploded as he held them, burning his hands badly. Still, he insisted that he play, and going into the final hole of his match he was 1-up.

After hitting a good drive, he had a 5-iron left to the green. He hit a good shot and watched anxiously as it covered the flag through the air. After a few seconds, he heard a sharp clang.

"Congratulations, boss, we hit the cup!" exclaimed his caddie.

For years, the dent left by Crawley's shot was a source of pride 333 to the Englishman. In fact, when it was finally removed he protested in print—with some justification.

The late Henry Longhurst was not only a golf writer of considerable note but also a broadcaster who covered golf for the BBC, CBS, and ABC. Late in his career, he decided to walk away from television. His friend, British golfer-turned-announcer Peter Alliss, asked Longhurst why he was quitting.

"Having sucked the orange dry, I saw no reason to chew upon the pits," Longhurst said.

The late Henry Longhurst was a celebrated and widely respected writer and television commentator. He was an Englishman who felt very much at home in the United States—or anyplace else where golf was played, for that matter.

Longhurst deeply loved the game, but toward the end of his life, be came to bemoan the track that golf was headed down. He detested golf carts and thought caddies should remain an integral part of the game. He was a traditionalist, in the best sense, and felt change should come slowly to the game.

One lovely spring afternoon, he was holding court on the veranda at Augusta National, drinking with friends and railing—in his own way—against the various outrages he thought were being inflicted on golf in the name of progress.

"Alas, it's still a wonderful game after all these years, the best there's ever been," he said. "The proof lies in the fact that whatever they do to it, they can't ruin it."

Longhurst, who is best known in the States for his work as a CBS Sports golf commentator, was an elegant and graceful writer.

On one occasion, when writing about the difficult par-3 18th hole at Killarney Golf Club in County Kerry, Ireland, he succinctly summed up the sheer beauty of the place.

"My, what a lovely place to die," he wrote.

Nick Price

Nick Price was born in South Africa but was raised in Rhodesia. He joined the Rhodesian Air Force at a time when the nation was rocked by a bloody struggle between the ruling white minority and the emerging black majority.

Now, Nick Price is not a particularly ideological person, but he saw his duty and resolved to do it. Having said that, he's not crazy, either.

During the induction physical, he was asked if he had any medical conditions that would keep him from serving.

"Well, I do have this skin problem," Price said.

"What's the problem with your skin?" he was asked.

"Bullets go through it," Price replied.

Nick Price, the winner of two PGA Championships and a British Open, is universally regarded as one of the nicest guys in golf. He's unfailingly pleasant and accommodating, which, given the demands on his time, makes him all the more remarkable.

In 1990, he hired Jeff "Squeeky" Medlin as his caddie, and the two enjoyed considerable success and developed a deep and abiding affection for each other.

At the 1994 British Open at Turnberry, Price came to the final hole needing a par to beat Jesper Parnevik by a stroke. After hitting a good drive, Price safely hit the green and began the traditional champion's walk to the green, with the gallery spilling onto the fairway, engulfing the players and their caddies.

When Price and Squeeky broke through the gallery, Price noticed that Squeeky was lingering behind.

"Come on, Squeek," he said. "Let's enjoy this together. We might never have the chance again."

And so the two friends walked together to the green, the roar of the enormous gallery echoing in their ears.

Sadly, Price's words proved all too prescient.

Squeeky died in 1997 after a courageous battle with leukemia.

DANA QUIGLEY

Dana Quigley is one of those success stories that make the Senior PGA Tour so appealing. A club pro from Massachusetts, he had long been a successful player in tournaments around New England. When he turned fifty, he decided to give the Senior Tour a shot.

He entered the 1997 Northville Long Island Classic and was a medalist in the Monday qualifying. He played well all week, and when he beat Jay Sigel in a three-hole playoff, his eyes filled with tears of joy and relief.

But a few minutes after receiving his trophy and $50,000 winner's check, he got a phone call from his brother, Paul, telling him that their father had died that afternoon after a ten-year battle with cancer.

"It went from being one of the greatest days of my life to the worst day of my life," Quigley said. "My dream was to come out on tour and be successful so my parents would be proud of me. I wanted to buy them a house on the water in Florida. I won, but I just didn't win soon enough. God works in strange ways. The day he took my father's life was the same day he gave mine back to me."

TED RAY

Ted Ray, who won the 1912 British Open and the 1920 U.S. Open, is most familiar to American golfers as the man who, along with Harry Vardon, lost to Francis Ouimet in a playoff for the 1913 U.S. Open at The Country Club in Brookline, Massachusetts.

On the day of the playoff, ten thousand locals flocked to the course (in no small part because the Open didn't charge admission fees in those days) to cheer on the twenty-year-old Ouimet—a Townie, as we say in Boston—who grew up on Clyde Street across from the 17th green. Now, it's safe to say that even the impeccably behaved Boston sports fans of the day knew little about golf or about how they should behave on the course, so there were bound to be a few disruptions.

At one point a rules official loudly admonished a man in the gallery—just as Ray prepared to hit his putt.

"Sir, are you going to talk or am I going to putt?" Ray asked sternly.

ALLAN ROBERTSON

In the mid-1800s, Allan Robertson of St. Andrews was believed to be the best golfer in Scotland and, therefore, the world. At a time when almost all golf was at match play, he was very nearly invincible. Of course, the fact that he was also a premier club and ball maker didn't hurt either.

One evening he was having dinner with a friend, Jamie Condie, a fine player and a member of one of Scotland's best-known golfing families. Condie kidded Robertson that for all his considerable skills, the real secret of his success lay in his equipment. The two men argued back and forth until finally they agreed to settle the debate with a match the following day. The terms were that the winner of a hole would get to take one of his opponent's clubs.

To his dismay, it didn't take long for Robertson to realize that he had been too generous in giving strokes to Condie. By the time they reached the home hole, all that Robertson had left were his two favorite clubs—his driver and putter. After putting out, he was down to his putter.

Bravely—or foolishly—Robertson agreed to play one more hole, this time with just his putter. A few minutes later, that was lost, too.

John D. Rockefeller

Oil baron John D. Rockefeller was a wildly enthusiastic, if eccentric, golfer. Just a few days after playing the game for the first time, he had four holes built at his estate, Pocantico Hills. Not satisfied with this, he ordered twelve more holes built and then brought in a series of local professionals to labor over his game.

Rockefeller and his playing companions rode bicycles between shots, the better to play as many holes as possible. He played year-round, and when it snowed he had a small army of people who preceded him around the course clearing away the snow.

Rockefeller was fanatical about instruction. For a time he determined that his slice stemmed from lifting his head during the swing, so he had a youngster follow him around screaming, "Keep your head down, sir!" during his swings. Another time, Rockefeller became convinced that his problems stemmed from faulty footwork, so he took to hammering croquet wickets over his feet to keep them in place.

For all his eccentricities, playing with Rockefeller could be a profitable experience. He routinely gave dimes to his playing companions.

CHI CHI RODRIGUEZ

Chi Chi Rodriguez grew up in Puerto Rico, and if his family wasn't poor, they were close enough to poverty to see what it looked like.

It's not surprising, then, that when he grew old enough to caddie, he jumped at the chance to earn some money for himself. Of course, it helped that he was fascinated by the game.

He was tremendously devoted to his father, who would sit with each of his children for fifteen minutes every evening when he came home from work. One night he was sitting with Chi Chi and he asked him how his school day had been. Chi Chi told him it had been great.

"Then he looked down at my shoes and saw grass clippings stuck to the sides," Chi Chi remembered. "He told me, 'Son, they don't have grass growing in the classrooms.' When he asked me where I'd been, I admitted I'd skipped school and gone to the golf course to caddie. He told me to give him the money I'd earned. It taught me two lessons: first, don't lie, and second, share what I had with others. They were two of the most important lessons I ever learned."

Beyond being one of the best-loved players on the Senior PGA Tour, Chi Chi Rodriguez is easily one of the most superstitious. In fact, he's elevated his collection of quirks, beliefs, and hunches to a veritable art form. There's no one who even comes close.

For starters, during any given round he'll carry a lucky walnut, tees in his lucky colors—whatever those colors are that week—lucky coins, and, last but not least, a rock blessed by the Pope. He always marks his ball with the "head" side up and never uses pennies, and if he has a birdie putt, he'll mark the ball with a quarter. If he sees a coin on the ground, he won't pick it up unless it's lying head side up.

When it comes to clothes, he always tries to wear green on Sunday because it's the color of money. It's also a good bet that he'll never wear red on Thursdays. And if he has a good round, he'll take the same route back and forth to the course for the rest of the tournament.

In one tournament, Rodriguez was staying in a house that had a palm tree planted outside the front door. When he came home after a poor first round, he noticed the palm tree and since this is a bad-luck omen in his native Puerto Rico, asked to have it removed. It was, and he shot rounds of 66 and 67 over the next two days.

Given all this, you'd expect that receiving a voodoo doll would positively unnerve him. Not at all.

"I was playing a tournament in Jamaica in late 1986," Rodriguez remembers. "I came back to my room and there was a voodoo doll on my bed. It had nails through each eye and each knee."

Did it work?

Apparently not, since 1987 was his best year on the Tour.

Chi Chi Rodriguez is a player who really made the most of his Senior PGA Tour career. He had won eight times on the regular Tour and was a member of the 1973 Ryder Cup team, but when he turned fifty, his career really took off. He has twenty-two wins and has emerged as one of the Tour's premier players. In fact, he's doing so well as a senior that he's come up with a plan to keep the party going.

"I'm going to set up a tour for players eighty and over," he explains. "You play three-hole tournaments, one hole a day. At the end of three days, the guy who can remember what he scored on each hole wins the $1 million first prize."

Chi Chi was playing in a pro-am with a partner who was extremely nervous. When they got to the first green, the amateur was making a series of extremely shaky practice strokes.

"Chi Chi, how do you think I should play this putt?" he asked.

"Whatever you do, partner, keep it low," Chi Chi said.

Chi Chi Rodriguez is passionate in his devotion to kids, especially underprivileged kids. He's especially interested in exposing them to golf, in no small part because it was his path out of wrenching poverty as a child growing up in Puerto Rico.

One day he was talking to a child who had demonstrated some skill for the game.

"What do you want to be when you grow up?" Chi Chi asked the child.

"I want to be a pro," the child said.

"Why?" Chi Chi asked.

"Because I want to win tournaments and become very rich and famous," he said. "I want everything."

"The problem with wanting everything, son," Chi Chi said, "is that it's never enough."

BOB ROSBURG

Most people today know Bob Rosburg as a commentator for ABC's golf coverage, but he was an outstanding player. He won the 1959 PGA Championship and he came close to winning a couple of U.S. Opens. Along the way, he developed a knack for walking off the course if the mood struck him.

Dave Marr remembered that he sent Rossie and his wife, Eleanor, a note when they celebrated their 18th wedding anniversary: "Eleanor, congratulations on performing a miracle. Rossie rarely goes all 18."

THE ROYAL AND ANCIENT GOLF CLUB OF ST. ANDREWS

For much of its early history, the Old Course at St. Andrews was closed on Sundays. One day a gentleman arrived and was miffed when he learned that he couldn't play. He got into a discussion with Old Tom Morris, the club's professional. After a few minutes, Morris had heard enough.

"Look, sir, the Old Course needs a rest, even if you don't," he said. "There'll be no golf played here today."

Prospective captains of the R and A are required to "drive themselves in" by hitting a tee shot off the first tee at the Old Course during the club's fall meeting. Some meet with more success than others.

In 1922 the Prince of Wales fortified himself for the task with a few stiff pops at the Grand Hotel's bar. He weaved his way through the mist, arriving at the tee where Andrew Kirkaldy, the honorary professional, prepared to tee his ball.

"This is an awful job," said the Prince.

"Just keep your eye on the ball, sir," said Kirkaldy.

If he did, he saw the most famous heel job in history, as the ball squirted sharply to the left, where it came to rest in the Valley of Sin fronting the 18th green.

"My God, if he holes it we've got a new course record," cried a member of the gallery.

Old Tom Morris, the first professional at St. Andrews, was a wonderful player who won four British Opens in the early years of the championship. But like almost all golfers, he occasionally had problems with his putting.

One time a friend sent him a letter. It was addressed simply:

To the Misser of Short Putts
St. Andrews, Scotland

Dealing with royalty can be a matter of some delicacy, as Willie Auchterlonie, the professional at the Royal and Ancient Golf Club of St. Andrews, discovered one day when he stepped onto the first tee to watch the Prince of Wales tee off.

A sizeable gallery had gathered around the tee, which didn't make the Prince any less nervous. He fidgeted nervously over the ball, finally took a mighty swing, and missed the ball entirely. There was an awkward silence.

"Well now, that's a fine practice swing, sir," Auchterlonie said. "Now just hit it."

Tom Kite was a member of the 1971 Walker Cup team. On the flight to St. Andrews, the twenty-one-year-old Kite talked with his veteran teammate Bill Campbell about the Walker Cup in general and St. Andrews specifically.

"I asked him whether St. Andrews was hilly or flat," Kite recalls. "He said, 'Yes.'

"After I played it for the first time in a practice round, I realized just how perfect his answer was."

Apparently, St. Andrews agreed with Kite. He won both his singles matches and teamed with Campbell to get a half in the foursomes.

American visitors to Scotland are often taken aback by the locals' strict, even passionate, devotion to the rules of golf. For them, the notion of something like "winter rules" is totally anathema to the spirit of the game.

Take the case of the American who sent his first drive on Scottish soil sailing out of bounds. He promptly teed up another ball and hit it down the middle of the fairway.

"In America we call that a 'mulligan,' " the American said to his caddie. "What do you call it over here?"

"Lying three," the caddie said, lifting the bag to his shoulder and striding off the tee.

An American tourist arrived for a late-afternoon round of golf at St. Andrews, but as luck would have it, the only available caddie was a stooped, elderly man who had already worked one loop that day. The American was apprehensive and told the caddiemaster that he didn't think the old man was up to a second trip around the Old Course, particularly since the Yank wasn't a very good golfer. The caddiemaster assured him that the caddie had the endurance of a man half his age, so off they went.

Sure enough, the American struggled with the gusting winds and capricious bounces. He didn't come close to breaking 50 on the outward nine, and things didn't get any better after they made the turn. Finally, it got to be too much for the caddie, who simply reached into the gorse and retrieved yet another errant drive. He put the ball in the bag and started walking back to the clubhouse.

"I'm sorry," the golfer said. "I was afraid you wouldn't be able to make it all the way around."

"Oh, I'm fine, sir," the caddie said. "But you've had enough for one day."

A hacker from America came to St. Andrews and, far from being inspired by the birthplace of golf, proceeded to top, shank, and slice his way around the course, despite the best advice his caddie had to offer.

After teeing off on 18, the two men walked over the ancient stone bridge that crosses the Swilken Burn. The American looked down and then told his caddie: "If that water was deep enough I'd throw my clubs in, dive in after them, and drown myself."

"That wouldn't be possible, sir," the caddie replied. "You couldn't keep your head down long enough."

THE RULES

One of the things that makes golf so special is the respect, even reverence, that the players hold for the rules. Still, that's not to say that there aren't times when players get a little frustrated with rules officials. Take the case of Simon Hobday.

Hobday, an easygoing South African who won the 1994 U.S. Senior Open at Pinehurst, once had an interesting conversation with an official.

"If I called you an SOB, would you fine me?" he asked.

"Probably," the official replied.

"Well, if I was thinking that you're an SOB, would you fine me?" he asked.

"No," the official replied. "How could I?"

"Good," Hobday said, with irrefutable logic. "Then I'm thinking you're an SOB."

A rules official at the North and South Women's Amateur at Pinehurst faced a difficult, if not impossible, rules decision.

An elderly matriarch, well into her seventies, picked up on a hole. Since it was a stroke-play tournament, the rules called for her disqualification. But she was in the last flight, with no chance of winning, so the official offered to make a deal.

"If you won't tell anyone, I won't either," he said. "Just give yourself a double bogey."

"I won't do any such thing," she huffed. "I insist on being penalized."

The official explained that the proper penalty called for disqualification.

"That's absurd," she replied.

The official tried another tack. He offered to penalize her two strokes.

"Too much," she said. "I'll take one stroke, young man, and I have no intention of standing here quibbling with you any further."

One stroke it was.

Ever hear of Burt Whittmore? Probably not, but if it weren't for a brush with the rules, he might well have won the 1898 U.S. Open at the Myopia Hunt Club near Boston.

He was in contention in the final round when he came to the 12th hole, a brutally difficult par 4. The hole was cut in the back of the severely sloping green. Whittmore's ball was on the front of the green. He hit the ball firmly, then watched in horror as it slid off the green and down a bank into the deep rough.

Things got worse very soon after that.

He and his caddie searched for the ball. So did his fellow players and their caddies. The gallery helped out, but to no avail. Burt Whittmore became the first and no doubt only player ever to lose an Open by losing a ball on a putt. In fact, he may be the only player *ever* to lose a ball on a putt.

Hale Irwin ran into an interesting rules question during the 1973 Sea Pines Heritage Classic. He hit a drive, then watched in disgust as it bounded into the gallery. Imagine his surprise when he discovered that the ball had somehow managed to wind up in a woman's bra. What was the right ruling?

Was the ball out of bounds? Yes, in a manner of speaking.

Was her bra a temporary immovable obstruction? You could make a good case for it.

Or how about ground under repair?

Whatever the arcane machinations of the rules, common sense

eventually prevailed. The woman discreetly removed the ball and Irwin got a free drop.

Want to know when you're having a bad caddie day? Just ask Raymond Floyd. Playing in the 1987 Tournament Players Championship, Floyd nailed an enormous drive and then looked on in horror as it rolled into his golf bag—for a two-stroke penalty.

For almost as long as there have been golfers, there have been problems with slow play and calls for draconian actions to help prevent it. Of course, some solutions are more drastic—and more successful—than others.

In 1930 Cyril Walker, the 1924 U.S. Open champion, was warned about his slow play. When he didn't pick up the pace, tournament officials disqualified him and ordered him to leave the grounds. He refused. They insisted. He still refused to go, so they called in the police and had him arrested.

The rules of golf strictly limit what amateurs can accept in prizes, and they most definitely don't include cash. So consider the dilemma faced by one Jason Bohn.

Back in 1992, the nineteen-year-old Bohn was playing in a charity golf event near his home in Alabama. He was one of just twelve participants invited to take a shot at a hole in one. The rules were simple. Each player got to hit one ball on a 140-yard par 3. Everyone failed, except Jason Bohn, whose hole in one earned him $1,000,000.

The problem was, if Bohn took the money, he had to give up his amateur status.

Some problem.

In about one nanosecond, Jason Bohn turned pro and became one of 1992's leading money winners.

Bill Campbell, the great American amateur who would one day serve as captain of both the Royal and Ancient Golf Club of St. Andrews and the United States Golf Association, learned a valuable lesson about the rules when he played in the finals of the 1952 Canadian Amateur.

Campbell and his opponent had been giving each other short putts throughout the match. Playing the 34th hole of the thirty-six-hole final, Campbell stood 2-up. Both players faced three-footers—Campbell for a par and the championship, his opponent for a bogey. His opponent made his putt and walked off to the next tee. Campbell's putt hung on the lip, and he raked it back to try it again, thinking he had halved the hole.

When he reached the tee his opponent asked him if he had made the putt.

"No, you saw that I missed it," said Campbell.

"No, I meant the little one," said his opponent. "I didn't give it to you."

Instead of being 2-up with two to play, Campbell found himself just 1-up. When his opponent birdied the next hole, the match stood all even. The match wound up going into sudden death, and Campbell—one of the game's true sportsmen—lost on the 37th hole.

Tom Weiskopf, Lanny Wadkins, and Lee Trevino were paired together in the 1981 PGA Championship at the Atlanta Athletic Club.

Following their round, they were in the scorer's tent going over their cards when Weiskopf questioned his card, which Trevino had kept. This is where things get complicated. Wadkins finished checking Trevino's card and passed it to Trevino to sign. Trevino signed Weiskopf's card and passed it to Weiskopf, who signed it. Wadkins signed his card, which Trevino had previously signed, and then—are you still following this?—Weiskopf signed Trevino's card where Trevino was supposed to sign his name. In a hurry to leave, Trevino looked at his card, saw the two signatures, and turned his card in. A short while later the mistake was realized and Trevino was disqualified.

In 1998, on the eve of the U.S. Open, the United States Golf Association hinted that it was planning to take action against the ball and club technology that had been developing so rapidly in recent years. Naturally, this created enormous outrage on the part of equipment manufacturers. It also led Rabbi Marc Gellman to muse what life might be like if the USGA had the ability to make rulings on nongolf matters.

Rabbi Gellman, along with his friend Monsignor Tom Hartman, was giving the invocation at the annual Metropolitan Golf Writers dinner in suburban New York. It was a receptive audience for the rabbi's thoughts.

"The USGA doesn't want golf to become too easy, so they want to change the rules," the rabbi said. "If they had their way, the Catholics would have to make hosts smaller because large hosts might make repentance too easy; Muslims would have their prayer beads checked for grooves that made them too easy to pray with; and Jews would have to reduce the size of dreidels [a child's four-sided, toplike toy] because the big ones are too easy to spin. I think the best thing they could do if they really wanted to make golf a better game is to ban lime-green pants. Now, that would be an improvement."

Until the early 1970s, simply saying you were thinking of turning pro was enough to cost you your amateur status. There's a story about the young man who wrote the United States Golf Association:

"Dear Sirs—I think I'd like to become a professional. How do I do it?"

"Dear Sir—You just did" was the USGA's reply.

One year Ken Venturi was playing in the San Francisco City Golf Championship, a match-play tournament that drew enormous crowds and the best players in California.

In one of his matches he hit his approach putt an inch from the hole and, assuming his opponent would give him the next putt, raked the ball away.

"Ken, I didn't give you that putt," said his opponent. "Since we're playing strictly by the rules of golf, I'm afraid you lost the hole."

"If that's so, it means I'm 3 down with five to play," said Venturi. "Are you sure you want to win like that?"

"Well, Ken, we are playing strictly by the rules," the man said.

"You're sure you want to win like that?" Venturi said.

"The rules are the rules, Ken."

"Okay, you've got fifteen clubs in your bag," said Venturi, heading for the clubhouse. "I win."

BABE RUTH

Babe Ruth and Ty Cobb were fierce rivals on the ballfield and, as it happens, skilled golfers. The Babe was about a six-handicap who could blast drives with the same power that made him a legendary home-run hitter. Cobb, a nine-handicapper, lacked Ruth's power, and while he could shoot some good scores, his volcanic temper made him woefully inconsistent.

Still, they were passionate golfers and, even after they left baseball, remained two of the biggest names in all of sports. Of course, none of this was lost on Fred Corcoran, the most skillful golf promoter of his time—or any other time, for that matter. Over the course of his career, Corcoran was involved with the PGA of America and the LPGA, got the World Cup off the ground, and was an agent for Sam Snead, Babe Zaharias, and Ted Williams.

In 1941, Corcoran convinced Ruth to challenge Cobb to a fifty-four-hole charity golf match for the "Ruth Cup." Cobb, who at fifty-four was six years older than Ruth, declined. Corcoran, not to be deterred, sent Cobb a telegram under Ruth's name and, for good measure, leaked it to some friendly writers.

"If you want to come out here and get your brains knocked out, come ahead. Signed, Babe Ruth."

Cobb, whose competitive fires hadn't been banked with the passing of time, had no choice but to accept. The game was on.

The first eighteen were played before a huge gallery at the Commonwealth Country Club in West Newton, just outside Boston. Cobb was on his game and won, 3 and 2. After the match, he couldn't resist giving his old rival a jab, for the benefit of the local papers.

"The fat man is getting fatter," he said. "He looks out of balance, like an egg resting on two toothpicks."

Not for nothing was Ty Cobb the most despised man in baseball.

Ruth came back to win the second match, played at Fresh Meadow Country Club in Flushing, New York, setting up the third and final eighteen at Grosse Ile Country Club in Detroit. Cobb wasn't going to take any chances.

He hired Walter Hagen as his coach.

He hired the club's assistant pro as his caddie.

And on the boat trip across Lake Erie, he made sure Ruth's glass was always filled with scotch.

The next day dawned hot and humid. Ruth, nursing a horrific hangover, was nauseous on the first tee and didn't feel any better by the time they made the turn—in part because he was five strokes back and in part because Cobb blew smoke from a particularly odious cigar in his direction every chance he got.

On the back nine, Cobb offered Ruth a bet to help him save face.

"How much?" Ruth asked.

"How about $50,000?" Cobb said. "You name it."

Wisely, Ruth settled for less—a lot less—and Cobb closed him out 3 and 2.

Babe Ruth was obviously an exceptional athlete, and his hand-eye coordination carried over to golf once he more or less got serious about the game.

One day back in the early 1930s, he and Dizzy Dean decided to have a little competition. Dean wasn't much of a golfer at that point, so The Babe agreed to give him five shots a side.

When Dizzy got to the first tee, Ruth made a gentlemanly offer. He asked Dizzy's wife to join them.

Everything went fine for the first couple of holes, but as soon as Dizzy began launching balls out into the trees, his wife felt it was her duty to help out with a suggestion.

"You're ducking," she said.

"What d'ya mean, I'm ducking?" he asked.

"Just what I said, you're ducking," she replied.

"Who invited you along anyway?" he asked, storming down the fairway.

The Babe traveled to Bermuda on vacation. As anyone would, he jumped at the chance to play at the Mid-Ocean Club, C. B. Mac-Donald's wonderful design. When he came to the elevated tee on the 370-yard 5th hole, he asked his caddie for the driver. The caddie knew better and advised Ruth to lay up and take the lake out of play.

"Give me the driver," said The Babe. "I could throw it on the green from here."

Fifteen balls in the water later, Ruth snapped the driver over his knee and walked in.

"I used to play with Babe Ruth in exhibitions," remembers Gene Sarazen. "Oh, he could hit that ball a mile, but he played Catholic golf—a cross here and a cross there."

THE RYDER CUP

In 1967, Ben Hogan, the captain of the American team, caused a stir at the pretournament dinner when he introduced his charges by simply saying: "Ladies and gentlemen, I'd like to introduce the twelve best players in the world, the United States Ryder Cup team."

With that, Hogan sat down and the Americans went on to prove that, if not exactly tactful, Hogan was nevertheless right on the mark. His team won, 23½-8½.

Twenty-two years later, at the Belfry in Sutton-Coldfield, England, the American captain, Raymond Floyd, stood up at the pretournament dinner and repeated Hogan's introduction. This took considerably more nerve than it did when Hogan said it, given the fact that the Americans had lost the previous two matches.

Miffed, European captain Tony Jacklin turned to a friend and said, "What am I supposed to say, 'I'd like to introduce the thirteenth-best player in the world, Seve Ballesteros?'"

363

In the 1931 Ryder Cup matches at Scioto Country Club, in Columbus, Ohio, Gene Sarazen faced Fred Robson in a final-day singles match. On a short par 3, Robson's shot came to rest twenty-five feet from the hole. Sarazen's tee shot flew over the green and into a nearby refreshment stand, coming to rest in a crack in the cement floor. Robson, who was struggling against Sarazen, surely thought this break would mark a change in his fortunes. At best, Sarazen would make a bogey. He might even be forced to concede the hole.

As Robson waited on the green, Sarazen studied the situation. At the last minute, he and his caddie moved a refrigerator out of the way. He lined up his shot, hit down sharply on the ball, and watched as it rocketed through a tiny window, landed on the green, and rolled to a stop ten feet from the hole.

It was more than Robson could stand. Shaken, he three-putted for a bogey and lost the hole to Sarazen's par. The match ended, not surprisingly, with a 7 and 6 Sarazen win.

In 1971, the Ryder Cup matches were held at Old Warson in St. Louis. One of the most imaginative pairings was that uniting Ireland's Christy O'Connor with England's Neil Coles. They were teamed in the lead foursomes match against Billy Casper and Miller Barber.

Foursomes, or alternate shot, requires a higher degree of strategy than four-ball or individual play. Of vital importance is deciding which player will drive on the even-numbered holes and which will drive on the odd-numbered holes. For example, if three of the par 3s are even-numbered holes, you'd want the stronger iron player to drive on those holes.

Knowing that if he and O'Connor could lead off with a win it would inspire their teammates, Coles was anxious to learn which holes he would be driving on. This would help him prepare mentally for the round. At dinner that night he asked O'Connor—known far and wide as simply "Himself"—what the order would be.

"It's no matter, really," said O'Connor. "We'll think about it on the overnight."

The next morning at breakfast, Coles asked again.

"Well, I have been thinking about it," said Himself.

"And . . . ," said Coles.

"And I'm still thinking," Himself said. "You're right, though. It is a vitally important question."

By the time they finally reached the first tee, O'Connor had very nearly exhausted himself with his thinking. Suddenly, the answer came to him.

"I know, Neil," he said. "We'll flip for it."

So they did, and went on to beat the Americans, 2 and 1.

The 1973 Ryder Cup matches were played at Muirfield in Scotland, where, a year earlier, Lee Trevino had won his second British Open championship. Naturally, this gave Trevino—then at the height of his game—considerable confidence in his Sunday-morning singles match against young Peter Oosterhuis.

"If I can't beat Peter Oosterhuis, I'll kiss the American team's asses," said Trevino.

Well, Oosterhuis proved surprisingly tough and the match ended in a tie. Somewhere, it is rumored, there is a picture of the American team standing in a line, facing away from the camera, with their pants dropped to their ankles, waiting for Trevino to make good on his promise.

GENE SARAZEN

In 1982, *Golf Digest* asked Dave Anderson, the Pulitzer prize–winning *New York Times* sports columnist, to collaborate with Gene Sarazen on a listing of the ten greatest male and female golfers of the century. Since Sarazen, then age eighty, had either played with or seen every great player of that span, he was the perfect choice.

Sarazen labored over the list, adding and deleting names, and moving people up and down in his rankings. Finally, worrying to the end, he came up with his lists. He ranked Jack Nicklaus first, followed by Bobby Jones, Ben Hogan, Walter Hagen, Harry Vardon, Gary Player, Sam Snead, Arnold Palmer, Lee Trevino, and in a tie for tenth, Byron Nelson and Tom Watson.

When it came to the women, Joyce Wethered was first, followed by Glenna Collett Vare, Mickey Wright, Kathy Whitworth, Betsy Rawls, Louise Suggs, Babe Didrikson Zaharias, JoAnne Carner, Donna Caponi, and Patty Berg.

When Anderson studied the lists, he noticed one glaring omission from the men's list—Sarazen himself. Why, he asked, did the first man to win all four of the modern professional major championships—the U.S. and British Opens, the Masters, and the PGA Championship—leave himself out of the rankings? Was it false modesty?

Hardly.

"My wife, Mary, told me I couldn't list myself," Sarazen said.

Later, however, Sarazen told Anderson that if he had ranked himself, he would have been "somewhere around eighth, ninth, or tenth."

One of the benefits of age is that it gives you a certain perspective on things. Take winning, for example. At the 1996 Masters, a writer asked ninety-four-year-old Gene Sarazen what he thought about two-time U.S. Amateur champion Tiger Woods.

"He's a good player," said Sarazen. "Of course, when I was his age [twenty] I won the U.S. Open and the PGA Championship."

Sarazen started as a caddie in Westchester County, just outside New York City. While at the Apawamis Club, one of his fellow caddies was Ed Sullivan. As he began to make a name for himself in local tournaments, Sarazen moved to nearby Westchester Country Club and went to work in the pro shop as an assistant.

One of his duties was to handcraft sets of clubs. Sarazen, the son of a carpenter, loved working on clubs. Upon completing his first set, he proudly presented them to the pro for his approval. The pro snapped every one of them in half and threw them on the floor.

Sarazen is a very proud and tough man and was a fierce competitor in his day. The tougher the conditions or the greater the challenge, the better he seemed to play.

When he entered the game, it was largely dominated by those of Scottish or English background. There was a great deal of prejudice against Italian-Americans like Sarazen. Sarazen took that discrimination and made it work to his benefit.

"Francis Ouimet and I were friends from the first, and when I arrived at Skokie for the 1922 U.S. Open, Francis asked me to join him, Chick Evans, and Jim Barnes, the defending champion, for a practice round. Barnes put up a big fuss and said he didn't want to play with me," said Sarazen.

"Well, after I won the Open there was a winner-take-all exhibition match arranged between me and Barnes. The night before we were supposed to play, Barnes asked me if I wanted to split the purse, which wasn't unusual in those days. I didn't want any part of it. I wanted to show him, and I did. I beat him, 6 and 5.

It might not be fair to say that Sarazen was cocky, but it would certainly be accurate to say that he never lacked for confidence. Following his first U.S. Open win, in 1922 at Skokie Country Club, he told the writers: "All men are created free and equal—and I am one shot better than the rest."

Gene Sarazen met British great Harry Vardon at the 1920 U.S. Open at Inverness, but only in passing. Vardon was one of the game's greatest players, and this was Sarazen's first major championship.

They were paired together at Sarazen's first British Open. Vardon hit first. When it was Sarazen's turn, he took the wind into account, but it never moved the smaller British ball.

"Will you look at that, the wind never touched that ball," Sarazen said to Vardon.

"No," Vardon said, "and the way you strike the ball, the wind won't affect it a bit."

Sarazen and 1928 U.S. Open champion Johnny Farrell traveled through Europe on an exhibition tour. They traveled to Rome, the birthplace of Sarazen's parents, and at the request of the United

States ambassador, they paid a call on Benito Mussolini, the country's dictator.

"When we arrived, I noticed a red carpet," Sarazen said. "I said to Johnny, 'See, they don't mind that I changed my name [from Saraceni]. They rolled out the red carpet for us.'"

The words were barely out of his mouth when workers began removing the carpet.

"We got there just after the Pope had left," Sarazen recalled, laughing.

When Gene Sarazen made his dramatic double eagle on the 15th hole in the final round of the 1935 Masters, many people believed he all but single-handedly put the tournament on the map. Certainly, it gave the Masters an enormous publicity boost, and even today it remains one of the game's most historic shots.

The magnitude of the shot wasn't lost on Sarazen, who went on to win the tournament the following day in a thirty-six-hole playoff with Craig Wood. In fact, he suspected that his friends Bob Jones and Clifford Roberts might be planning to do a little something to commemorate the event. He thought a plaque embedded in the fairway where he played the shot from would be perfect. He asked his caddie, Stovepipe, if he'd heard any rumors.

"Well, Mr. Gene, I sure did see some fellas go down there this morning," he said, pausing for effect. "They filled that divot in just as neat as can be."

Gene Sarazen, then seventy-one, traveled to Troon for the 1973 British Open.

Playing the par-3 8th hole—the "Postage Stamp"—Sarazen made the sixth ace of his career.

"I'm glad they got this one on film," he said. "When I die I'm going to bring it with me and show it to Hagen, Armour, Jones, Ouimet, and the boys."

Gene Sarazen's game was simple and solid and held up for a remarkably long time.

One day, when he was in his early seventies, he and his longtime friend Ken Venturi agreed to take on two Tour pros who were visiting Marco Island to work on their games under Venturi's watchful eye.

Venturi, then in his mid-forties, was no longer playing much competitive golf, but he and Sarazen proved to be a formidable pair. They won handily and then retired to the clubhouse for lunch. When it came time for them to leave, Sarazen thanked his opponents for the game and offered them a chance to get their money back.

"Good luck fellas," Sarazen said. "Come back again when you can play a little better."

Sarazen's career paralleled the growth of golf around the world. He was an ambassador, traveling to the four corners of the Earth to play exhibitions and tournaments. It was a profitable learning experience for Sarazen.

"My first visit to Japan was unlike anything I'd ever experienced before," Sarazen recalled. "I was playing a match and I hit my ball into a bunker. I played it out, and after I walked out of the trap, I looked back and there were people in there measuring where my feet had been placed. I felt like a science project."

When Gene Sarazen became one of the hosts of "Shell's Wonderful World of Golf" in the 1960s and early '70s, he was introduced to a whole generation of people who had never seen him play. One of the most poignant moments in the long history of the series came when Sarazen sat down for a visit with Bob Jones. Jones was virtually crippled by this time, and it was a testimony to the two men's deep friendship that Jones agreed to the interview.

In the course of the interview, they marveled at the similarities in their lives.

They were born seven weeks apart. They were married—to women named Mary—one week apart. They both played in their first U.S. Open in 1920.

There was a pause in the conversation, then Jones looked at Sarazen and said: "We didn't do too bad, did we?"

SCOTLAND, THE BRAVE

Golf historians can debate the origins of the game, but the Scots insist that it was born on the linksland of St. Andrews, was nurtured by the Scots themselves, and grew to take on the character of these proud people.

That's their story, they're sticking to it, and God help anyone who wants to argue the point. After all, the Dutch can point to a few old prints of guys in black frock coats and funny hats hitting balls along frozen rivers. The Scots can point to a line of British Open champions dating back to the mid-1800s.

When golf began to take hold in America in the late 1800s, it only made sense that the early club professionals would be Scots. One of the most prominent was Willie Campbell, a native of Musselburgh, a town hard by the coast near Edinburgh.

Campbell went to work at The Country Club in Brookline, Massachusetts, in 1894 for the princely sum of $300 a year. Campbell would work at TCC in the spring and fall and would work at the Essex Country Club on Massachusetts' north shore, where many members of The Country Club spent their summers.

One day a Boston writer, anxious to learn the finer points of the game, asked Campbell whether American golfers resorted to Scottish or American profanities on the course.

"Golfers are gentlemen," Campbell said. "They dinna' swear or invoke the name of the Lord in vain."

"Not even when they find themselves in a bunker?" the writer asked.

"Ah, well, in a bunker even a gentleman is human," Campbell said. "And a man wouldn't be human if he didn't swear in a bunker."

"Shell's Wonderful World of Golf"

The old "Shell's Wonderful World of Golf" series took the game's best players to some of the most exotic locales around the globe—sometimes with unexpected complications. "One year we went to Guatemala for a match between Gardner Dickinson and Mason Rudolph," remembers Fred Raphael, the executive producer for the series. "After we checked into the hotel, Jimmy Demaret, who was one of our announcers, poured himself a drink and was looking out his hotel room window at the scenery. All of a sudden there was a roar and a nearby volcano erupted. Jimmy called my room and said, 'Fred, either they have the best damn whiskey in the world here in Guatemala, or I just watched the top come off one of their mountains.'"

When Fred Raphael was starting out with the Shell series, he was the first to admit he didn't know much about golf. But he did have plenty of contacts in New York, and one of them was a director named Lee Goodman, who not only had excellent credentials but also knew a little bit about the game.

One afternoon Raphael and Goodman met Herbert Warren Wind, the celebrated writer who was collaborating on the series, for lunch. In the course of the meeting, Goodman was explaining camera angles and locations to Wind, who listened intently. Goodman was using a shoot he had done with Sam Snead as an example.

After several minutes, Wind asked Goodman where the Snead match had been played.

"Match?" Goodman said. "What match? It was an Alka-Seltzer commercial."

The "Shell's Wonderful World of Golf" series was the brainchild of Monroe Spaght, the president of Shell in the United States. An avid golfer, he was enthralled by the idea of a television show that would highlight golf around the world (and, coincidentally, Shell's worldwide presence).

Since the show was his baby, so to speak, he took a paternal interest in its development—sometimes obsessively so.

"Mr. Spaght was very protective of the show, particularly in our first year," recalls Fred Raphael. "He reviewed every show before it aired. In one case, Herb Wind and I met Mr. Spaght and some executives from [Shell's advertising agency] Kenyon and Eckhart for lunch. Mr. Spaght said he was very pleased with the show we had sent him, but there was just one problem: he said there was a split infinitive in the voiceover and he wanted it removed because he didn't want to 'get letters from eighth-grade teachers across the country.' "

Fine.

Raphael, Wind, and—naturally—the ad guys would have been delighted to remove the offending split infinitive. The problem was, Mr. Spaght didn't tell them just where it was in the show. Finding it proved to be more difficult than anyone could have imagined, and to make matters worse, they were working on a very tight deadline since the film had to be sent to the network.

Herb Wind screened the film twice, to no avail. It should be noted here that Herb Wind is a Yale graduate who enjoyed many successful years at both *Sports Illustrated* and *The New Yorker*. In other words, Herb Wind would know all about split infinitives.

Desperate, Raphael called in an English professor from Columbia and paid him $75 to screen the film. The professor also came up empty, although he did write a note on Columbia letterhead staking his reputation on the fact that there wasn't a split infinitive to be found anywhere.

With time running perilously short, Raphael urged the account executives to call Mr. Spaght with the news that, with all due respect, perhaps he was mistaken.

Now, Mr. Monroe Spaght didn't get to be Mr. Monroe Spaght by listening to account executives tell him he was, well, hearing things.

"They called me back and said, 'If he says it's in there, it's in there, so find it,'" Raphael recalls.

Working on the theory that desperate times call for desperate measures, Raphael called Mr. Spaght's office, only to learn that he was in London for the week.

"I figured that since Mr. Spaght wouldn't see the film and the Kenyon and Eckhart guys wouldn't know a split infinitive if it bit them on the nose, I told the production guys to cut the commercials back in and ship the film," Raphael remembers. "While they were editing the commercials into the film, a kid who was cleaning the editing room said, 'There it is.'

"'Where?' I asked.

"'In the commercial,' the kid said."

"We were filming a show in France one year and had to use a crew that didn't speak much, if any, English," recalls Fred Raphael. "I knew we were in trouble when I asked one of the cameramen if he was able to follow the flight of the ball.

"'Oui, Monsieur Fred,' he said with this huge smile on his face.

"On the next hole I asked him if he'd missed the ball, and he smiled just as widely and said, 'Oui, Monsieur Fred.'"

The trucks carrying the cameras on the Shell series were heavily camouflaged with leaves and branches so they wouldn't be obvious to the viewers. As a general rule, this worked fine, except for a few memorable occasions.

During the filming of one match in Ireland, a couple of women in the gallery felt the need to answer nature's call and relieve themselves. Since they were a considerable distance from the clubhouse, they decided to take advantage of the large, nearby stand of foliage.

This was all well and good until the truck drove off down the fairway, leaving the women exposed to nature and the rest of the gallery.

"One year we had Doc Middlecoff in one of our matches," recalls Fred Raphael, the producer of "Shell's Wonderful World of Golf." "Doc was a very deliberate player. He'd fidget and waggle, move around, change clubs, and start all over again until he felt comfortable and ready to play his shot. This meant that we had to do a lot of cutting to get the show to fit. When he saw the film of his match he was sure he'd learned the reason he played poorly.

" 'Did you see that, Fred?' asked Doc. 'My pre-shot routine was way too fast. I was out of my rhythm.' "

SHINNECOCK HILLS
GOLF CLUB

Shinnecock, located on the eastern end of New York's Long Island, was one of the founding clubs of the U.S. Golf Association. It hosted the second U.S. Open in 1896; in 1986, it hosted the Open for just the second time. That year, Raymond Floyd shot an inspired final round to edge Lanny Wadkins and Chip Beck. The Open returned in 1996, to the delight of players and purists who regard the course as one of the world's finest tests.

How good is Shinnecock?

"I knew as soon as I played my first practice round that I could win the Open at Shinnecock," said Raymond Floyd. "It's a pure golf course. There's nothing that anyone can do to trick it up. It's perfect as it is."

That Shinnecock membership has traditionally been drawn from the swellest of New York's society swells never had much of an impact on its longtime professional, Charles Thom, an immigrant from Scotland. Thom served as pro from 1905 to 1966 and stayed around as pro emeritus until his death at age ninety-eight.

He once dismissed a particularly influential member as a man who "couldn't find his ass with both hands if you gave him a one-hand head start."

On another occasion, Thom watched a foursome flail their way through the tall grass that separates the 9th and 18th holes. After a few minutes, he couldn't take it any longer.

"I don't know where you think you're going," he shouted down the hill from the clubhouse, "but you sure as hell need a new map."

But Thom is best remembered for his frustration as he tried to teach a wealthy Wall Street speculator how to play. The man proved to be every bit as inept as he was enthusiastic. He was willing to pay Thom any amount of money for lessons if only he could become respectable on the golf course. It didn't take Thom long to realize that there might not be enough money in the world to get the job done.

One day, Thom blurted out in exasperation: "You'll make this a lot easier on both of us if you'll just keep your mind on the ball instead of your damned money."

Shinnecock's rambling clubhouse was designed by the famous New York architect Sanford White. White is almost as well known for his death as for the exquisite quality of his work.

White, a fixture of New York society, was having dinner with a Broadway showgirl, Evelyn N. Thaw, when her husband walked in, pulled a revolver, and fired three rounds into White, killing him.

The killer, a millionaire named Harry K. Thaw, was sentenced to seven years in an "asylum for the criminally insane." The hardship of the sentence was lessened by the fact that his time was spent in his own lavishly decorated suite of rooms.

Upon his release, Thaw traveled to Florida for the winter. There, he was exposed to the work of an architect whose Spanish-inspired motifs were particularly garish and jarring.

On his first day in Florida, Thaw is reported to have looked around in shock and revulsion and exclaimed, "My God, I killed the wrong architect."

Show Business

Anyone who has ever watched one of W. C. Fields's movies knows what remarkable hand-eye coordination he had. He was a skilled juggler and masterful around a pool table. He was also a good golfer, and he appeared in one of the instruction films Bobby Jones made after his competitive career ended. True to form, though, Fields never let golf get in the way of his drinking.

"I always carry a bottle in my bag in case of an emergency," he once told a writer. "Fortunately, I also carry a snake in my bag in case I need to invent an emergency."

Over the years the Los Angeles Country Club has tried to avoid publicity in the most publicity-mad city in America. Its North Course is known as "the best course that's never hosted an Open" because the membership didn't want all the attention.

Perhaps it's not surprising, then, that the club has long avoided having members from the world of show business. Witness the case of Randolph Scott.

After his acting days were over, Scott became a successful businessman in Los Angeles and several of his friends sponsored him for membership at the LACC. As part of the admissions process, he was required to meet several board members, one of whom thought he looked very familiar.

"You're not an actor, are you, Mr. Scott?" the man asked.

"No," quipped Scott, "and I've got the films to prove it."

In 1952, Katharine Hepburn and Spencer Tracy filmed the classic movie *Pat and Mike*. The golf scenes were shot at Riviera Country Club in Los Angeles.

Hepburn, as it happened, was quite a good golfer in her own right. Early in the shooting, the scene called for her to hit a twenty-foot putt. She studied the line, set up over the ball, and drilled it into the heart of the cup on the first take. Naturally, she was thrilled.

"No, no, no," cried the director, George Cukor. "You're supposed to miss it. Do it again. And don't try so hard this time."

Actor Victor Mature was surprised and more than a little amused when he learned that a Los Angeles newspaper had reported that he had been quietly buried in a private funeral service the previous day.

"If that's true," he told a writer for another paper, "then I'm the only guy who ever made six double bogeys on the back nine on the day of his funeral."

383

Phil Harris won the first Crosby he played in. It was 1951 and he was teamed with Dutch Harrison—a pairing of kindred spirits if there ever was one.

They came to the 17th hole on the last day, and Harris knocked in a huge putt of some eighty feet. The gallery went wild.

"You take it from here, Dutch," said Harris. "I'm heading for the bar."

He left, and Harrison made a routine par on 18 for the win.

CHARLIE SIFFORD

One of the great benefits to the stunning success of Tiger Woods is the reflected light that shines on minority golfers who went before him—players like Ted Rhodes, Bill Spiller, Lee Elder, and Charlie Sifford.

While many talented black golfers never had a chance to play the Tour, Sifford did and carried himself with distinction. Like Elder, his struggle was heightened because he played at a time when the civil rights movement was shaping—and shaking—America, to the considerable resentment of many. The racism was occasionally subtle; but more often than not, people didn't bother with the subtleties.

In 1965, Sifford entered a tournament at the Pensacola (Florida) Country Club. Prior to the first round, he walked into the clubhouse dining room and ordered breakfast. He was just about to begin eating his meal when a man approached.

"Excuse me, Charlie, but you can't eat here," he explained, nervously. "This is a private dining room. Please don't give us any trouble."

Charlie Sifford was mortified. But rather than cause a scene, he quietly took his breakfast and went to the locker room to eat. A few minutes later he was joined by Bob Rosburg, Ken Venturi, and Frank Stranahan, who ate with him—sending a powerful signal to the members and tournament officials alike.

Charlie Sifford, who helped integrate the PGA Tour and won the 1967 Hartford Open and 1969 Los Angeles Open, knew what he was getting into when he turned pro in 1948.

"In 1947, I talked to Jackie Robinson about my plans to try and play on the Tour," recalled Sifford, who also won twice on the Senior PGA Tour. "He looked me right in the eye and asked me if I was a quitter. I told him I wasn't.

"'Good,' he said. 'If you're a quitter, quit now, because you'll never make it.'"

J. C. SNEAD

For most of his career Jesse Carlyle Snead went by his initials, but for a brief stretch he let it be known that he'd prefer to be called "Jesse." That was fine, until he suddenly announced that he was going back to "J.C."

"How come?" a writer asked.

"Because Jesse isn't playing worth a damn," he answered.

J. C. Snead is best known as Sam's nephew, but he's an accomplished golfer in his own right. His sport of choice was baseball, at which he was good enough to land on a farm team of the old Washington Senators before turning pro and joining the Tour. He won

eight times on tour, but his best chance to win the prestigious Players Championship was literally blown away one year.

"I was paired with J.C. when the tournament was played on the original Sawgrass course," remembers Tom Watson. "The wind was unbelievable. Signs were being blown down. We came to 17 and J.C. was in contention. The hole was playing straight downwind, which made it almost impossible to hold the ball on the green. You weren't even thinking about getting it close to the hole, which was cut on the top level of the three-tiered green.

"Well, J.C. hit the most beautiful little shot in there that you've ever seen. We were all watching the ball get close to the hole when the wind gusted and knocked J.C.'s hat off. The hat started rolling and flip-flopping down the fairway. Pretty soon it was getting near the green. It was like watching an accident in slow motion. You knew what was going to happen next, but you couldn't believe it. The hat reached the green, rolled up all three levels, and hit J.C.'s ball. He had to take a penalty stroke because the hat counted as part of his equipment. It's still the most unlucky thing I've ever seen on a golf course."

Waiting to tee off one day in a pro-am, J. C. Snead was taking some practice swings, trying to get the feel for a new move he was going to try out on the course. When the starter announced his name he walked over, teed up his ball, and got into position to hit it. Then he stepped away from the ball.

"What's the matter, J.C.?" one of his pro-am partners asked.

"I forgot what I was going to try," he laughed.

SAM SNEAD

Sam Snead grew up in the small town of Hot Springs, Virginia, in the shadow of the famous Homestead Hotel. One day when he was seven, Sam wandered away from home and found himself at The Homestead, where a woman asked him if he'd like to caddie for her. He wasn't quite sure what being a caddie entailed, but when he learned he could earn a little money, he was all for it.

Off he went with the woman, and when they finished she took his hat and filled it with pennies and nickels.

"I looked real hard for a dime, but there wasn't one," Sam said.

With a new job and a hat full of money, Sam set off for home, a two-mile walk. When he got there he could hardly contain himself.

"Look, Mom," he said, proudly holding his hat out for her to see his riches. "I earned all this money caddying, and it's all for you."

What was her reaction?

"She was real pleased to see that money," Sam recalls. "But that didn't stop her from taking that switch out and giving me a good licking for wandering off and scaring her half to death."

When he was a boy, Sam fashioned his first club from the limb of a swamp maple. Later he attached an old clubhead to a buggy whip and found he could hit the ball huge distances—too far on at least one occasion.

"I used to skip Sunday school because I hated sitting in one place for all that time," he remembers. "One day, during church, I was out hitting rocks with my club and I hit one right through the church window. I ran up into the hills and hid there all day, scared to death. Folks had an idea it was me but they never did prove it."

Years later he made amends by buying a new organ for the congregation.

The legendary tale of Sam's carving his first club from the limb of a swamp maple had its veracity challenged many years later by a guest at The Greenbrier.

Sam remembers, "I bet him that I could go out that day and carve me a club out of a tree limb and break 80 with just it and a putter. Well, he couldn't get that bet down fast enough. It was the easiest money I ever made."

"My uncle Ed was probably my favorite relative growing up," Sam recalls. "We did everything together. We'd pitch horseshoes, go hunting and fishing, play a little golf. We'd spend all day together. He'd get so mad at me when I beat him. He'd chase after me, and if he caught me he'd rub his knuckles across the top of my head. I think that's why I went bald so soon. One day Unk and I went fishing. He'd staked out a real good spot and was just hauling those fish in. I couldn't catch cold. So I found an old log, climbed on it, and floated out where I could get my line at his spot. He was as mad as a wet hen. I think he chased me all the way home.

"Unk and I used to play up at the Goat course, which ran straight up the mountain. They finally made it into a ski slope. He hit it off into the woods and was slashing around all over the place. When he finished I asked him what he had made. He said, 'five,' which was the highest score he could get because it was as high as he could count. I told him I counted six because of the whiffs."

With the passage of time it's easy to forget what an awesome player Sam was in his prime, or even in his early days on tour. The long-sleeved shirts he wore in the 1930s would routinely shred at the shoulder seams from the sheer force of his swing.

In the 1936 Hershey Open, Gene Sarazen watched Sam hit one 300-yard drive after another. After his round, the writers asked Sarazen what he thought.

"I've just seen a kid who doesn't know the first thing about golf," Sarazen said. "And I don't want to be playing when he learns."

Sam didn't know it at the time, but he played a pivotal role in Harvey Penick's decision to abandon full-time tournament play and focus on teaching.

"I was playing in the Houston Open one year and the players were all talking about this fellow from the Virginia mountains," Penick said one day. "They said they'd never seen anyone hit the ball quite like him. I went over to take a look. They were right. Not only had I never seen a ball hit like that, I'd never heard a shot sound like it did when Sam hit it. It came off the clubface with a crack, like a rifle shot. At that moment, I decided that the life of a teaching professional looked pretty good to me."

Sam joined the Tour in 1937 and almost won the first U.S. Open he played in—that year's Open at Oakland Hills.

After finishing the final round he went to the clubhouse, where he ran into Tommy Armour.

"Congratulations, laddie," said Armour. "You've won your Open."

The writers surrounded Snead, forgetting that Ralph Guldahl was still on the course with a chance of catching the young Virginian.

"I don't know, fellas," said Sam. "Goldie's out there, and all he needs is a couple of birdies to win. I don't want to jinx myself."

Jinx or not, Guldahl did what he had to do, making two birdies on the last six holes to win.

"After Goldie made that putt you could have fired a shotgun off in the locker room and not hit anyone but me," said Sam. "That's how fast the newspaper boys cleared out of there."

Early in his career Sam was paired with the Scotsman Willie Mac-Farlane, the man who beat Bobby Jones in a playoff to win the 1925 U.S. Open championship. Sam was just making a name for himself on tour at the time, and when MacFarlane noticed he was paying careful attention to MacFarlane's club selection, he decided to teach the youngster a lesson.

They came to a par 3, and MacFarlane took his time selecting a club, making sure that Sam saw exactly which club he pulled. When the time came to play the shot, he "dead-handed" it—that is, took something off his shot. The ball came to rest just under the hole for a birdie putt.

Sam pulled the same club for his drive, knocking the ball over the green.

"My boy," said MacFarlane as they walked to the green. "Never go to school on another man's club, or ye'll never make a penny in this game."

While his golf swing was largely self-taught, Sam's brothers were fine players, and Sam respected their opinions.

"They knew my swing like the backs of their hands," Sam remembers. "One year I showed up at Augusta and I was hitting the ball all over the lot. I was just disgusted. I couldn't figure out what I was doing wrong, so I hopped in my car and drove home to Hot Springs. I rounded up Homer, Jess, and Pete, and we went over to The Homestead course. I hit one ball and they told me I was getting the club laid off at the top. They got me fixed up in just one swing, and I got back in my car and drove back to Augusta. The next day Bob Jones was watching me warm up, and he was amazed at the difference. He asked me who had helped me, and I told him. He just shook his head and asked where he could find my brothers."

Even with Sam's truly incredible record, it's sometimes difficult to put in perspective just how awesome a player he was in his prime. Here's a good indication.

Sam entered the navy in 1942 and for much of the war was stationed in San Diego. While he had to play a lot of golf with officers, he managed to keep his game in shape by regularly playing against two fellow sailors. One was a scratch golfer and the other was a plus-2, which put him on a par with some of the Tour's better players. Sam used to play their best ball. He seldom lost.

In 1946, at the urging of his sponsors, Wilson Sporting Goods, Sam traveled to St. Andrews for the first British Open played following the war.

Postwar Scotland and Sam were not an ideal pairing. The weather was cold and damp. The Old Course was unlike anything he'd ever seen before. The Scottish burr was alien to Sam, who grew up in Virginia's mountains. The food was barely tolerable and, as a final insult, his prize for winning the oldest championship in the game came to a mere $600 in American money. The trip to Scotland had cost him almost $2,000.

After the awards ceremony, a British writer asked Sam if he'd be back to defend his title the following year at Hoylake.

"Are you kidding?" Sam said in disbelief.

So Sam traveled to St. Andrews for the 1946 British Open. As the train pulled into St. Andrews station, he looked out his window across the Old Course, the most venerated course in the game.

"Look yonder at that farm there," he said to his traveling companion, Lawson Little, pointing to the course. "It looks like that might have been an old golf course that's gone to seed."

Not surprisingly, his comments found their way to the British press, which had a field day at Sam's expense.

Sam went on to win, and when the ceremonies finished, his caddie, Scotty, approached, begging him for the ball he won with.

"Mr. Snead, if you could find your way to part with that ball I should treasure it all my life," he said.

"I gave him the ball, and he went right down the street to the nearest pub and sold it to the highest bidder for fifty quid," Sam recalls. "He made more money than I did that week."

Over the years Sam has developed an undeserved reputation as a hustler, which doesn't make sense if you think about it. First of all, just playing with Sam Snead would make most people so nervous they couldn't play to their handicap; and even if they could, he was so talented he could probably beat them anyway.

The truth of the matter, though, is that by his own admission he has to have a little something riding on a match just to hold his interest. Usually that means a $5 Nassau. Sometimes it means more. Much more.

"I used to play down in Boca Raton during the winters," says Sam. "These two fellas came along one day and wanted to play for a little money. They were both good players, 5s I think. I nicked 'em for about fifty in the morning and they wanted another shot in the afternoon, so we raised the stakes. I was playing real good at the time and won about $700. Well, they were pretty well-off, and even though I was beating them pretty good they were pretty close matches and we were having a lot of fun. We decided to make a week of it. We played a different course every day. I set four course records that week. The worst round I had was a 67. I won $10,000 that week, and we parted as the best of friends."

Sam always enjoyed playing as long as there was a little money riding on the match. It didn't have to be much, just enough to hold his interest. Otherwise, he often said, he'd "rather be out fishing."

He had a reputation as a hustler, but nothing could be further from the truth. He'd always give people their handicap, properly figuring that just playing the Great Sam Snead was enough to throw anyone off their game.

Although he won most of his friendly matches, he did lose on occasion. In one case, it cost him $20. At the match's conclusion, he reached into his pocket and handed his opponent a $20 bill.

"Sam, do me a favor and autograph it for me," the man said.

"What for?" Sam asked.

"I want to take it home, frame it, and put it on my office wall," the man said. "Otherwise, nobody will believe I beat you."

"Here, give me that $20," Sam said, taking the bill back from the man. "I'll give you a check."

For much of his career Sam was affiliated with The Greenbrier resort in West Virginia. For many years the resort hosted a Tour event, the Sam Snead Invitational.

One year, in the mid-1950s, the tournament coincided with the release of *Follow the Sun*, the movie based on Ben Hogan's recovery from a near-fatal automobile accident. The movie featured cameo appearances by a number of players and starred Glenn Ford—not that you'd know that from the marquee on the movie theater down the street from The Greenbrier. It read: "Follow the Sun starring Sam Snead."

One of Sam Snead's best friends on the Tour was Johnny Bulla, but it was a friendship that almost proved very costly for Snead.

"Johnny used to promote a ball named the Po-Do, which was sold in Walgreens drugstores," Sam remembers. "They sold millions of 'em, which angered the big equipment makers because it was the first ball sold outside pro shops. It especially angered Mr. Icely, who ran Wilson, because it cut into the sales of their Hol-Hi ball. Mr. Icely did all he could to run John off the Tour, but he wouldn't give in. Finally, one time when I was in Chicago for a tournament, Mr. Icely asked me to come to his office. He told me that Wilson was paying me a lot of money and he didn't want me traveling with John anymore. I looked him square in the eye and said, 'Mr. Icely, I appreciate all you and Wilson have done for me, and you can tell me where to play and what clubs to play, but no one is gonna tell me who my friends are going to be.'"

Sam was playing in a tournament on the day of the memorable 1948 presidential election between President Truman and Thomas

Dewey. When the early returns began to come in, Fred Corcoran told Sam, "Dewey's leading."

"What'd he go out in?" Sam asked.

Another time Sam was in the clubhouse when Corcoran came in and announced, "Bing Crosby won the Oscar."

"Is that match or medal?" Sam asked.

Sam Snead always said that "golf didn't get complicated until I put on shoes." Fred Corcoran, his agent, was always looking for ways to promote Sam. At the 1942 Masters, Corcoran told the writers that Sam could really tear the course apart if only—you guessed it—he could play barefoot. Before Clifford Roberts or Bob Jones could find out about it, Sam was out playing a practice round in his bare feet. He birdied two of the toughest holes on the course, and the story made all the papers the next day.

Predictably, not everyone was happy about it. No one was more outspoken than Gene Sarazen, who called it a publicity stunt.

"Hell, Gene, if it wasn't for publicity stunts you'd still be back on a banana boat someplace," said Jimmy Demaret.

Edward, Duke of Windsor, was a passionate golfer. He once asked Sam's longtime agent and friend, Fred Corcoran, if he would arrange a round of golf with Sam. Naturally, Corcoran obliged and the two men had an enjoyable round.

A few days later, the Duke telephoned Corcoran and asked if he might send a check to Sam in appreciation. Corcoran said that was very nice, but he was sure Sam would rather have an autographed photograph of the Duke. Later, when Sam found out, he quickly set the record straight.

"Next time take the check," said Sam. "If I want to start a picture collection of a bunch of kings, I can go down to Woolworth's and buy some bubble-gum cards for a nickel."

Not surprisingly, young players could find Sam Snead an intimidating player to deal with. Not that he tried to be brusque or tough, but he was, after all, one of the game's greatest players.

When Bob Toski joined the Tour in the 1950s, he was in awe of Snead's game, particularly his skill in the bunkers—for which he's always been underrated.

"I knew I couldn't just go up and ask him for a lesson, but I also knew that he wouldn't turn down a bet," remembers Toski. "I used to bet him milk shakes that I could get ten balls closer to the hole than he could. I hardly ever beat him, at least at first, but I learned to be a pretty good bunker player just by watching Sam. I paid for a lot of milk shakes, but it was the best investment I ever made."

Tom Kite was another player who took advantage of Sam's competitive instincts to become a better player.

"Sam was still playing a fair amount on tour when I came out in 1972," Kite remembers. "I introduced myself and asked if I could play with him in his practice rounds. We didn't play for much, just enough to keep his interest, but it was an education that I couldn't have gotten any other way. I remember going back home to Austin

and asking Harvey Penick, my teacher, whether it was possible for a player to develop all the shots Sam had and then hit them in competition. Mr. Penick disappointed me a little by saying 'probably not.' But he was right."

Sam was playing a practice round at Augusta National with Tom Kite and young Bobby Cole from South Africa, who was playing in his first Masters. Sam hit a fine drive on the 13th, the dogleg left par 5. As Cole prepared to play his shot, Sam said, "You know, junior, when I was your age we'd drive the ball right over the corner of those trees."

Cole hit a towering drive that crashed two-thirds of the way up into the pines.

"Of course, Bobby, when I was your age, those trees were a hell of a lot smaller," Sam said, as he walked off the tee smiling.

Because Sam played so well for so long, he had a chance to compete against players who were the same age as his sons. While Sam was intensely competitive and rarely gave the other guy an edge, he did give some of these young players a bit of advice from time to time.

One day a young player asked if he could join Sam for a practice round. Sam agreed and, just to make things interesting, a little bet was made on the round. After a few holes, Sam took the player aside.

"Son, don't call anyone you're trying to beat 'Mister.'"

Many—in fact, most—of Sam's acts of kindness to other players have gone unreported, but here's a good example of his generosity.

He was paired with Johnny Miller in the 1974 Los Angeles Open. It was the year Miller broke through and became a dominant player, winning eight times and ending the year as the Tour's leading money winner. But in Los Angeles, he wasn't in contention and wasn't very interested in being there. As the two men walked together down one of the final holes, Sam decided to give Miller some advice.

"Look, Johnny, I wouldn't say this if I didn't think you're a good guy," Sam said. "These people paid good money to come out here and see you play your best. This round may not mean much to you, but it means a lot to them. You're going to be a great player, and it would be a shame if you got a reputation for dogging it. You owe it to these people and you owe it to yourself."

That night Sam got a phone call in his hotel room. It was Johnny Miller thanking him for the advice.

Sam Snead is deeply respected by his fellow players not only for his playing ability and his remarkable record but also for his knowledge of the golf swing. They often seek him out for advice.

"One time I was in an awful slump and happened to play a practice round with Sam," Raymond Floyd remembers. "When we finished, I said, 'Sam, I know there has to be a secret. There has to be something you know that I haven't figured out yet.' He kind of looked around, like he wanted to make sure there was no one who would overhear us. Then he said, 'Junior, you've got to turn. You've just got to make a good turn.'

"I said to him, 'That's it?'

" 'That's it, junior,' he said."

Sam Snead always insisted that if he was even a halfway decent putter he would have won twice as many tournaments as he did. In truth, he was one of the greatest lag putters in the game's history, in no small part because of his remarkable feel for distance and touch.

One day, when this was brought to his attention, he argued that maybe he was an okay approach putter but "no one ever missed more short putts than I did."

"Maybe that's because no one ever had as many short putts as you did, Sam," countered Doc Middlecoff, Sam's friend and fellow Hall of Famer.

In hockey, a "hat trick" is when a player scores three goals in one game. In the old days, fans would toss their hats down onto the ice in tribute to the player. Sam Snead scored a hat trick of sorts one year in Canada.

"We were playing this par 3," he recalls. "It was 245 into the wind, and most of the boys couldn't even reach the green. I took a driver and hit the prettiest little hook in there that you ever saw. The ball hit on the front of the green and started rolling like a putt. It ran up over a ridge, and I lost sight of it. When I heard the crowd roar I figured it was close, but when I saw them start throwing their hats onto the green, I knew it was a hole in one."

A writer once asked Sam if he always shot at the pin or whether he liked to be safe and play to the fat part of the green. Sam looked at the man as if he were crazy.

"Well, I shoot at the pins," he said.

"Why?" the writer asked.

"'Cause that's what they're there for," Sam replied.

For proof, he could have cited his record for holes in one. He's made thirty-five in all—and he's made them with every club in the bag, from a driver and a 1-iron through a pitching wedge.

"I've always been flattered when people ask for my autograph, but I can't even imagine what it must be like for Sam," Dave Marr once said as he watched Sam work his way through a crowd of fans. "He's been signing autographs for sixty years. That's an awful lot of autographs."

And interrupted dinners.

One night Sam was having dinner with a writer friend when a woman approached and asked for his autograph. Sam was very polite, asking her if she played golf, where she was from, and so on. When he handed her the autograph, she thanked him. She should have quit while she was ahead.

"We've always loved watching you, Mr. [Gay] Brewer," she said, as she returned to her table.

What made this all the more incredible was that it took place in Sam Snead's Tavern, in his hometown, Hot Springs, Virginia.

Few, if any, players have ever played in as many pro-ams as Sam Snead has. But for all the poor, long-suffering hackers he's seen, one stands out above all the rest.

"I played with this old bird one time," says Sam. "He was a nice guy. I could tell he wasn't much of a player, but he was so nice I just hurt for him. I tried to help him relax, but it was no use. He hit his first drive out of bounds. He whiffed twice on the next hole. I'd never seen that before or since, come to think of it. He picked up on every single hole until we got to this real short par 4. He hit a good tee shot, and it wound up about fifty yards from the green. I think it hit a sprinkler head or something. He was getting a shot on every hole, so I was licking my chops. I figured he just might get us a birdie and that would settle him down. Well, he sort of shanked it and topped it all at the same time. Whatever happened, the ball wound up a few feet from the hole. He hit his first putt twenty feet past the hole and then knocked the next one back another twenty feet away. Well, he was shot then. He asked me if it would be all right if he picked up. I said, 'Yes, partner, I think you can.'"

The first time Sam Snead saw Pete Dye's course at Harbour Town, with all its railroad ties and bulkheads, he was asked his opinion of the design.

"It's a nice course," said Sam. "But it's the first course I ever saw that could burn down."

In 1980, Sam Snead won the Commemorative, one of the first events on the PGA Senior Tour. In his press conference, a reporter asked him if he realized that he'd become the first player in history to win Tour events in six different decades.

"Is that right?" asked Sam. "How long are decades these days?"

"One day I'm out fishing, and because it's so hot I'm wearing a baseball cap instead of my straw hat," says Sam, beginning a story that shows his ability to laugh at himself. "I see this old-timer looking me up and down, trying to figure out who I am. Finally he comes up and says, 'Excuse me, you're somebody famous, aren't you?'

" 'Well, I believe you might have heard of me,' I replied.

" 'You're a golfer, right?' he said.

" 'That's right,' I said.

" 'I knew it,' he said, all excited. 'You're Ben Hogan!'

"He ruined my whole damn day."

While Sam would seek out his brothers—Homer, Jess, and Pete— for help when his swing wasn't quite right, the truth is that like most players of his generation, he was largely self-taught. It helped that he was a great natural athlete and had a keen eye for adapting what he saw in other sports to the game of golf.

One afternoon, when he was in his seventies, Sam was watching a baseball game on television when a player hit a towering home run. The player's swing was replayed in slow motion and the announcer mentioned the man's outstanding arm extension that generated so much power.

"As soon as he said it, a light went off in my head," Sam recalled. "I realized that as I had gotten older I had gotten a little lazy and hadn't been extending my arms when I hit the ball."

The next time Sam went out to play, that was the only swing key that he focused upon. He was playing the Lower Cascades course with some friends, and to say that the key worked is an understatement. He tied the course record—a feat made all the sweeter because the record had been held by Sam's nephew, J. C. Snead.

LEFTY STACKHOUSE

Lefty Stackhouse had a temper. A considerable temper. As a matter of fact, as tempers go, he could have given the golfing world two or three a side and still been the best in history.

The stories about him are legendary. According to one, he missed a putt and, in the heat of the moment, hit himself in the head with his putter. The blow staggered him, sending him briefly to his knees, at which point he tried gamely to rise, only to collapse in a heap near the cup. Other stories are remarkably similar, except that they have Lefty punching himself in the head and knocking himself out. I tend to go with the latter. After all, who'd take a chance on ruining a perfectly good putter by smashing it against his head?

Other Lefty Stackhouse stories tell of the times when, after hitting a particularly grievous hook, he'd smash his right hand against a tree trunk or thrash it through a thorn bush, screaming obscenities at it as though it had a life of its own, independent of his brain and nervous system.

But the greatest of all the Lefty Stackhouse stories is the one that finds him playing in an exhibition tournament in Knoxville to sell war bonds. Everyone who finished the tournament would win something, and on hand to present the awards and help attract the crowds was Tennessee's greatest legend, World War I hero Sergeant Alvin York. York, a deeply religious man who disapproved of golf on the Sabbath (or anything else except church, for that matter), had a fanatical abhorrence of alcohol. It was pure fate, then, that he chose to follow a group that included Lefty Stackhouse, a man who approved mightily of both golf and distilled spirits on any day the combination presented itself.

Stackhouse, freed from the pressures of having to play well to earn a check, began drinking liberally from a bottle of Coca-Cola laced with alcohol. Soon the combination of his drinking and the heat began to take its toll. On one of the closing holes, he bent over to read the line of his putt—an unnecessary effort since, at this point, he could barely see the ball, let alone anything as sublime as the line. Spent by his efforts, he passed out and had to be carried to the clubhouse.

"That poor man exhausted himself," said a stunned York. "I had no idea this golf was such a strenuous game."

Lefty Stackhouse was a talented golfer, but he's probably best known for a fairly volcanic temper. Now, there are times when getting mad can help you play better, but that was seldom the case with Lefty.

Playing in the final round of a tournament that he had a chance to win, he hit a wild hook off the tee on a par 3 and watched as it sailed out of bounds. He slammed down his club and raked his right hand through a nearby rosebush, cutting it badly.

Still, that wasn't enough. He glared at his left hand—which equally offended him—and growled, "You're next."

"People are always writing about old Tom's temper, but let me tell you something, I'm not even close to Lefty Stackhouse," Tommy Bolt once told a writer friend. "Lefty was playing in a pro-am down in Texas one time, and he and his partner were doing just fine until they came to this one hole. Lefty's ball was just off the green, but his partner was close to the hole and looking at a birdie, so Lefty picked up. His partner three-putted for a bogey, and Lefty got so damn mad he punched himself in the head. He started bleeding so bad, he had to go back to the clubhouse and get himself bandaged up. Old Lefty was a beauty, that's for sure."

There are players with tempers. There are players with fierce tempers. Then there is Lefty Stackhouse, who was the standard all others are held against.

He came to one tournament and noticed that True Temper, the shaft manufacturer, had sent a representative out with a set of clubs fitted with their latest shaft. Lefty asked the man if he might borrow the clubs for a practice round. The man, apparently not aware of Lefty's reputation, thought it might help promote the shafts.

Wrong.

A few hours later, Stackhouse finished his round and ran into the True Temper man.

"How were the clubs, Mr. Stackhouse?" he asked.

"I don't think they're for me," said Lefty, dropping a matched set of broken shafts at the man's feet and walking away.

CRAIG STADLER

When Stadler was a kid growing up in San Diego, he was part of a group that took lessons from two-time PGA champion Paul Runyan. Years later, after Stadler had won a U.S. Amateur and twelve PGA Tour events, including the 1982 Masters, a writer asked Runyan about his early impressions of Stadler. Runyan said he thought Stadler was one of the shyest youngsters he'd ever seen.

Several years later, an interviewer asked Stadler about Runyan's assessment.

"Actually, I thought he would have said that he thought I had a bladder disease," Stadler said, laughing. "Paul is a sweetheart and a very good teacher, but sometimes I'd get confused when I tried to follow what he was telling me. Pretty soon every time he came down the line on the practice tee and was about to get to me, I'd tell him I had to go to the bathroom. I didn't want to hurt his feelings, but I didn't want to get any more confused, either."

Craig Stadler shot a 79 in the first round of the 1998 Masters. As he walked toward the clubhouse, a writer asked him what number he had in mind for Friday.

Now, one thing you should understand about Craig Stadler is that any answer to a question like that, at a time like that, is probably going to be fairly concise. This was no exception.

"Nine-thirty," said Stadler, not breaking his purposeful stride.

"Nine-thirty?" the writer asked.

"Yeah, the nine-thirty flight out of here tomorrow night," Stadler said.

Not quite. The next day Stadler went out and shot a 68 and made the cut by a comfortable three strokes.

CURTIS STRANGE

Two-time U.S. Open winner Curtis Strange is one of the game's really good guys. He's also one of its toughest competitors—one of the toughest that ever lived. Lee Trevino nicknamed him "The Piranha" because "if he gets a chance he'll eat you up." He's also candid and honest. For a time in the 1980s, he decided to skip the British Open. When Peter Andrews, an editor at *Golf Digest*, asked him why, he explained: "I like the British Open and I like playing over there. The problem is that every time I turn around some son of a bitch is telling me I have to play there, so I don't." Perfect.

Curtis's father, Tom, was a professional who worked for a time in Sam Snead's pro shop at The Greenbrier. He died from cancer when Curtis and his twin brother, Allan, were just fourteen. Anyone who was around the pressroom after Curtis won his first Open, in 1988 at The Country Club, saw a side of Curtis that until then had been seen only by his close friends and family.

"From the time I was nine, everything my father taught me about the golf swing is still with me," he said to a hushed crowd of writers, many of whom had known Curtis since his days as an amateur at Wake Forest University.

"In 1976 I was the low amateur at the Masters and was brought into the pressroom for an interview," says Curtis Strange. "Usually they have one of the Yates brothers conduct the interview, but this time, for some reason, it was an older member, with white hair, a moustache, and an unbelievable southern accent. The reporters asked me a few questions but they really were more concerned with what was going on out on the course.

"There was a long pause and everyone thought we were done; then the member says, 'Curtis, I have a question. You went to Wake

Forest on an Arnold Palmer scholarship. How'd it feeeel to play with Arnold in the first round?'

" 'Sir, I didn't play with Arnold in the first round,' I told him.

" 'Oh,' he said. 'Well then, how'd it feel to play with the great Jack Nicklaus in the first round of the Masters tournament?'

" 'Well, sir, I didn't play with Jack in the first round,' I explained.

" 'Well then, Curtis, just who did you play with in the first round of the Masters tournament?' he asked.

" 'Gay Brewer,' I said.

"There was a pause for a few seconds—maybe longer—then David Lamb, a reporter from Jacksonville, asked, mimicking the member's southern drawl, 'Tell us, Curtis, how'd it feeeel to play with Gay Brewer?' "

TEMPER, TEMPER

Clayton Heafner was a fine player. Like many fine players, he fought a hook. And he fought his temper. Very often, the hook and the temper managed to win.

"Clayton could really play, but every so often that old right hand of his would take over and he'd hit some of the ugliest hooks you'd ever hope to see," Sam Snead remembers. "He was leading a tournament one time when he hooked one out of bounds. You could just tell he was going to explode. Damned if he didn't walk over to this tree and punch it. I think he broke his hand, too."

"Clayton Heafner was what you'd call a brooder," Sam Snead remembers. "He'd get something under his skin and it would fester. He'd think about it and think about it, and the more he did, the madder he'd get. One time he was driving to a tournament at a course he didn't really like. Naturally, all that time in the car gave him a chance to work up a nice little rage. When he reached the course he told the tournament officials he was pulling out. When they asked him why, he didn't bother to make up an excuse. He just told them their course was a goat track and then stormed off. That earned Clayton a nice little fine from the PGA, but at least he got it off his chest."

"I was playing in an outing one day and I saw a guy absolutely lose it," Dave Marr once recalled. "It was one of those deals where I stood on a par 3 and hit a shot for each group. This guy gets up there and dead-shanks it into a pond next to the tee. Man, you could just see the red come up into his face. He took his club and threw it into the pond, then he reached over, picked up a golf bag, and threw that in, too. People were in shock. I said, 'I can't believe you did that.' One of the other guys said, '*You* can't believe it! It was my bag!' "

Lefty Stackhouse showed up for a tournament, but his clubs had somehow gotten lost along the way. This by itself had put him in a grim mood, and things didn't get any better when he played poorly with the set he had borrowed from the pro shop. By the time he finished his round, he could no longer contain himself—or think of any reason to treat the borrowed set any differently than he would his own. He marched over to a nearby stump and—very carefully—broke each club over it.

Lefty Stackhouse was driving to a tournament in his Buick Road-master when the car suddenly gave out. He wiggled wires, adjusted hoses, checked clamps, and, failing to get the car up and running, went berserk. He began by kicking the car and wound up punching the windshield until it shattered.

Several years later, Stackhouse was giving a lesson to a particularly inept pupil. Finally the frustration became too great and he began shaking his fist for emphasis. Inexplicably, it began to swell grotesquely. Stackhouse rushed to the hospital, where doctors removed shards of glass left from his punchout with the Buick.

"People talk about my temper, but old Tom didn't have anything on Lefty Stackhouse," Tommy Bolt once recalled. "I may have thrown a club now and then, but I never ruined an entire set. One time, back in the old days when they had hickory shafts, Lefty came in from a round and burned his whole set. He just made a little bonfire for himself and torched them. Now, that is a temper."

Ivan Gantz was a wild man by any standards. He was known to miss a putt and then do a perfect belly flop into a nearby bunker. He also had a habit of punching himself in the head when he missed a putt. Still, that was an improvement. One time he hit himself in the head with his putter and knocked himself out cold.

TITANIC THOMPSON

It would be inaccurate, and also unfair, to dismiss Alvin Clarence "Titanic" Thompson, who died in 1974, as simply a hustler or gambler. He was a keen student of both the odds and human nature, and he used that knowledge to his best advantage. He was a fine player who realized early on that the disparity between tournament purses and the money he could easily lift from the unsuspecting was too great to pass up.

"Titanic asked me once if I thought he could beat anyone playing left-handed if he got nine-and-a-half shots a round," remembers Paul Runyan. "I told him I thought that was quite possible. He went to Dallas and played several rounds in the 80s to set the trap. He then offered to play left-handed with strokes. He won $5,500 the first day and naturally said it would only be sporting to give the boys another chance. They bit, and he wound up winning over $20,000. That night he was leaving a casino, and a caddie tried to rob him. He shot him with the .45 he always carried, killing him instantly. I should add that it wasn't a lucky shot. Ti was an extraordinary shot."

Once, when he was in Illinois for a tournament, Thompson met a farmer driving down a road with a truckload of watermelons. He stopped, counted the melons, and bought the entire load on the spot. The only stipulation was that the farmer had to drive past a hotel in town where Ti knew there would be gamblers staying. At the appointed hour, as the farmer came down the road, Thompson bet the gamblers that he could guess the exact number of watermelons. They bet, he gave them the number, and he made a small fortune.

Jim Thorpe

Jim Thorpe left college, where he had earned a football scholarship, to concentrate on golf. To make ends meet, he worked for a few years in a General Motors plant near Baltimore. After a while, he figured that the only way to really improve his game was to get involved in some of the money games around town. One of the best players—and biggest gamblers—was a guy named Joe Pew, who favored bets of $500 a nine.

Thorpe knew that if he could beat Pew it would (1) prove to himself that he really did have a game good enough to make it on the PGA Tour; (2) establish him as a money player around town; and (3) help stake him to a shot at his Tour card.

There was just one small problem: Joe Pew liked to see the money up front, and Jim Thorpe had exactly $104 to his name.

"I went to the bank and got a $50 bill and fifty-four ones," Thorpe explains. "I rolled the bills up, put the $50 on the outside, and wrapped an elastic band around them. Man, I looked like a Rockefeller. I got to the course and sort of flashed the roll to Joe, but told him I had to stash it because we were being watched.

"We went out and played, and when we got to 18 all I needed was a half to win a grand," he continues. "The problem was that I only had one kind of shot, and that was a hook. I mean, I really had three kinds of shots: a hook, a big hook, and a hook that would go from here to there and keep running forever. This hole had trees all down the right side. There wasn't enough room for me to start the ball off the tee. My drive hit into those trees and came shootin' back at me. I thought to myself, 'Good-bye, money,' especially after Joe hit himself a good drive.

"I sort of knocked it up there towards the green and then Joe hits it three feet from the hole," Thorpe goes on. "I got up and skulled a pitching wedge. It was goin' about a hundred miles an hour when it hit the flag. The ball dropped straight down into the hole for a three. Man, I took that money, said 'Thank you very much,' and got out of there as fast as I could."

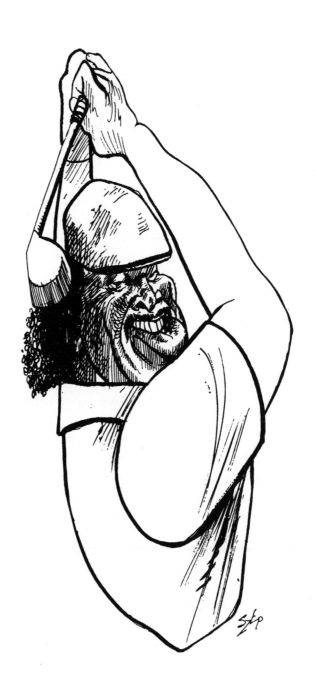

After fine-tuning his game with his own money on the line, Thorpe decided to try his luck on the Tour. But first there was the matter of raising the money he needed to give himself a real shot. Luck—and a certain amount of skill—took care of that.

He was playing in a local pro-am that was offering a car to anyone who made a hole in one. He made one, learned the car was worth $8,000, and sold it on the spot. After paying some bills, he headed for the qualifying school.

When he made it to the Tour, Thorpe became a particular favorite of Lee Trevino, who was generous with advice. The first time he was in contention to win a tournament, Trevino approached him on the putting green prior to the last round.

"Just remember, the other guys are just as nervous as you are," Trevino told him.

"Oh yeah?" said Thorpe. "Then there's goin' to be three guys throwing up on the first tee in a couple minutes."

"I was in the locker room after one of my rounds in the 1978 PGA at Oakmont," remembers Thorpe. "Arnold [Palmer] was there and he had had a good round. He saw on television that Nicklaus had finished at 8 over. It was just pouring rain outside and Arnold said, 'Watch, Jack is 8 over and it's raining. That means they'll wash the round out.'

"Just then Jack walked around the corner and gave Arnold that look.

" 'Yeah, Arnold,' Jack said, 'just like they used to do for you.'

"Arnold turned bright red and they just kind of glared at each other for a second," said Thorpe. "I turned to the guys near me and said, 'Lord, let's get out of here. God and Jesus Christ are about to go at it.' "

JEROME TRAVERS

Jerry Travers was one of the great American players in the early part of the twentieth century. From 1906 to 1915, he won four U.S. Amateurs and a U.S. Open—one of only five amateurs to win the Open.

To say that Travers marched to the beat of his own drummer is to put it mildly. In the years he was at the height of his game, he twice failed to enter the Amateur and he never entered the Open after his win in 1915.

Like Bob Jones, who retired from championship play at a young age, Travers all but quit serious competition while he was quite young—age twenty-eight. The difference was that Jones retired because he had won the Grand Slam and had nothing left to accomplish. No one is quite sure why Travers retired when he did.

The keys to Travers's success were his phenomenal putting and his uncanny ability to focus, to the exclusion of everything going on around him. Witness his match with Francis Ouimet in the finals of the 1914 U.S. Amateur at Ekwanok Country Club in Manchester, Vermont.

"I was fortunate enough to beat Jerry, 6 and 5, and after I putted out, I waited for Jerry to come over and congratulate me," Ouimet remembered. "Instead, he walked right past me, took his driver from his caddie, and walked off to the next tee. One of the officials ran after him and asked if he was planning to play the bye holes. 'Why,' Jerry asked, 'is the match over?'"

WALTER TRAVIS

Walter Travis was one of the game's greatest amateurs at the beginning of the twentieth century. Between 1900 and 1904, he won three U.S. Amateurs and a British Amateur at a time when the amateur championships were every bit as prestigious as—and maybe even more so than—the respective opens. That Travis finished second in the 1902 U.S. Open at Garden City Golf Club on Long Island is all the more remarkable when you realize that he didn't even take up the game until he was thirty-five.

Travis, who was born in Australia but lived in America, could be difficult—to put it mildly. He didn't care whom he offended, and sometimes he seemed to go out of his way to annoy people. He was seldom without one of his truly nasty black cigars clenched tightly between his teeth. It's not clear what people found more irritating about Travis—his cigars or his personality.

Not surprisingly, then, Travis was a fierce competitor. Even his most vocal critics would give him that much. His win in the 1901 U.S. Amateur was not only one of his greatest triumphs but also one of his most nerve-racking.

The championship was played in Atlantic City, New Jersey, and Travis won the thirty-six-hole qualifying medal by three strokes. By the luck of the draw, however, he faced a difficult route to the finals.

He faced Charles Blair MacDonald—who could be equally difficult—early in the match-play rounds and managed to beat the winner of the first U.S. Amateur. In the semifinals he came up against the formidable Findlay Douglas. Douglas, who had won the U.S. Amateur in 1898 and had lost in the finals of the previous two championships, ranked with Travis as one of the premier amateurs at that time. The match figured to be a classic, and thousands of spectators came from all along the East Coast to watch it. They weren't disappointed.

The lead and momentum shifted back and forth between the two players until, at the end of thirty-six holes, the match was tied. Travis won on the second hole of sudden death.

The final promised to be every bit as tense, as Travis would face Chicago's Walter Egan, who had cruised to an 11 and 10 win in his semifinal. But the finals would have to wait. That evening, news came that President William McKinley, who had been shot eight days earlier, had died. The country went into an official state of mourning.

When the final was finally played a week later, Travis's competitive edge showed. He won easily, 5 and 4, in the longest U.S. Amateur championship in history.

Walter Travis was a keen judge of talent. At the 1916 U.S. Amateur at Merion, he closely watched the fourteen-year-old Bobby Jones in his third-round loss to the defending champion, Robert Gardner. After the round, a writer asked Travis what Jones needed to do to improve.

425

"Well, he can never improve his shots," Travis said. "But he has a great deal to learn about playing them, and when he does, he will be all but unbeatable."

Travis was right.

The rest is history.

Along with his ever-present cigar, Travis was known to take a drink now and then. In fact, he relished a good, stiff pop or two. Once, however, on the eve of an important tournament, he decided to give abstinence a try. It was a short-lived effort.

"I conceived the idea that my game would be improved if I stopped drinking and smoking, so I cut out both," he explained. "I found that while it made no difference in my long game, my work on the greens was nothing short of childish. I couldn't putt at all. I have never since allowed even golf to interfere with either my smoking or drinking."

Spoken like a true champion.

Travis set a record by shooting rounds of 75-74—149 in the final two rounds of the 1902 U.S. Open at Garden City Golf Club. He finished in a tie for second place, six strokes behind Laurie Auchterlonie.

As an amateur, Travis was ineligible for his $100 prize money. Instead, he asked USGA officials to use $75 of the prize money for a trophy and give the remaining $25 to his playing companion, Alex Smith, for his "thoroughly sportsmanlike spirit throughout the championship."

LEE TREVINO

Lee Trevino grew up in tremendous poverty in Dallas. He lived in a sharecropper's house with his mother and grandfather.

"We had dirt floors, and there was no plumbing or electricity," Trevino recalled. "Hell, I joined the marines when I was seventeen. The barracks were the first place I ever lived that had running water and lights. I thought I was staying at the Ritz-Carlton."

"I grew up playing on a public course in Dallas called Tenison Park," Trevino recalls. "It was so tough out there that people would skip a stretch of holes away from the clubhouse for fear of getting robbed.

"One day these two guys are out there playing a match, and the bets are flying fast and furious. One guy's out $1,000. Just then, these two robbers pop out of the trees with guns.

" 'Here,' the guy who was losing said, handing over $1,000 to his friend. 'We're even.' "

Lee Trevino didn't come out on tour until he was twenty-seven, but he had learned he could handle the competition a few years before when he was working in the shop at the Horizon Country Club in El Paso, Texas. A group of members arranged for Raymond Floyd, twenty-two, to come down and play against a young unknown. Floyd, who was the Tour's Rookie of the Year, was used to playing money games and was looking forward to a $3,000 match against a player he'd never even heard of.

When Floyd arrived at the club, Trevino took Floyd's bag from his car, shined up his shoes, and asked if there was anything else he could do for him.

"Just tell me who I'm playing," said Floyd.

"Me," said Trevino.

Floyd took one look at Trevino and decided he didn't even need to see the course.

They went out that afternoon and Floyd shot a 67. Trevino cut him by a shot. Floyd suggested they play another nine. Trevino said he had to go park carts, shine shoes, and clean clubs. Floyd just shook his head and went off to shoot doves.

The next day they went at it again, and again Trevino won, this time 66-65. Again, Floyd suggested they play another nine, and again Trevino said he had to go park carts.

On the third day, Floyd came out and shot a 31 on the front. The match came down to the final hole, and Floyd won by a shot. Somebody asked Floyd if he wanted to play again the next day.

"No, thank you," he said. "I can find much easier ways to make money."

For several years, Lee Trevino skipped the Masters. He believed that Augusta National was ill-suited to his game because he wasn't a high ball hitter and didn't feel comfortable drawing the ball. Also, he never really felt comfortable at the club.

In 1971, he decided to take Masters week off but at the last minute decided he wanted to play—just not at Augusta. So he entered a PGA sectional tournament in El Paso.

To no one's surprise, he won the tournament and the princely sum of $125.

Like many people gifted with a sharp sense of humor, Lee Trevino knows how to turn it into a weapon when it's called for. A classic case occurred at the 1984 PGA Championship at Shoal Creek in Birmingham, Alabama.

Two things should be noted here: first, Trevino's caddie, Herman Mitchell, is a large black man whom Trevino is enormously fond of and loyal to; and second, the tournament was played amid a swirl of racial controversy because Shoal Creek was unapologetically segregated.

At any rate, as Trevino and Mitchell were walking toward a tee, some genius in the gallery called out, "Hey, Lee, what do you feed your caddie?"

"Rednecks," Trevino called back, not breaking his stride, "and he's hungry."

One day Trevino stood on a tee waiting for the pairing ahead of him to clear the green. To check the wind, he bent over and tore up a little grass, tossing it into the air.

"Excuse me, Lee," somebody from the gallery asked. "Why do you do that?"

"I don't know," Trevino joked. "I see the other guys doing it and I figure I should, too."

One afternoon Lee Trevino was cutting the grass in the front yard of his Dallas home. A woman drove up, rolled down her window, and asked how much he was being paid for yard work.

"Nothing," he said. "The lady of the house lets me sleep with her."

The woman drove off, probably in shock.

Before the Senior Tour really took off, a writer asked Lee Trevino if he had any goals for when his playing days were over. Trevino thought about it for a second.

"When I turn sixty I'm going to get me one of those old blue blazers, sprinkle it with dandruff, spill some soup on my tie, and then go run the USGA," he joked.

About the time Lee Trevino came on the Senior Tour he hired Chuck Rubin, Tom Watson's agent and brother-in-law, to represent him. Chuck had never shown a great deal of interest in learning the game, but one day he told Trevino he'd like to come down to Florida for some lessons.

"Chuck, I get $40,000 a day for an outing," Trevino said with a laugh. "How many days' worth of lessons do you want?"

Lee Trevino is a good friend of former President George Bush. One night Trevino and his wife, Claudia, were invited to dinner at the White House. Following dinner, they were all out walking one of the Bushes' dogs around the White House lawn. They approached a group of tourists standing outside that tall iron fence that surrounds the White House, and President Bush introduced Trevino to them.

"You don't have to tell us who he is, Mr. President," said one. "In Australia, he's more famous than you are."

Harry Vardon

England's Harry Vardon, winner of six British Opens and the 1900 U.S. Open, was a man of few words who did not suffer fools gladly. It's easy to imagine, then, how testy he might have become at times during a promotional tour of the United States. Vardon was a genuine celebrity, even in a country where golf's appeal was in its infancy.

During one stop on his tour, a new golfer asked Vardon if he consciously tried to keep his left arm straight on his backswing.

"No," Vardon said.

"Do you think it's important for a beginning golfer to keep his left arm straight?" the man asked.

"No," Vardon said. "As a matter of fact, I rather like playing against people who insist upon keeping their left arm straight. I find that they seldom think of anything else."

Vardon was paired with Bob Jones in the 1920 U.S. Open at Inverness. Both went out in opening round 76s. In the second round Jones chose to play a pitch-and-run into the 7th hole but skulled the shot, sending it racing over the green and into the back bunker. From there, the best he could salvage was a bogey 5. As he walked to the next tee, he sought to ease the tension by speaking with Vardon, who had remained speechless until that point in the round.

"Mr. Vardon, did you ever see a worse shot than that?" Jones asked.

"No," he said. Period.

A leader of the Women's Christian Temperance Union once urged Vardon to give up drink as an example that golfers might follow.

"Madam, I believe that moderation is essential in all things, but never in my life have I been beaten by a teetotaler."

After dominating golf in Great Britain, Harry Vardon came to America and staged a series of exhibitions that helped popularize the game in this country.

Following one exhibition in Chicago, a man approached Vardon and asked him a question.

"Mr. Vardon, if I may be so bold, who was the best left-hander you ever saw?" the man asked.

"Frankly," Vardon answered, "I never saw one that was worth a damn."

KEN VENTURI

In 1954 Ken Venturi was an amateur playing in his first Masters paired with Ben Hogan. After they both putted out on the first green, Hogan told Venturi to please call him Ben instead of Mr. Hogan.

They played along and the twenty-two-year-old quickly impressed Hogan with his nerve and shotmaking. Venturi had the honor on the difficult par-3 4th hole and hit a 3-iron onto the green. After watching, Hogan checked the wind and then hit a 3-iron as well, putting it into the front bunker.

"Let me see that club," Hogan said to Venturi. "My God, you've got a bag of 1-irons. It serves me right for watching an amateur."

"I guess this means you want me to call you Mr. Hogan," Venturi joked.

Following the round, Hogan asked for Venturi's address and later sent him a set of clubs.

When Ken Venturi was a young man his confidence in his golf game bordered on cockiness. His father, a down-to-earth man of uncommon wisdom, didn't exactly approve of his son's attitude.

In 1950, Ken won the San Francisco City Championship—a hugely popular win over an impressive field. At home after the match, he was telling his parents how well he had played. If he wasn't bragging, it was the next-best thing. Finally his father had heard enough.

"Son," he said. "When you're really good, other people will tell you. You won't have to tell them."

No amateur has ever won the Masters, but Ken Venturi came close in 1956, when he led going into the final round.

At that time, it was a tradition that Byron Nelson played with the leader on the last day. That presented a problem.

"Cliff Roberts came up to me Saturday night and said that since Byron was my mentor they thought it would be better if I didn't play with him in the last round," Venturi recalls. "Nobody thought Byron would coach me or anything, but they didn't want my win to be tainted in any way. He told me I could play with anyone else I wanted. I thought about it and decided I wanted to be paired with Sam Snead. I figured that since I'd learned from Byron and polished my game with Ben Hogan, what could be better than playing with Sam when I won my first Major."

Roberts tried to dissuade Venturi.

"He said it was up to me, but he thought Sam could be tough," Venturi remembers.

The final round was played in windy, difficult conditions. Venturi continued to play well from tee to green, but his putting failed him and he finished second behind Jackie Burke, who was the only player to break par in the last round.

When he returned home to San Francisco, a newspaper reported that Venturi had been critical of the way Snead treated him on the course. Naturally, this caused an uproar at Augusta National and throughout the golf world, even though Venturi insisted that the quotes were inaccurate. Some twenty years later, he put the issue to rest.

The occasion was a black-tie dinner at the Waldorf-Astoria hotel in New York. Both Snead and Venturi were being honored, and when Venturi rose to speak, he recounted the painful last round of the 1956 Masters. He spoke movingly of how he struggled to maintain his composure as the tournament slipped from his grasp. Then he turned to Sam.

"After the tournament, a newspaper reported that you gave me the treatment in the last round," he said. "That's not true. You went about your business and let me go about mine. That's as it should be. I wanted to play with you because I felt that, if I was lucky enough to win the Masters, it would be an honor to walk up the 18th fairway at Augusta with you. And I want to say this right now for the record: if I had to do it again, I'd still choose you, Sam."

In early 1956 Ken Venturi and fellow amateur Harvie Ward played Ben Hogan and Byron Nelson at Cypress Point in what many people feel might have been the greatest golf match ever played.

Hogan and Nelson were both just shy of their forty-fourth birthdays, and while neither was at the peak of his game, they both remained formidable foes. Venturi, twenty-five, and Ward, thirty, were arguably the two best amateurs in the country. Venturi had just beaten Ward for the San Francisco City Championship and in a few months would finish second in the Masters before turning pro later that year. Ward was the U.S. Amateur champion and would successfully defend his title later that year. He had also won the 1952 British Amateur. A three-time member of the Walker Cup team, he would finish fourth in the 1957 Masters.

All the players were at Pebble Beach for Bing Crosby's pro-am, and early in the week George Coleman, a wealthy Oklahoma businessman, hosted a cocktail party at his home near the lodge. Coleman got into a conversation with Eddie Lowery, a successful San Francisco car dealer who was a patron to both Ward, who worked for him, and Venturi. Lowery, who had caddied for Francis Ouimet in the 1913 U.S. Open, was so impressed by Venturi and Ward's play in the city championship that he said he believed they could "beat any two players in the world, pros included." Coleman asked him if he was willing to bet on them, and they settled on a bet of $50,000.

"I'll take Nelson and Hogan," said Coleman, and the match was arranged for the next day. By the time they teed off, the bet had been reduced to a more realistic, if less dramatic, $50.

The match began with very few spectators—a bogus tee time had been announced at Pebble Beach in an attempt to avoid publicity—

but word got out, and a large crowd soon gathered. By the end of 10 holes, Venturi and Ward were 9 under par—and 1-down.

"It was just an amazing display of golf," Venturi remembers. "It seemed like everyone was topping everyone else. Every hole was being halved with birdies.

"My recollection is we halved every hole from 11 through 15," says Venturi. "I know Ben and I halved 15 with birdies, and Harvie and Byron did the same thing on 16 and 17. They were still 1-up on 18. I made an uphill twelve-footer for a birdie on 18 and Ben had a tough ten-footer with a right-to-left break to halve me and win the match. Byron said, 'C'mon, Ben, knock it in.' Ben said, 'Don't worry, I'm not going to let us get tied by a couple of amateurs.' He didn't."

Hogan shot a 63, Venturi a 65. Nelson and Ward each had 67. The best ball of the foursome was 16 under par.

"Harvie and I were the best of friends and—maybe this was being a little cocky—but we really believed we could take on the world," says Venturi. "You know, now that I think back on it, that's about what we did."

439

Ten years later, Venturi's and Hogan's lives had changed dramatically. Hogan's magnificent career was past its prime, his last hurrah having come in 1960 at the U.S. Open. It wasn't that Hogan's singular shotmaking had failed him, but putting had increasingly become not only problematic, but even torturous. Venturi, whose career had produced fourteen victories, including a win in the 1964 U.S. Open, was struggling from the effects of carpal tunnel syndrome, a condition that affects sensation in the hands.

"In 1966, the Open came to the Olympic Club in San Francisco, my hometown," Venturi says. "I was paired with Ben, and when we got to the second hole, a good par 4, Ben put it in there about twelve feet to the right of the hole. He got over the putt and just froze. He couldn't take it back. Finally, he said to me, 'Ken, I can't take it back. I can't hit it.'

"I just looked at him, gave a little laugh, and said, 'Who cares, you've beaten everyone long enough.'

"I'd like to say he made the putt, but he came close. A couple holes later, we were walking down the fairway after we hit our tee shots and he said, 'Thanks.'

"'For what?' I asked.

"'You know what for,' he said."

When his career went into a tragic slump in the early 1960s, Ken Venturi became despondent and talked of quitting the Tour. He was broke, discouraged, and ashamed of the way he was playing. Once the brightest of young stars, he was now humiliated almost every time he teed it up. After returning to San Francisco, he told his father he was going to quit the Tour.

440

"Ken, you know I'll support whatever you decide to do, but just remember one thing," the older Venturi said. "Quitting is the only thing it doesn't take any talent to do."

Ken decided to give it one more try. He went to work on his game like a man possessed. He drove himself to get back into shape, despite the pain from injuries sustained in a recent automobile accident. He practiced relentlessly. Finally, as the 1964 season approached, he began to see glimmers of hope. Improvements were slow, coming in tiny increments, but they were coming nevertheless, and his confidence was returning.

That summer he capped his comeback by winning the U.S. Open at Congressional—a win most people rank as the most inspirational in Open history.

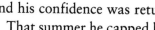

Few stories in any sport are as moving as Ken Venturi's. One of the top amateurs in the 1950s, he turned pro and quickly became one of the Tour's genuine superstars. But a series of injuries sent him into a despairing collapse, to the point where he came close to quitting golf altogether.

As his frustrations multiplied, Venturi, at age thirty-three, felt he had reached the absolute bottom. One evening he went to the basement of his house and prayed.

"I just asked God please not to let me go out this way," he recalled. "It wasn't that I had to win. I had gotten past that. But I needed to prove that I could still play, that I hadn't wasted everything I once had."

Venturi made a vow. He would work hard to get himself and his game back into shape for one more season; 1964 would be his make-or-break year. The year did not begin with much promise, and by the time June came around this enormously proud man was reduced to begging sponsors for exemptions into their events.

"I called Bill Jennings, who ran the Thunderbird Tournament in Westchester County. I felt my game was finally coming around, and I pleaded with him for a spot in his tournament. He had one left and gave it to me."

Venturi, who had struggled all year, played his way into contention. As he was leaving the clubhouse for the final round, he overheard a father telling his son, "That's Ken Venturi. He used to be one of the great players."

Venturi made a promise to himself. He would prove the man wrong. When he came to the 16th hole, a long dangerous par 3, he considered playing the safe shot rather than attacking the pin and risking a big number. He thought about that man and his son. Then he thought about one other thing.

"I told myself that this was it," Venturi recalls. "If I backed off now I knew I would be backing off for the rest of my life."

Venturi pulled out a 3-iron and rifled it at the flag. The shot was perfect, and while he missed his birdie putt, he had proven something to himself and to all those around him. His third-place finish set the stage for one of the greatest triumphs in golf history: Ken Venturi's win in the 1964 U.S. Open.

When Venturi arrived in suburban Washington, D.C., for the Open, he sought out a Catholic church. Alone in the church that evening he prayed, again asking God to give him the confidence and strength that he needed. He also asked for some sort of sign that his prayers had been heard.

That sign emerged on the eve of Saturday's final two rounds, when he received a letter from a friend, Father Frank Murray. The letter began:

"Dear Ken:

For you to become the 1964 U.S. Open champion would be one of the greatest things that ever happened during the year in the United States.

There are so many people in this country and in the world that need the encouragement and inspiration that your winning would give them.

Most people are in the midst of struggle. If not with their jobs, then it's their family life, or their health, or their drinking, or their frustrations. For many there is the constant temptation to give up and to quit trying. Life seems too much, and the demands too great. . . ."

Saturday's thirty-six-hole final round was brutal. The heat and humidity hovered near 105 degrees. Venturi, paired with young Raymond Floyd, went out in 30 strokes. On the 14th hole his body began to tremble from the intense heat. On 17, as he stood over a two-foot par putt, he hallucinated, seeing three holes. He putted for the middle hole and missed. Another bogey on 18 left him with a 66 and a three-round total of 208.

In the clubhouse between rounds, he was advised by a physician not to play the second eighteen. "Ken," said Dr. John Knowles, "if you go out there you could very easily die."

"Doc," said Venturi, "I'm already dying. I've got no place else to go."

Venturi went out and gamely fought on, playing largely on instinct and emotion. He went out in 35, and as he stood on the 10th tee Joseph C. Dey, the director of the United States Golf Association, told him he had the lead.

"There's a scoreboard over there if you're interested, Ken," said Dey.

"I'm not interested," Venturi said. "I can't change what's up there, and I can't control what the other guys are doing. One shot at a time is all that interests me."

As he left the 17th tee, Venturi knew he still had the lead, but again he was on the verge of collapse.

"Joe, you can put two strokes on me for slow play, but I've just got to walk slowly," he told Dey.

"Ken, it's all downhill to the 18th green," said Dey. "Now how about holding your chin up, so when you come in as a champion you'll look like one."

When he sank the winning putt on the 72nd hole, Venturi threw his arms into the air and then collapsed in tears. "My God," he said softly. "I've won the Open."

A few minutes later, in the scorer's tent, he tried to check his score, knowing that a mistake could cost him the Open. Fear swept over him as he was unable to focus on his card. Then he heard a voice from over his shoulder.

443

"Sign it, Ken. It's fine," said Dey, who had walked every step of the final round with Venturi, the new U.S. Open champion and a man who had come back from the dead.

Vince Lombardi, the legendary football coach of the Green Bay Packers, went to the last day of the 1964 U.S. Open. As he and his wife, Marie, were walking past the first green, they paused to watch Ken Venturi putt out. Venturi's putt hung on the edge of the cup, and the exhausted golfer stared at it, willing the ball into the hole. After a few seconds, it dropped.

"My God, his eyes are dead," said Lombardi. Instead of moving along to watch another group, Lombardi and his wife followed Venturi for the rest of his dramatic round.

For the rest of his coaching career, Lombardi would use the example of Venturi's courage and determination as a way to rally his teams.

As a youngster growing up in San Francisco, Ken Venturi idolized Byron Nelson. One day Nelson came to town to play an exhibition and Ken went out to watch. On one hole, Ken worked his way through the gallery and inside the ropes. As Nelson prepared to hit a shot, Ken raised his little camera to snap a picture.

"Son, you should get back outside those ropes," Nelson said kindly.

That night Ken raced home and excitedly told his mother the good news.

"Mom, Byron Nelson spoke to me!" he said.

444

"What did he say?" she asked.

"He told me to get back outside the ropes," Ken said.

"Ken, that's not speaking to you, that's telling you what to do," she said.

"Yeah, but he was saying it just to me," Ken answered.

Ken Venturi polished his game under the wise eyes of Byron Nelson and Ben Hogan, which, if you're going to have your game polished, is about as good as it gets.

Early in their friendship, Hogan paid the young Venturi a compliment that gave him a huge boost of confidence.

"In the 1958 Masters, we were all sitting around upstairs in the old locker room having lunch," Venturi recalled. "I was down at one end of the table and Ben was up at the other, near the door. Sam Snead walked in and asked Ben if he had a game for that afternoon. When Ben said he didn't, Sam asked him if he wanted one.

" 'Sure, I'll take Venturi and we'll play anyone in the world,' Ben said.

" 'I can find an easier game than that,' Sam said."

It was fitting that Nelson captained the only Ryder Cup team Ken Venturi played on in his injury-ravaged career. The 1965 matches were played at Royal Birkdale in Southport, England. While the Americans would go on to win 19½-12½, a turning point came in an alternate-shot match that paired Venturi and Tony Lema against Neil Coles and Brian Barnes.

On a par-5 hole late in the match, Lema hooked his second shot behind a bunker, leaving Venturi a delicate pitch off a downhill lie to a pin cut just over the bunker.

"I'm afraid things don't look very good for your side, Prime Minister Harold Wilson said to Nelson. I don't favor your man Venturi's chances with this shot. I believe the match may go even here."

"That may be, Mr. Wilson," replied Nelson. "But I've got ten men on this team, and if I had to pick one man to play this shot for me, it's the man playing the shot right now."

Venturi's pitch finished stiff to the pin.

"My, Mr. Nelson," said Wilson. "You do know your men, don't you?"

Ken Venturi was very close to his father, and their relationship did much to fuel his drive to become one of the game's great champions.

"My father understood people and what makes them tick," Venturi remembers. "When I won the San Francisco City Championship—which was really a big deal in those days—he said to me, 'So what? Do you have any idea how many cities there are in this country?' When I won the California Amateur, he said, 'That's

nice, but there are forty-seven other states that have championships.' Even after I won the U.S. Open, he wasn't that impressed. He told me that it wouldn't count for that much unless I backed it up with another win—which, fortunately, I did.

"But after I won the 1966 Lucky International in San Francisco, I began to have problems with my hands. I went to the Mayo Clinic, and the doctor was very honest with me. He told me that gangrene had set in and it was very serious. He told me to go back home to San Francisco and get my affairs in order. He said that there was a very good chance that some of my fingers might have to be amputated.

"When the time came for me to leave San Francisco and go have the surgery, my father drove me to the airport," Venturi continues. "I told him what the doctor had said. He was quiet, then he hugged me and said, 'Ken, it doesn't matter if you never hit another golf ball. You were the best I ever saw.'"

One of Venturi's colleagues and friends is Jack Whitaker, who remembers a particularly memorable round the two men played at Winged Foot.

"We had finished a taping and decided to try and squeeze in a round," says Whitaker. "Kenny didn't have his clubs, but we borrowed a set from the pro shop and I gave him a beat-up old sweater I had tucked away in my locker.

"We went out and Kenny was 1 or 2 under through eight," Whitaker continues. "On 9 he hooked his drive into the left rough. I didn't think he had a shot, and I'm pretty sure our caddie didn't think he had one, either. After Kenny studied his options, he pulled out an 8-iron and hit the prettiest little shot you've ever seen. The ball shot out between two branches and then began hooking back towards the green. The ball wound up about fifteen feet from the hole.

"The caddie looked at the ball and then back at Kenny. Finally he asked, 'Are you a pro?' Kenny smiled sort of sheepishly and said he was. The caddie said, 'If you come back here tomorrow dressed like that, we can make a lot of money for ourselves.' "

Ten years after his win at the U.S. Open, Ken Venturi came to Winged Foot to play in the 1974 Open. Beset by injuries, he was only playing the Tour sporadically, devoting most of his time to his work as a commentator for CBS Sports.

He struggled at Winged Foot and was never really in contention. As he trudged up one of the final fairways, a man in the gallery said to a friend, "If I was him I'd quit."

"Yeah," the friend replied. "But if you were him, you'd have quit ten years ago, too."

Lanny Wadkins

Lanny Wadkins often works on his game with golf professional Dick Harmon, the son of the late Masters champion Claude Harmon.

One day Lanny traveled to Houston for a session with Harmon. As luck would have it, Claude was down visiting his son and joined them on the course. On one hole, Lanny hit a 3-wood off a downhill lie to a green guarded by water.

"Tell me, son," Claude said to Dickie, "just what is it you plan to teach this young man?"

When they finished on the course, the elder Harmon did have one piece of advice.

"Lanny, just make sure you vary your route to the bank," he suggested.

Early in his career, Lanny Wadkins played a fair amount of golf with Ben Hogan, another man who didn't mind playing for his own money. Midway through one of their matches, with Lanny ahead, they had to return to the clubhouse. A few days later Lanny received a check in the mail from Hogan for $15.

Several weeks later Lanny received a telephone call from Hogan's secretary asking if he had cashed the check.

"No, ma'am, and you tell Mr. Hogan not to worry about it," he told her. "It's never going to be cashed, and it's probably going to be framed."

CYRIL WALKER

England's Cyril Walker was thirty when he won the 1924 U.S. Open at Oakland Hills, beating Bobby Jones by three strokes. He was so thrilled by his victory that he paid his caddie the astonishing sum of $500—the amount of the winner's purse.

Several months after winning the Open, Walker arrived on the first tee at the Los Angeles Open.

"Mr. Walker, are you the winner of any state opens?" the starter asked him.

"All goddamn forty-eight at once," he replied sharply.

Despite his win at the Open, Walker wound up as something of a sad—even tragic—figure.

Whatever money he earned as a player was lost in a failed real estate venture in Florida. In 1937, fourteen years after his greatest victory, the U.S. Open returned to Oakland Hills. The club invited Walker back to honor his victory and put him up in one of the area's best hotels. When the tournament ended, Walker refused to leave the hotel. His last years were spent as a caddie—a fine pastime for someone who loves the game but not for an Open champion.

THE WALKER CUP

The United States holds an enormous edge in Walker Cup victories, 31-4-1. One of those victories came in 1969, when the Americans won, 10-8, at the Milwaukee Country Club. There were six halved matches, and the U.S. won several matches with clutch play on the 17th and 18th holes.

After the match, America's Vinny Giles tried to console Britain's Michael Bonallack.

"You know, if these had been sixteen-hole matches you guys would have been in great shape," Giles said.

"No," Bonallack said, sighing. "I think we would have found a way to screw up 15 and 16."

TOM WATSON

Tom Watson and Jack Nicklaus have enjoyed a wonderful rivalry over the years, dating back to their historic duel at Turnberry in the 1977 British Open. In 1982, when Tom Watson chipped in on the 71st hole of the U.S. Open at Pebble Beach, it allowed him to edge Jack Nicklaus—who was the first player to congratulate Watson when he walked off the final green.

Watson and Nicklaus were paired together in the second round of the 1991 Masters. Watson played his way into the lead that day, and as the two men approached the 18th green, the enormous gallery rose and gave the two a huge ovation. Watson slowed to let Nicklaus catch up.

"Go ahead, Tom," Nicklaus said. "You go first."

"No, Jack," Watson said. "Let's walk up together."

"But you're leading the tournament," Nicklaus argued.

"Yeah, but you're Jack Nicklaus," Watson said.

TOM WEISKOPF

The 1974 U.S. Open was played at Winged Foot Golf Club in Mamaroneck, a suburb of New York City. The week before the Open the Tour was in Philadelphia, and most of the players drove straight to New York when the tournament finished. Tom Weiskopf was one of them, although his route was a little more circuitous than most.

Before leaving Philadelphia, Weiskopf checked to make sure he had the directions to Winged Foot. So far, so good.

And he also had the directions from Winged Foot to the house he was renting in nearby Bronxville. Okay, fine.

What he didn't have were the directions from Philadelphia to Bronxville. So he did the only logical thing. He drove to Winged Foot, arriving at midnight. Then he checked the directions and drove on to Bronxville.

"Jack [Nicklaus] and I always used to go over and play our practice rounds together beginning the week before the British Open," Weiskopf recalls. "At Carnoustie in 1975 we went out one evening after dinner, which was fairly normal since it stays light for so long. We were on the second green when we heard Australian Jack Newton [who would lose to Tom Watson in a playoff] and [Irish professional] John O'Leary calling to us from the tee. When they caught up with us, Jack Newton said they wanted to challenge us to a game. Nicklaus made it a practice of not playing for anything during practice rounds because he was never shooting for a score but trying to fit his game to how the course would play that week.

"Now, you have to keep in mind that even though we were playing in the evening, we had a gallery of several hundred people. Newton kept badgering Jack, saying things like 'You are supposed to be the two best players in the world but you're afraid to play us,' and so on. On the 3rd hole Newton made a birdie, then he ran in a forty-footer for another birdie on 4. When it went in he looked over at Jack and asked if we wanted a press. Now, until that point we hadn't even said we wanted a game, but Nicklaus looked over at Newton with a look I don't ever think I'd seen before or since. He said, 'Jack, we're not two down yet.' With that, he ran in a ten-footer for a birdie.

"All of a sudden, the game was on. We decided to play $10 automatic one-downs. On the fifth tee Jack took me aside and put those steely blues on me. 'Tom,' he said, 'if you've ever really tried I want you to try now. I want to bury these guys.' He was scary.

"I've never seen Jack quite as intense as he was that night. Between us we made twelve birdies and an eagle over the next fourteen holes. And that doesn't count what happened on the 8th hole, which is one of the hardest par 3s you'll ever see.

"Nicklaus hit first and got his ball on the green. The pin was hidden behind some mounds, and I shot right at the flag. We couldn't see it land, but the gallery applauded politely, so we figured it was safe. When we reached the green, we could see three balls but not mine. Finally Nicklaus went up and found my ball in the hole.

" 'Can you believe it?' he said. 'You made a hole in one and nobody said anything?'

"With that, he walked over to these two old Scots sitting on their shooting sticks.

" 'Were you there when Tom hit his shot?' Jack asked them.

" 'Aye, Jack,' one of them replied.

" 'Did you realize it went in the hole?'

" 'Aye, Jack,' the guy said. 'But isn't it only practice?' "

One evening during the 1979 British Open at Royal Lytham and St. Annes, Tom Weiskopf, Ed Sneed, and writer Dan Jenkins went to dinner at the Clifton Arms hotel. Weiskopf ordered an expensive bottle of wine but upon tasting it decided it wasn't quite right.

"Dieter, bring us some ice and some club soda," Weiskopf told the maitre d'.

Dieter arrived a few minutes later with the ice and soda, and Weiskopf blended them with the wine.

"Now that's a good glass of wine," he said, beaming.

In 1980 Tom Weiskopf came to the 12th hole in the first round. The pin was cut in the easiest position—front left—and, for a change, there was no wind to complicate matters. Weiskopf, a player who lived for the Masters, took an 8-iron, hit the green, then watched in dismay as the ball checked back off the green and rolled into the water. He took a drop, hit again, and watched as the ball tumbled into the creek. By the time the smoke had cleared he had made a 13, the highest score on either a par 3 or par 4 in Masters history.

As she watched her husband's hopes wash down Rae's Creek, 457 Jeanne Weiskopf began to cry. A friend, Tom Culver, put his arms around her and asked, "Jeanne, you don't suppose he's using new balls, do you?"

Tom Weiskopf is one of the finest ball-strikers the game has ever seen. But like so many skilled shotmakers, his putting has seldom been a match for the rest of his game.

In 1994, in his second year on the Senior Tour, he got a lesson from Lee Trevino that gave him a tremendous shot of confidence. He went into the U.S. Senior Open at Pinehurst with a lot of optimism about his play on the greens—even though he had putted horribly the week before.

"I feel like I'm the best putter in the world," he told a friend. "All these years I thought putting was the hardest part of the game. I was wrong."

The next day Weiskopf walked off the practice green and was approached by a fan, an older man.

"How's your putting, Tom?" the man asked.

"Super," said Tom. "I feel like I'm the world's greatest putter."

"Are you the same Tom Weiskopf that I saw on TV last weekend?" the man asked.

Even when he was well past his prime as a competitor, Ben Hogan was idolized by his fellow players.

"In 1967, I was playing in a tournament at the Champions Club in Houston," remembers Tom Weiskopf. "Jeanne and I hadn't been married that long and she really didn't know that much about golf. We were sharing a house with Bert Yancey and Tony Jacklin. After Friday's round, Jeanne called to get the Saturday pairings. She called out and said I was playing with 'Al Geiberger and somebody named Ben Hogan—who's he?' We just cracked up.

"Anyway, the next day both Ben and I shot 67s, but the thing I remember is that when guys would finish their rounds they'd come out on the course to watch Ben. You never see that. Never. After I finished, I went back to the house and players began coming by. They wanted to know what it was like to play with Ben. They asked what club he hit here or what kind of shot he played there.

"Finally, Jeanne said, 'I don't know why you guys find Ben Hogan so interesting. He hits every fairway and every green. Tom is much more interesting to watch. He drives it into the trees. He hits into the rough and the bunkers. It's a thrill a minute with Tom.'"

Following a round in the 1980 British Open at Muirfield, Tom Weiskopf and his wife, Jeanne, were with some friends in the Greywalls hotel watching the BBC's Open coverage.

"I was criticizing the BBC, and I noticed that Jeanne kept motioning me to be quiet, but she was being very subtle about it," he recalls. "Finally, this woman who was with us got up and left.

"Tom, do you know who that woman is?" she asked me.

"I give up. She's the Queen of England," I said.

"Close—she's her sister, Princess Margaret."

Well, I felt pretty bad, and when the princess came back I went out of my way to be polite. We were having a very nice conversation, and she mentioned that her father loved to play golf.

"That's nice," I said. "What did your father do?"

"He was the King of England," said the princess.

Jeanne was horrified, but the princess took it pretty well. Heck, she still tells the story all the time.

JOYCE WETHERED

Joyce Wethered, now Lady Heathcoat-Amory, is arguably the greatest female golfer in British history and, some would say, in all of golf. She won, among other titles, four British Women's Championships and five English Women's Championships.

Like every outstanding player, she was graced with both athletic skill and an almost superhuman ability to concentrate, as Cecil Leitch, one of her greatest rivals, explains:

"As Miss Wethered was preparing to putt for the win and the title of 1920 English champion, a long train suddenly rattled by, making the most horrible noise. She appeared quite unbothered by the train, in fact, appeared almost in a trance, quite unconscious of any of her immediate surroundings. Later, I asked her if the train had not bothered her. She replied by asking, 'What train?' Remarkable. Utterly remarkable."

KATHY WHITWORTH

Kathy Whitworth's eighty-eight victories make her the most successful golfer in LPGA history. While she never won the U.S. Women's Open, she won just about everything else worth winning before winding down her playing career and concentrating on teaching. In the end, the pressure of competition and other people's expectations finally got to be too much.

"I was talking about it with Ben Hogan one time," Whitworth recalled. "He said that the more you win, the easier people think it is to win, while just the opposite is true. He compared it to water dripping on a stone. You wouldn't think that water could damage something as hard as a stone, but eventually the water wears it down. That's how it was for me. I just found I couldn't take the steady pressure any longer. I knew it was time to get out."

The Wild Kingdom

Sam Snead, who spent his boyhood hunting and fishing in the Virginia mountains, has maintained his passion for outdoor sports ever since. One day he was explaining to a group of writers how he used to catch trout by hand.

"You'd have to be pretty quick," one writer said.

"Nope," said Sam. "All you have to do is think like a trout."

"One day I was playing golf down at Pine Tree in Florida," Sam recalls. "I looked off there in the trees and saw this little bobcat. I used to catch them by hand when I was a kid, so I decided to give it a try. You have to get them by the scruff of the neck, just like a house cat, or you'll get scratched up pretty good. Well, I got him and put him in the side pocket of my golf bag. When we got back to the clubhouse, one of the fellas started to take my bag off the cart. I asked him to get my sweater out of the bag. He opened the zipper a few inches and that cat set to screeching and growling and scratching. I never did see anyone move as fast as that old boy did."

In the 1980s, a real estate developer in Florida came up with a clever marketing approach. He lined up several players on the then-fledgling Senior Tour to help promote one of his developments. In return, the players would be given either houses or condominiums on the property.

One of the players involved was Sam Snead. Sam loved nothing better than to go out and play a few rounds with his retriever,

"Meister," at his side. Meister is an exceptionally well-behaved dog, and Sam's playing partners always readily accepted him.

Apparently, however, not everyone living near Sam's new property was happy about having Meister out on the course, and Sam was told that the practice had to stop.

"Well, if Meister's not welcome neither am I," said Sam, who promptly sold his property and moved.

A player named Jim Stewart was getting ready to tee off in the first round of the Singapore Open. As he reached into his bag for a club, he heard a hissing noise. He emptied the bag and, to his horror, saw an enormous cobra fall out along with his clubs. Immediately he grabbed an iron and killed the snake. Tournament officials were understanding and let him move back his starting time.

Playing in the Nigerian Open one year, Philip Walton found himself facing a tricky shot from underneath a thick tree branch that would restrict his swing. He took his stance, made a couple of practice swings, and punched the ball out. As soon as Walton hit the ball, his caddie pointed out that a large snake was resting on the branch.

"Are you mad?" Walton screamed. "That snake could have fallen on me. Why didn't you tell me the snake was there?"

"I wanted you to hit a good shot and not worry about the snake," said his caddie.

Gordon Brand, Jr., was playing in Nairobi and noticed several monkeys in a stand of trees close to a tee. He and his playing partners gathered some nuts from the ground and threw them toward the monkeys. The next day, when Brand's group came to the same hole, they were showered with nuts by the monkeys.

Tom Sieckman is an American who honed his game on the foreign tours. He eventually got used to the variety of foreign courses and playing conditions, but frequently some of the local customs would leave him at a loss for words.

"I was playing a tournament in Asia and the promoters arranged a party for us," says Sieckman. "When it was time to eat, they brought out a dish that I didn't recognize. In fact, I'd never seen anything quite like it. I asked the host what it was.

464

" 'Monkey brain,' he said."

Sieckman begged off.

MORRIS WILLIAMS

Most golf fans know that Tom Kite and Ben Crenshaw grew up competing against each other as teenagers in Austin, Texas, and later as students at the University of Texas. But as good as they are, many people believe that Morris Williams was as good, if not better.

Like Kite and Crenshaw, Williams was a pupil of the late Harvey Penick. At age thirteen, Williams became the youngest person ever to win the Austin City Championship and went on to dominate area golf.

Like Kite and Crenshaw, Williams went to the University of Texas, leading his team to the Southwest Conference titles in 1947, '49, and '50. In his senior year he finished second in the NCAA individual competition.

After graduating, Williams joined the air force and won every interservice tournament he played in, including the worldwide air force championship in 1959. Not long after winning that tournament he was killed in a crash during a training flight.

465

"I was at Austin Country Club when I got the call telling me that Morris had been killed," remembered Harvey Penick. "I had to be the one to break the news to his father, and it was the hardest thing I've ever had to do in my life. He was the sports editor of the Austin paper. When he came into the newsroom he asked me what I was doing there. I started to tell him but broke into tears. I barely managed to get the words out and Mr. Williams collapsed in my arms."

WIVES AND LOVERS

"We took a mulligan."

—PGA TOUR PRO BILL KRATZERT,
on his marriage, divorce, and
remarriage to his wife, Cheryl

There are some reasons for getting a divorce that are better than others. Take the example of the man who had given his wife his entry for the U.S. Open. Things hadn't been going very well in their marriage for some time, and in the midst of yet another heated argument, she told him that instead of mailing his entry to the USGA, she had thrown it away.

That was more than the man could stand. He picked up the phone, called his lawyer, and started divorce proceedings.

Lee Trevino played pretty well from tee to green in the 1984 British Open at St. Andrews, but his putting was atrocious. His wife, Claudia—whose late father was a golf professional—thought she knew what the problem was but broached the matter with great diplomacy and a certain spousal delicacy.

"Honey, what kind of putter does Seve use?" she asked after watching Ballesteros edge Tom Watson for his second British Open title.

"A Ping," Trevino answered.

"And what kind of putter is Tom Watson using?" she asked sweetly.

"A Ping," Trevino replied.

"Oh," Claudia said. "And what kind of putter is Freddie Couples using?"

"He uses a Ping, too," Tevino answered.

"Can I ask you something else?" she asked.

"Sure," Trevino said.

"When are we going to get one?" she asked.

Pretty soon, as it turned out.

"We flew from Scotland to the Dutch Open," Trevino recalls. "I went into a pro shop and saw a Ping that looked pretty good to me. I bought it, banged it on the floor to flatten the lie, and went out and shot 13 under par to win the tournament. It worked like a charm."

In fact, it worked so well that a few weeks later Trevino, then forty-three, went out and won the PGA Championship at Shoal Creek by four strokes.

Claudia was credited with an assist.

Winged Foot Golf Club, in the New York City suburb of Mamaroneck, has been a home away from home for its members since it opened in the early 1920s. In fact, for some members, it's more like home than home itself. Take the case of the man who got to the club early, played thirty-six holes, then had dinner and several happy hours relaxing with the guys in the grillroom.

Alas, his reverie was interrupted by a phone call from his wife, who was curious why he was still there and not back home in New York.

"I'm sorry, honey, but the car broke down," he said.

"But you took the train out this morning," she said.

There was a moment of silence.

"Well, that's my story and I'm sticking to it," he said.

One fine day Donald Trump, the New York real estate developer and darling of the tabloids, decided that his then girlfriend, Marla

Maples, should learn to play golf. So off they went to Winged Foot, where Marla changed into new golf clothes and headed toward the practice tee for a lesson from one of the assistant pros. All of this would have been uneventful if the route from the pro shop to the driving range had not taken her past the men's grill.

When she reached the practice tee, she was delighted to see that it was virtually deserted.

Not for long.

In the time it takes to finish a beer and change back into a pair of spikes, the range had become packed with men who had decided their swings needed a little work.

"My wife always said she wanted to marry a millionaire," joked Chi Chi Rodriguez one day. "Well, I have to give her credit. She made me a millionaire. Of course, I used to be a multimillionaire."

When Nick Faldo was divorced from his first wife, a friend asked if he'd always been unhappy in the marriage.

"No, I was very happily married for two years," he said. "Unfortunately, we were married for seven."

Reporters asked former First Lady Barbara Bush for her reaction to the news that her husband was going to play in the Bob Hope Desert Classic along with President Clinton and former President Gerald Ford.

"Isn't there already enough violence and bloodshed on television?" she said.

Men-cnly golf clubs are becoming increasingly rare in the United States, but one that remains staunchly so is Bob O'Link, outside Chicago. A member once described the club this way: "It's like a family club without women."

In the early years of their marriage, before their children were born, Sam and Audrey Snead traveled together. It didn't take long for Sam to give his wife a valuable piece of advice.

"Audrey, if I come home with sand in my cuffs, don't ask me what I shot," Sam said.

The wife of a young PGA Tour pro sat in the bleachers behind the practice tee and watched her husband grind away in the hot summer sun. Finally, the boredom—and the heat—got to be too much. She motioned for his caddie to come over.

"How much longer do you think he's going to be?" she asked.

"Until he gets it right," the caddie said.

"Oh God, can't he just stop when his hands begin to bleed?" she asked.

Want a recipe for domestic misery? Want to all but guarantee that your marriage will be whistling south faster than Amtrak's "Sunshine Special"? Have your wife caddie for you. Or worse yet, if you play in the LPGA Tour, sign up your husband. Or boyfriend. The historic landscape is littered with relationships that were shattered on the shoals of the player-caddie/wife-husband team.

Just ask Amy Alcott.

"The funniest thing I ever saw on the golf course involved a player whose husband caddied for her when she first came out on tour," Amy recalls. "It was in the late '70s. We were playing in Dallas, and the woman was in contention going into the final round. She got off to a terrible start and couldn't recover. By the time we made the turn she was 6 over, she was history, and she and her husband were barely talking. We got to the 10th hole, which was a par 3, and there was a 5-wood and a 3-iron resting against the bench where her husband had left them. Up by the green was a pitching wedge and her putter. But no husband. The next hole was a par 4. He left her driver on the tee and her 5- and 6-irons down in the rough near the landing area. He left her sand wedge up by the green since he was sure she'd hit it into a bunker. On the next hole, he left her 3-wood on the tee and her 4-iron in the left rough, where he was sure she was going to hook the ball. By the time we reached the 13th hole, he was pretty sure she had all the clubs she'd need, but just to be on the safe side he left her 9-iron on the tee. Now she's carrying eleven clubs. She's so mad she can barely see straight, and it's all I can do to keep from falling down laughing. We finished the hole and he was waiting on the tee. I don't think they said a word to each other for the rest of the round. It wasn't too long before they decided he'd retire from caddying—at least for her. It probably saved their marriage."

Want to know the record for futility as well as patience? It's 166 strokes—on a single hole—and it belongs to a woman who was playing in the 1912 Shawnee (Pennsylvania) Invitational. She hit her tee shot on the 130-yard, par-3 16th into the Binniekill River. As she watched the ball cascade down the rock-strewn waters, her husband urged her to jump in a nearby rowboat. As he rowed, she tried valiantly to hit the ball back to shore. With her husband cheering her on, she finally succeeded. Unfortunately, she was about a mile downstream. Not to be deterred, she played back through the woods—counting every single, miserable, humiliating stroke. Finally, she holed out—166 strokes later.

Hubert Green was playing in the final round of the 1977 U.S. Open at Southern Hills in Tulsa when, with four holes to play, he was told that officials had received a threat on his life.

He was given three options: first, he could leave the course immediately and withdraw from the championship; second, he could request a suspension of play; or third, he could continue under a police guard. Green elected to play. Remarkably, he was 1 under par for the next three holes and then made a four-footer for bogey on 18 to edge Lou Graham by a stroke.

Later, writers asked him how he could remain so calm under such pressure.

"I just figured the threat came from an old girlfriend of mine," he joked.

Archie Compston was a fine player from England and a member of several Ryder Cup teams in the 1920s and '30s. Like many skilled golfers, he didn't come naturally to teaching when his playing days were over. He was often impatient, especially with beginners, and he didn't have what doctors refer to as a good bedside manner.

One day he was giving a lesson to a woman who was every bit as imperious as old Archie. Finally, she'd had enough of his attitude and hit him on the leg.

"You've finally bloody got it!" he yelled. "Now try it on the ball."

Golf, like life, is more complicated these days. Take this story from a public course in Atlanta.

A gentleman made a starting time for himself and his wife. He asked if there was a dress code and was told it was pretty informal. When they arrived at the course, it turned out he was a cross-dresser and was wearing a tennis dress.

It gets worse.

Apparently he must have looked pretty good in the dress because as they prepared to hit, a man approached the two and asked if they'd mind if he joined them.

The cross-dresser turned and looked at the man.

"Not at all," he said, in a deep baritone.

Arnold Palmer is, to put it mildly, strong-willed. But he met his match when he married Winifred Waltzer.

His early days on tour coincided with the early years of their marriage. He was successful almost from the beginning, but money was tight in those days, and to help make ends meet, they towed a twenty-eight-foot trailer from one tournament to the next.

It should be noted here that Winnie came from a family that, if not rich, was certainly comfortable—not a background that would prepare a young bride for crisscrossing the country in a trailer.

One memorable journey proved to be one memorable journey too many for the young Mrs. Palmer.

The young couple had just finished a tournament in North Carolina and decided to return home to Latrobe, Pennsylvania. Naturally, nothing would do for Arnold but to take a shortcut he knew. Winnie was skeptical, but being young and in love, she said okay.

Along the way, they almost killed a cow in a collision and came close to running off the road twice—on their way up and then on their way down a mountain. When they reached Latrobe, the young Mrs. Palmer put her foot down.

"That's it!" she said. "I'm never getting back in that trailer again."

"But Winnie . . ." Palmer protested.

"Never," she said.

End of discussion.

The value of an understanding and supportive wife cannot be overstated, but in some cases logic and common sense override even the strongest wifely devotion.

Consider the case of Kathy Shearer, wife of Australian professional Bob Shearer, who called the clubhouse during the 1980 Atlanta Classic and asked what her husband shot.

"63," came the reply. "No, Shearer. S-H-E-A-R-E-R," she replied.

"My wife, Louise, was a very patient and supportive person, but even she had her limits," remembers Byron Nelson. "I told her I needed to buy a new driver and she said, 'Byron, I haven't had a new dress in three years. Don't you suppose you could fix up one of the drivers you already have?' Sure enough, I fooled around with one of them and it worked pretty good."

Good enough to let him win everything in sight for the next twelve years.

One evening there was a large dinner-dance at an exclusive club in North Carolina. In the course of the evening a great deal of liquor was consumed and a man and a woman, who were not married to each other, became bored with the activity on the dance floor and decided to take a walk. One thing led to another and they wound up in a greenside bunker but not in what one might call an unplayable lie.

Suddenly, a guard showed up with an enormous flashlight and asked a simple question: "Are you members?"

"Yes," they replied as they scrambled to rearrange their clothes and retreat to the clubhouse.

"No, you're not," the guard shouted, chasing after them. "No member of this club would leave without raking the bunker."

TIGER WOODS

Tiger Woods, who won the U.S. Amateur in 1994 and 1995 while still a teenager, was paired with Curtis Strange in the second round of the 1995 Masters. On the 5th hole Woods crushed a drive that measured 347 yards.

"Tiger, I'm just gonna retire and watch you play golf," said Curtis.

"You've been a hero of mine since I was a kid," Woods said respectfully to the two-time U.S. Open champion.

"You ain't a kid anymore," said Curtis.

By the time he was fourteen, Tiger Woods was already a favorite in most of the tournaments he entered. That was certainly the case in 1990, when he entered the U.S. Junior Amateur Championship at the Lake Merced Golf and Country Club near San Francisco.

But Woods lost in the semifinals to Dennis Hillman. After the match, he was angry and frustrated—perhaps as only a kid can be. But the anger lasted for only a few moments, until he saw his father standing by the green. Tiger walked over and gave his father a hug.

"Dad," he said. "I really love you."

He would be back the next year to win the first of his three U.S. Juniors.

Tiger Woods's record-setting win at the 1997 Masters was dramatic on a variety of levels. Not the least of which was the fact that it marked the first time a non-Caucasian won this prestigious tournament played in the heart of the Old South.

When Woods entered the clubhouse for the traditional dinner honoring the new champion, the members stood and applauded. But more important—and poignant—was the other group of people who stood and showed their appreciation for his accomplishment: the mostly black waiters and kitchen staff, who basked in the reflected glow of all that Tiger Woods had accomplished that historic week.

If you think Tiger Woods was under a lot of pressure when he won the 1997 Masters, or when he won three U.S. Amateurs, or when he outgunned Sergio Garcia to win the 1999 PGA Championship, just consider the pressure he felt at the PGA Tour's 1997 Awards Dinner.

He was awarded the Arnold Palmer Award by the Great Man himself, and as he approached the podium, Palmer stopped Woods in his tracks—and sent a chill through the audience.

"Wait right there," Palmer said, motioning to Woods to pause. "I have something to say. You have an enormous responsibility. When I think of when I started playing this Tour so long ago and how much it's changed, it is amazing. I think we should be thankful, but we should also be careful. Remember how we got here and the guys who helped get us here. You guys are playing for so much money. Always remember that you have an obligation to protect the integrity and traditions of the game. It is important. When I see bad conduct, it truly disturbs me."

Then he signaled for Woods to come stand next to him.

"It's all right here," he said, placing his hands on Woods's shoulders. "The responsibility is all on your shoulders. Protect the game. It's beautiful."

WORLD WAR II

The members of the Hilversum Golf Club in Holland were understandably nervous when during the German occupation a German officer's staff car pulled in front of the club. The officer entered the clubhouse and politely asked if he might enjoy playing privileges for the duration. Not surprisingly, his request was granted.

For the next several months the officer, who always conducted himself impeccably, came to the club and played alone. He never entered the clubhouse; never asked for any special treatment.

One day a corps of German engineers arrived and marked hundreds of the club's magnificent old oaks for removal to be used in the fortification of Hitler's "Atlantic Wall." The officer arrived for his afternoon game, saw the markings on the trees, and immediately got into his limousine and left. He returned several hours later with a unit of troops who posted signs around the property that read, "*Achtung! Es ist verboten . . .*" signed by order of the Commandant of the Gestapo.

Years later, the members of the Hilversum Golf Club tried, to no avail, to locate the mysterious officer and thank him. He was never heard from again.

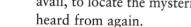

Ben Wright

British-born golf commentator Ben Wright is part of an increasingly rare breed—a television journalist who got his start in newspapering. His entry into television came in the early 1970s when fellow Englishman Henry Longhurst was taken ill and CBS's golf producer, Frank Chirkinian, went looking for a replacement Brit. He found Ben, who's been a regular member of the CBS broadcast team until recently.

As a young man, Ben Wright enjoyed driving race cars—until he was involved in a serious accident. The accident caused serious damage to his mouth, and he was required to wear false teeth.

One morning, in Los Angeles for the telecast of the L.A. Open, he was seized with a coughing fit. Somehow, his upper plate fell into the toilet just as it was being flushed. To his utter shock, he watched his teeth—and possibly his career—head for the Los Angeles sewer system. There were just scant hours before he was scheduled to go on the air.

In a panic, he called the production truck and explained his dilemma. CBS found a dentist nearby, who came up with a temporary replacement plate to get Wright through the telecast.

Of course, if he thought he was going to get off that easily, he was sadly mistaken. As he began to record his taped hole opener ("I'm Ben Wright, and I shall be reporting play from the . . ."), his producer told him to look at the monitor, where a set of windup false teeth went chattering across the screen.

BABE ZAHARIAS

It could be argued that Babe Zaharias was the finest woman athlete in American history. After a brilliant career in track and field, she turned to golf. Her greatest triumph was in 1954, when she came back from cancer surgery to win the U.S. Women's Open at Salem Country Club outside of Boston.

Zaharias was married to George Zaharias, a popular wrestler. He was dark-haired and handsome and something of a sex symbol among women wrestling fans, of which there were surprisingly many in those days. Still, Babe couldn't resist needling him.

"George, when we got married you were a Greek god," she said. "Now you're just a goddamn Greek."

Not surprisingly, the Babe was a confident, even cocky, athlete. It's also no surprise that this didn't always sit well with her fellow golfers. For example, how thrilled would you be if you were sitting in the locker room before your round and the Babe walked in and asked—as she often did—"Which one of you girls is gonna finish second this week?"

"In my rookie year I was paired with Babe in a four-ball tournament," recalls Peggy Kirk Bell, who would go on to become both a top touring pro and a teacher. "I was naturally very nervous, and I told Babe that I'd do my best and hoped I could help her enough so we could win.

" 'Win!' she roared, 'of course we'll win. We can't lose. I can beat any two of these girls on my own. You just come along and have a good time.' "

The Babe was playing in a pro-am, and one of her partners was obviously unnerved by playing with Babe in front of a big gallery.

He got over the ball, made several nervous waggles, and accidentally knocked the ball off the tee. He apologized, reteed the ball, and began the process all over again. When he finally connected, the ball shot off to the right, squarely struck a tree, and headed back toward the tee, prompting Babe and the other players to scatter.

"Sir, let me give you a piece of advice I learned when I first took up this game," she said. "The first rule of golf is 'Always make sure the ball winds up in front of you after you hit it.' "

A writer once asked Babe what she did when men tried to hit on her.

"It depends on my mood and what the guy looks like," she quipped. "Sometimes I let him and sometimes I kick the hell out of him."

And she actually did just that one day in a clubhouse bar. She had played badly and was in no mood to be bothered. But the man was persistent, and the next thing he knew, he was spread-eagled on the floor. Babe went back to her bar stool and finished her drink in peace.

Babe Zaharias was diagnosed with colon cancer in 1953, and few people expected her to return to championship competition. In the hospital, she prayed for a chance to return to golf, and in 1954, she won an emotional victory in the U.S. Women's Open at Salem Country Club. It was her third Women's Open title.

Sadly, however, her recovery was short-lived. The cancer returned, and she and those around her knew that she had less than a year left to live.

On Christmas Eve 1955, she was in Fort Worth visiting with friends. As darkness fell, she asked to be driven to Colonial Country Club. When they reached the 2nd green, the Babe, dressed in pajamas and a robe, got out of the car and walked slowly to the green. There, she knelt and slowly ran her hands over the surface, then returned to the car.

"I just wanted to see a golf course one more time," she said.

Index